"While not usually a fan of true crime stories, this book entertained me on a deeper level — as one can almost feel both the frustration and dogged dedication of the primary story-teller, Detective King. He and co-author Burch have taken a stunning series of historical crimes, perpetrated by one man, and transformed them into an interesting page-turner. The research is solid, but presented in a fashion that is never boring, rather it draws the reader into the complex lives portrayed on these pages. It is highly recommended, not only as entertainment, but for the life lessons gleaned from those charged with upholding the law, and the criminal mind determined to thwart their efforts."
— T. Hall, Birmingham, Alabama, Amazon Five Star Review

"I appreciated the detailed raw reality of this true crime story presented largely through the lens of a key detective on the case, Jim King. This story would make a very interesting movie. If you like true crime stories, this one is well worth a read."
— Eleece, Amazon Five Star Review

"I grew up in the DC area, when this guy was operating there. I remember the headlines - and remember being amazed at the newspaper stories; but, WOW! the real, full story - even more amazing. Very well researched and well written. The truth IS more amazing than fiction."
— William Lilly, Lino Lakes, MN., Amazon Five Star Review

"This book is a well thought out page turner."
— Peter Smith, Amazon Five Star Review

"Wow...if this doesn't get made into a movie! A non-stop great read."
— Margot Peter "Savvy Grams," Amazon Five Star Review.

"I really enjoyed the true story of this book's main character Bernard Welch, who out foxed and eluded authorities on numerous occasions throughout his storied career as a a master thief, murderer, and rapist! The book is well written and keeps your interest from start to finish! A great read I highly recommend!"
— Will Sheehy, Amazon Five Star Review

"I really enjoyed it. Well researched without becoming boring. An almost unbelievable story, yet it's true. Very entertaining. Finally a book worth owning."
— Ernie S., Amazon Five Star Review.

"Mr. Burch, and Detective King did an excellent job researching the activities of Bernard Welch, and the crime spree
— Gina, Amazon Five Star Review

Ghost Burglar

Ghost Burglar

The True Story of Bernard C. Welch Jr.
Master Thief, Ruthless Con Man,
and Cold-Blooded Killer

Jack Burch
and
James D. King

SAVAGE PRESS
A Superior Publishing Company

P.O. Box 115 • Superior, WI 54880
(218) 391-3070 • www.savpress.com

Published by:

Savage Press
P.O. Box 115
Superior, WI 54880

Phone: 218-391-3070
E-mail: mail@savpress.com
Website: www.savpress.com
         www.ghostburglar.com

Cover Art/Illustration: Linda Siegel - SHE Designs
Layout/Book Design: Debbie Zime - Dezime Graphics

Printed in the USA

To Joanna, Deanna, Dan, and Amanda;
and to Marion, Alex, and Johnny.
To Mike, who believed in us,
and Jessica, who made every word count.

And to a good and courageous man,
Dr. Michael Halberstam.

Preface

Bernard C. Welch Jr. was a high school dropout and a lifelong con artist who became the most prolific and successful burglar in history. Welch managed to flummox police departments and federal agencies across half of the United States for more than twenty-five years, stealing tens of millions of dollars, robbing countless individuals, and living in the open by posing as a wealthy antique dealer and investor. He had an expensive suburban Washington, DC, home with an indoor pool, Mercedes Benz autos, two million dollars in a stock brokerage account, and a summer home in Duluth, Minnesota, all amassed while living under a dozen aliases as an escaped convict. Even after he was captured, convicted of first-degree murder, and sentenced to 143 years to life, Welch found a way to break out of an allegedly escape-proof federal prison and continue his life of crime.

Ghost Burglar is not only the account of a crafty master criminal, but also the story of a veteran police officer who pursued him. I had worked in the TV news department of a Fox affiliate in Minneapolis during Welch's one-man crime wave in the late 1970s. As I dug into Bernard Welch's activities in Duluth, Minnesota, my research eventually led me to Detective James D. King. The more I learned about the incredibly twisted criminal life of Bernard Welch, the more I was convinced that this was a story worth telling, and I realized that Detective King was the one to help tell it. Detective King was a police detective in Montgomery County, Maryland. He worked with other regional police departments on the "Standard Time Silver Burglar" investigation from start to finish. Despite his own personal tragedy during this time, Detective King relentlessly pursued Bernard Welch. Shortly after Welch's arrest in 1980, Detective King stated in a *Washington Post* interview that pursuing this elusive and dangerous burglar "was like chasing a ghost."

The research and writing for *Ghost Burglar* took four years. Detective King's own personal notes and recollections offer readers a unique insight into this historic manhunt. Our other extensive sources include court transcripts and records, police reports, newspaper reports, and magazine articles. We interviewed many people who encountered Bernard Welch during his life of crime—defense attorneys, federal prosecutors, US Marshals, FBI agents, police detectives, prison officials, court reporters, antique, art, and coin dealers, neighbors, and others. Because of Welch's notoriety, many individuals interviewed for this book shared information only because they were promised anonymity. In some instances, victims' names have been changed.

All details that research can verify are true. Where there were no records, we include details, descriptions, and statements based on the facts that are known. Because people tend to remember the details of events differently, wherever there were conflicting recollections, we did our best to keep the content and dialogue true to what actually happened. The sense, sounds, smells, pathos, emotions, dirt, and police work are authentic.

In the words of Detective King, "I know it's real. I lived it."

Jack Burch

Prologue

On the evening of November 10, 1980, near Washington, DC, Bernard Welch began his work in the darkened home of Special Agent Phillip A. Chaney, a ten-year veteran of the Federal Bureau of Investigation. While Agent Chaney and his family were out, Welch found the telephone box and cut the wires. With the phones and possible alarm system disabled, he broke into the home and removed the following: a pair of Smith & Wesson handcuffs with a leather holder, an FBI badge and holder, an ammo pouch, a necklace with a cross having a diamond in its center, and a charm bracelet. Two Smith & Wesson revolvers were also stolen. One was a .357 Magnum; the other was a Model 60 stainless steel five-shot revolver in .38 police special caliber. This handgun was almost new, with a dull, brushed finish and wooden grips. The two-inch barrel and compact cylinder made this an ideal concealed weapon or a backup gun for plainclothes detectives. Agent Chaney and family returned at 8:30 p.m. and discovered the burglary.

At 4:45 p.m., Omelan Antonovych and his wife Tatiana left their home at 5041 Loughboro Road NW to buy winter coats. They returned at 6:30 p.m. and discovered that their back door was open and had been jimmied in two places. When they tried to call the police, they discovered the phone lines had been cut. Looking through the house, they found that dresser drawers in the bedroom had been dumped on the floor, and many items were missing: money, jewelry, wristwatches, and sterling silver trays and bowls. Also taken was a very distinctive pair of cufflinks.

At 6:30 p.m., Monique Lass and her two children left their home at 5347 MacArthur Boulevard NW to meet her husband, Karl Lass. They all had dinner with some friends and returned at 1:00 a.m. on December 6. Upon arriving home, they saw that the kitchen door had been pried open and the house ransacked. Missing were a wallet, money, jewelry, and credit cards. The total loss was $7,300.

At 7:30 p.m., sixteen-year-old Monica Koval left her home at 5318 MacArthur Boulevard NW with some friends. When she returned at midnight she noticed one of the home's rear windows had been forced open. It was obvious to her that the house had been robbed. Scared and alone, she left, but eventually returned and tried to call the police. The line was dead, so Koval went next door and used the neighbor's phone to contact law enforcement officials. Missing jewelry totaled $5,275.

Early on the morning of December 5, Julio Heurtematte Jr. left his house at 5208 Lowell Street NW and headed to work. He and his wife Jeanne returned two days later on Sunday afternoon, December 7, and discovered that their belongings had been strewn around in "complete disarray." Jewelry, money, and sterling silver serving pieces were gone, as well as two small solid silver pigs.

At 8:15 p.m. a narrow beam of light moved through the house in the Palisades area of Washington, DC. It swept the living room slowly before stopping on a bright reflection. The shadowy form behind the light moved in for a closer look, plucking a silver dish from the table, his gloved hand quickly flipping it over to scan for a hallmark. Not up to standard, the serving piece was abruptly set down and the ghostly figure moved upstairs.

As the penlight sought better prizes in the darkness, a Chevrolet Monte Carlo eased into the driveway at 2806 Battery Place NW. The intruder wasn't aware of the homeowners' return because the driver had turned off the car lights before swinging onto the blacktop in front of his garage. Michael Halberstam was a beloved doctor; his professional life was caring for others. This compassion extended to even the smallest action in his personal life, such as shutting off the headlights so they wouldn't shine in his neighbors' windows as he made the sweeping turn through the house-lined cul-de-sac. He and his wife, Elliott, had left a cocktail party early, as Michael had wanted to catch a movie. Elliott insisted they head home to feed the dogs.

The intruder tensed when he heard the car doors slam outside the house, and he quickly doused the penlight. Wraithlike, he moved quickly to the window facing the street. In the backlighting of the streetlamps, he saw a tall figure exit the Monte Carlo and head quickly toward the house. Another figure moved around the garage toward the backyard.

"Shit!" the burglar hissed. The lone stairway ended right next to the front door. He was trapped.

The doctor came in the front door of their home as his wife strode across the backyard to feed Iris and Jake, their two dogs.

The burglar, an average-sized man in soft, dark clothing and a black knit cap, had been in difficult circumstances many times before on a job. The prospect of a confrontation did not frighten him. In his long criminal career, Bernard C. Welch had always come out on top.

Instinctively, Welch reached inside his quilted ski jacket and slipped the penlight into a chest pocket. His right hand felt for the weapon stashed in the inside pocket of his jacket and emerged grasping a snub nose revolver. Welch moved down the stairs toward the foyer with the compact .38-caliber five-shot leading the way. His left hand pulled up a dark blue bandana tied around his neck. The bandana covered his mustache and nose so only his eyes and the white skin around them showed. He was hoping he could slip past the homeowners and get out the front door undetected.

Turning the lights on, the lanky homeowner strode into the entryway and stopped to shuffle through the mail lying on the hall table. A creak from the staircase caught his attention as he stepped into the living room. He froze. Elliott came back up the steps to the sliding glass door and saw her husband standing motionless, alert. Michael caught her eye and whispered tensely, "Elliott, there's someone in the house!"

At that moment, Welch announced, "Lie down on the floor, or I'll blow your fucking head off!" The tone was cold and demanding. Halberstam stood transfixed, unmoving. A second later, Welch repeated the command, louder, "LIE DOWN NOW, OR I'LL BLOW YOUR FUCKING HEAD OFF!"

Halberstam knew enough to obey. He lowered himself to the carpet. His wife crouched where she was, making herself small beside the sliding door. She could see Michael laying face down on the floor and then caught sight of a shadowy figure heading out the front door. In the semi-darkness, her husband lay still for a moment, then rose and darted after the burglar.

When the doctor jumped him on the sidewalk outside, Welch's eyes widened in disbelief. In the past, everyone he pointed a gun at complied. But this big guy came right at him, grabbing his gun-hand and clutching for his throat. Welch instinctively jerked his head back, and the big man ended up grabbing a handful of bandana. With his left hand, the doctor gripped Welch's wrist so the gun pointed straight out, away from his body. The men grappled, arms extended, one seeking control of the weapon, and the other fighting hard for its release.

Halberstam was taller, heavier, and stronger than Welch. His lunge had pushed the smaller man back against the garage door. For the first time in years, Bernard Welch felt fear. If he failed now, he would spend the rest of his life in jail. Welch resorted to a tactic he learned in prison, quickly bending his legs and lowering his body to pull the big man off balance. As the big man lurched forward, Welch bent his head down further and butted the taller man's chest, causing the doctor to stumble backward with an explosion of breath. This offered just enough leverage to jerk the gun free.

But the doctor was still grasping the bandana and began shaking Welch back and forth, hitting the burglar's head on the wall behind him. Welch was desperate. He quickly swung the short-barreled gun toward the big man. The muzzle of the pistol flashed brightly with three shots, which pierced the doctor's coat but missed his body. Ignoring the shots, the doctor continued banging his attacker's head against the wall.

Welch was losing. If he could not end this fight soon, he would be on the ground, unconscious. His only chance was the weapon he still clung to. Just able to move the gun close to the doctor's chest, he pulled the trigger. The doctor bent away from the blast, but he did not let go of Welch's kerchief. Welch pulled the trigger again.

With the last shot, Halberstam let go and slumped back against the garage with an expression of shock on his face. Welch did not wait to see what Halberstam would do next. It was time to get the hell out of there.

Bernard Welch ran toward the darkness at the end of the cul-de-sac. He could hear a woman yelling somewhere behind him and knew the cops would be coming soon. Better get back to his car and leave quickly, but not too quickly. He cut through two yards and a driveway and scrambled under some bushes to break free onto Eskridge Terrace NW. He stopped, winded, his head hurting. He tucked the empty gun into the rear pocket of his jeans before continuing on.

Welch took a few deep breaths, got his bearings, and headed down Eskridge to Dana Place NW. At Dana, he took a left turn and continued walking rapidly toward his car.

"Don't attract attention. Just drive away, like a normal, law-abiding citizen," he reminded himself. No one would ever suspect a white guy in a new $40,000 Mercedes Benz.

Dr. Halberstam felt huge, hammer-like blows to his chest and left side. The two slugs had taken the wind out of him. His breathing was affected, and it was hard to get air. He tried to diagnose the damage by touch. He felt a warm wetness under his left arm, blood. Soon, the blood loss would send him into shock. His blood pressure would drop and the doctors would have to waste time stabilizing his vital functions before operating. Reflexively, he placed his right hand over the bullet holes. Direct pressure would help slow the bleeding and, if his lung was pierced, stop his diaphragm from sucking in outside air. From the location of the wounds, he surmised that, of his vital organs, only his left lung had been struck. He could not feel any exit wounds on his lower back. That was fortunate, as he knew they were usually bigger and messier than entry wounds.

The doctor, in the shock of the moment, did not realize that one bullet had, in fact, exited his upper back. Dr. Michael Halberstam, respected cardiac surgeon, father, husband, and son of the esteemed Halberstam family, was mortally wounded.

As he focused on controlling his breathing, Halberstam heard his wife's voice from the front door area. He looked toward the open doorway where his wife stood. He stepped away from the garage and moved toward her, bending slightly to the left, favoring his side.

"Elliott, help me."

His left side was hurting more now that he was walking. Muscle damage, he thought, and swelling was beginning. He could put up with that until he got to the Sibley ER, only a mile away. It was the hospital where he worked, and it had a great thoracic surgery team.

His wife came to him quickly. In the glow of the exterior house lights, he could see her face lined with fear and concern. As she approached, she touched his left arm, asking tensely, "Michael, what happened?"

"The guy that was in the house shot me," he said calmly, like he had just hit his thumb with a hammer. He had to act fast, be decisive, and stay detached. His life depended on it.

He began to feel a little light-headed. Feeling more wetness seeping down his left side, he pulled out his shirttail, wadded it against the wound, and applied pressure with his right hand. The sooner he got in the car and moving toward the hospital, the better. Sibley was only five minutes away. He could do that. It would be faster than calling an ambulance.

"Let's go," he said gruffly as he opened the car door and slid into the driver's seat.

He fished his keys out of his coat pocket and started the car left-handed. Elliott ran around to the passenger side and jumped in as the engine started. Halberstam shifted into reverse left-handed, winced, backed out, and sped toward the hospital.

They had gone about three blocks when he noticed a figure loping along the sidewalk. His headlight beam spotlighted his assailant. The dark ski jacket and black knit cap were the same, and there was a bandana around his neck.

"That's the guy!" Halberstam exclaimed, turning quickly. The '73 Chevy hopped the curb, and the doctor aimed his Monte Carlo straight at the career burglar whose luck had run out.

Welch heard the bang as the front wheels hit the curb and a wheel cover popped off. He turned, saw the headlights, and tried to outrun the crazy son of a bitch who was trying to kill him.

Halberstam did not hit Welch squarely. The left headlight of the big Monte Carlo hit Welch a little right of center on his backside, flinging him into the air, the impact instantly increasing his speed by thirty miles per hour. Due to the angle of contact, Welch flew several feet above the ground, spun to his left, hit the side of a house twenty feet away with a distinct thud, and rebounded. The Chevy passed beneath while he was airborne. Welch hit the lawn limply, rolled over once, and lay still.

The car continued on across a second lawn, turning toward the street. Halberstam looked grimly into his rearview mirror. In the red illumination of his taillights, he watched Welch hit the ground and remain motionless beside some bushes. He didn't think the guy was dead, but he would definitely need hospitalization.

Bright sparks flew out from the bottom of the car as its metal frame scraped across the sidewalk and over the curb. As the Chevy reentered the street, the doctor swerved the vehicle to straighten it out and stepped on the accelerator. He made a squealing right turn onto MacArthur Boulevard without stopping for the stop sign. The hospital was only half a mile away now.

The doctor's ears were buzzing, and he had to squint to focus on the road. The steering wheel was slippery with blood. He had forgotten to put his right hand back over his wound. The car's path wavered. He missed the right turn that would take them to the hospital's ER entrance. His wife was saying something. What? He tried to answer but could not. His eyes closed.

Dr. Halberstam never saw the tree he hit. He was unconscious when his wife exited the steaming ruin of their car and flagged down a passing motorist for help.

Detective Sergeant William Rollins of the Washington, DC, Metropolitan Police Department was on duty December 5, 1980. He was dispatched first to the Halberstam home but then proceeded directly to the vicinity of University Terrace and Dana Place. Jack Mulford, a private citizen, claimed he heard the gunshots and thought he knew where the shooter was. Mulford led police to 5026 Dana Place NW, where they discovered Bernard Welch sprawled out near a barrel planter.

Patrol Sergeant Robert Cermak joined Rollins as they approached Welch, who was groaning in agony. The officers did not see a gun in plain sight, so Detective Rollins, correctly assuming Welch was right-handed, stepped on Welch's right hand with his boot while Sergeant Cermak secured him with handcuffs. Because of his banged-up condition, Welch was transported by ambulance to Sibley Hospital for an examination under guard.

A hasty pat-down of Welch's pants pockets had produced four French coins and two sterling silver pigs. When the officers did a wider search of the area where Welch was lying, they also found a pair of brown cotton work gloves, a slotted screwdriver with a blue handle, a penlight, and a Smith & Wesson five-shot revolver with brown wooden grips. The handgun had five expended cartridges in the cylinders. Sergeant Cermak also made note of tire tracks in the front yard at 5026 Dana Place.

Detective Rollins rolled this one over in his mind—no wallet, no identification, and the shooting victim runs down the shooter. Odd case so far.

Back at Sibley, Dr. Halberstam was in the operating room. Elliott was in the waiting room, where a District of Columbia police officer found her.

"Mrs. Halberstam?" the officer started. "I'm Sergeant Simmons, Second District. You saw the guy your husband hit with his car? He did that because he was the guy who shot your husband, right?"

She nodded yes. The police officer explained that the suspect had been found on the front lawn of a home in her neighborhood. He had been arrested and transported to Sibley. He would be given a quick examination in the ambulance, after which he would be driven across town to a secure ward at DC General Hospital.

Sergeant Simmons informed Elliott that, for now, the suspect could only be charged with possession of an unregistered weapon. With only that charge, he could make bond and disappear before more serious charges could be placed. If Elliott could step outside to the ambulance and state whether this was the same person her husband had hit with his car, then the suspect could also be charged with burglary and attempted murder. The additional charges would keep him in jail until a court bond hearing on Monday.

Elliott agreed to look at the man.

The police officer led her outside to the ambulance bay. She followed him over to an idling DC Police Department ambulance. There was a younger police officer standing beside the white emergency vehicle.

"Open 'er up, Hank," the sergeant ordered with a wave of his hand. The young officer opened the side access door.

The sergeant walked to the door and pointed inside the lit compartment. "Recognize this guy, Mrs. Halberstam?"

Elliott stepped up to the opening. A man lay handcuffed to the metal frame of a gurney. He had rumpled dark hair and a mustache. He wore blue jeans and was covered with a blue ski jacket. A black stocking cap rested on the floor. Elliott looked hard at this man. His eyes were closed, and his middle-aged face was creased with pain. She recognized the blue coat, black cap, and the mustache. No question, he had been the one in the headlights when Michael yelled, "That's the guy!"

"Yes, that's him," she said. "That's the son of a bitch that did it. He's the one my husband said shot him and we hit with our car."

"Hank, make a note. At 2120 hours, the victim's wife positively identified this John Doe as being the shooter."

Elliott stepped back, and the sergeant closed the door. The ambulance pulled away with the young cop riding in back with the unidentified suspect.

The suspect was then transported to DC General Hospital where doctors noted a severe abrasion and a large bruise on his buttocks. Further inspection of his blue jeans and ski jacket revealed $142 in cash, two Susan B. Anthony dollar coins, a buffalo nickel, a pair of Fuller wire snips, and a key for a Mercedes Benz.

Detective Russell Drummond took the Mercedes key to the 5000 block of Dana Place NW and discovered a late model silver-gray Mercedes sedan with Virginia plates UGB-355 parked directly across the street from 5026 Dana Place. The key opened the car door. Drummond relocked the door and radioed a request that a police crane take the vehicle to police headquarters for impounding. The subsequent search of the Mercedes yielded 169 stolen items that had been taken from area homes that had been burglarized earlier in the evening of December 5.

Dr. Halberstam never learned that his self-diagnosis was correct, but incomplete. The bullets had missed his vital organs, except for the one that entered his left lung. That bullet hit a rib and angled upward, nicking the aorta before exiting his back. Each time his heart pumped, more blood surged out of the damaged artery and into his chest cavity. He died on the operating table of internal bleeding before the surgeons at Sibley Hospital could repair the damage.

Dr. Michael Halberstam, a modest and compassionate man, a civic leader, and one of the finest heart surgeons in Washington, DC, would never know the vital role he played in capturing the most prolific and elusive burglar in American history.

On April 28, 1940, Genevieve Welch gave birth to a baby boy in Rochester, New York. She and her husband, Bernard, named their first child Bernard C. Welch Jr. and called him Bernie. Bernie entered the world just eighteen months before his father left to serve in the US Army when the United States entered World War II. When Bernard Welch Sr. arrived back home in upstate New York after the end of World War II, he immediately began looking for work and a home for his young family. Fortunately, the United States had entered a postwar period of significant economic and manufacturing growth, and a grateful nation created many services and benefits to welcome home its victorious military veterans. Bernard Sr. quickly landed a job on the film processing line of the Eastman Kodak Company.

In 1946, Genevieve bore a second child, Marilyn. The Welch family also moved into the Rochester-area veterans housing project. Part of the federal government's plan to offer affordable housing for returning GIs, the housing projects only cost forty-two dollars per month, but had very little to offer beyond functionality. The cheap, multiple-family buildings were constructed on concrete slabs and looked like two-story army barracks, housing ten units under a single roof. All of the buildings, lined up like the rank and file of a military formation, were cinder block construction with a skim coat of cement on the rough surface, which was then whitewashed, making for a spartan, though functional structure. The interior walls, ceiling, and appliances were also white, necessitated by the meager lighting. Brown linoleum flooring covered the bare concrete slab throughout the home. Every unit was eight hundred square feet with two bedrooms and one bathroom. Although the Welches had a completely adequate house, they hardly had a home.

Bernard Welch Sr. had his steady job at the Kodak processing plant, but he didn't sign up for any of the educational opportunities that the GI Bill afforded. Instead of trying to improve his family's lot, Welch spent his time drinking and gambling. More often than not, some portion of his paycheck was lost. When he did stay home, Welch liked to hit the bottle. His drunken tirades allowed him to vent his anger at his wife, his bosses, the cops, politicians, the city of Rochester—any burr that was under his saddle at the moment. His weekend drinking bouts also allowed him temporary escape from the bizarre family life his wife was creating.

Genevieve Welch was an eccentric woman who, like her husband, found her own way to escape the dismal realities of everyday life. She did not care how others viewed her or how her actions affected them. She entertained her kids with recitations of fairy tales mixed with her own fanciful myths. Her stories were detailed and populated with characters whose names she conjured out of thin air. Her tales and descriptions were so vivid that they took on a life of their own. Genevieve also corresponded with a long list of pen pals on a regular basis. They all lived in exotic locations, far from her dreary corner of the world. Genevieve's pen pals were the special people to whom she sent long, chatty letters. She spoke affectionately of her pen pals to Bernie and Marilyn, the neighbors, the folks at the grocery store—anyone who would listen. Genevieve preferred living in her private world of fanciful stories and foreign pen pals. As time went on, she ensconced herself more deeply in this fantasy world.

Genevieve's withdrawal, coupled with Welch's absences and beer-fueled benders when he was home, meant there was little parental supervision for Bernie and Marilyn. They were left to their own devices to look out for themselves.

There were no playgrounds or swings in the housing project. Bernie and Marilyn played on the worn grass and the dirt between the units. Swimming pools were unheard of. The only water was an occasional mud puddle or the rivulets created by a downpour. The kids found ways to entertain themselves with only a ball or a stick and their imaginations. They played cops and robbers and cowboys and Indians. These fantasies gave Bernie and Marilyn a welcome escape from their dreary, disappointing reality of secondhand clothes, a beat-up bike, and dolls with missing parts. Bernie and his little sister grew very close during these early years. With their eccentric mother and drunk father, it felt like it was them against the world.

Spencerport, New York
1951 to 1958

In 1951, the family moved out of the veterans housing project and into a shabby, crumbling house in Spencerport, New York. Half the linoleum was ripped off the kitchen floor and most of the paint had peeled from the exterior siding. The Welches had neither running water nor flush toilets. There was a well with a hand pump at the kitchen sink and an outhouse in the backyard. Now the family had more room, but the chaos and the clutter in their home never seemed to disappear.

In Spencerport, Bernie's father eventually earned a reputation for being a drunk and a gambler. Although with limited funds, he was just an amateur at both.

Bernie's mother grew more and more reclusive, constantly corresponding with her mysterious pen pals and eventually filling their home with over two dozen cats. Cats were everywhere, adding to the already noxious odors in the house. Bernie would always remember his mother's selfless devotion to her cats instead of her children.

Domestic life and housekeeping were about as primitive as it could get. One of Bernie's responsibilities was to walk to the local market and haul two big buckets of tap water back to the house. They used this for cooking and drinking water. The well water that came into the kitchen was loaded with iron and smelled of rotten eggs.

Bernie also devised other ways to provide for his family, though these ways weren't as legitimate as visiting the local market for water. He supplied the household milk. Bernie would go to a nearby farmer's field, and making sure he was out of sight, he milked the nearest cow by hand. In another effort to keep their family fed, he and Marilyn would travel to local potato fields at night. They would dig up potatoes by moonlight and flashlight, stealing them for the household meals.

While Bernie formed a close bond with his sister, he had an uncomfortable relationship with his father. His dad's liquor-fueled escapes from reality irritated Bernie. He learned that people lubricated with alcohol said things they would regret later. This distaste for drinking and drunks stayed with him throughout his life.

Even though their relationship was strained, Bernie managed to pick up a few useful skills from his father. Because the family couldn't afford to hire anyone for repairs around the house, young Bernie was required to help his dad with general repair projects. Commercial film processing required extensive mixing of chemicals, so Welch's film processing job at Eastman Kodak familiarized him with pipes and plumbing. At work, Welch Sr. was often called upon to perform minor plumbing repairs like fixing a leaking valve. He noticed and was impressed by the respect bestowed upon the full-time plumbers working at the Kodak facility. Bernie's dad repeatedly told him that plumbing was a skill with which a man could make a comfortable living.

In fact, Bernie got a lot of satisfaction from working on fix-it projects with his dad. They got along well when they had a project to work on and little conversation was required. Bernie liked small, short-term projects and the feeling of satisfaction in seeing them completed. He was a quick study and a keen observer with a knack for looking at a problem and quickly working out the solution. His almost photographic memory enabled him to remember nearly everything he was shown.

Although Bernie was learning a reputable trade and enjoying it, household projects didn't pay. By the time he was ten years old, Bernard Welch Jr. was seized by a desire to have better, nicer things. He wanted toys that weren't broken, better clothes, and most importantly, money to spend freely. He started shoplifting to get the things he wanted.

He started small. He loved candy, but his family could never afford it. At the end of the school day, he'd visit the local drug store and practice stealing candy. Before long, Bernie adeptly calculated when the store staff was watching and when they weren't. He quickly became proficient at his new game.

But Bernie's new habit had a downside. When a family doesn't have much money, one of the last problems to be taken care of is tooth decay. Most government subsidy programs in the 1950s would supplement food and general health care requirements, but as far as dental care was concerned, the poor were on their own. Bernie's penchant for shoplifting candy meant he developed cavities but received little or no dental care. His teeth began the long, slow process of rotting.

Although Bernie was an astute observer and a quick study in plumbing and shoplifting, he didn't fare too well in school. He found concentrating on the subjects unbearably boring, and as a result, his grades were lousy. Being more of a loner than a joiner, he never got involved with school activities. Every school day was a challenge for Bernie, trying to outwit teachers, cops, shop owners, truant officers, and the kids at school.

Instead of studying for school, Bernie began honing his outdoor skills. He spent much of his time camping and hunting, testing his navigational skills through the woods, and becoming a crack shot with his dad's old .22 rifle. He also tried his hand at fur trapping, skinning the skunks, muskrats, and foxes he caught and selling their pelts.

At age sixteen, Bernie had only made it to ninth grade. One day, he felt he was wrongly accused of talking in study hall. When this was combined with his other school rule infractions, the penalty would be daily afterschool detention until the end of the grading period. This was too much for Bernie. He dropped out of school.

To fill his time now, Bernie picked up odd jobs around the area during the day. At night, he ran his trap lines. Bernie earned a reputation as being one of the best trappers in the county, but he also thought nothing of killing game out of season. Nobody talked much about the poaching until he was caught by a deputy sheriff with an illegal deer carcass. In his first official run-in with the law, he was put on notice by the sheriff's office that he was being watched.

Knowing that the police were on to him, Bernie headed out of town. At only seventeen years old, he spent the winter of 1957 in the foothills of the mountains in Adirondack Park, about 150 miles east of the family home in Spencerport. He wintered over in a tent and spent his time trapping beaver, mink, and otter. There was suspicion that he also stole from other people's trap lines and broke into summer cabins, but he was never brought up on charges.

By the spring of 1958, Bernie had sold enough pelts to buy a new red Ford Thunderbird convertible. Now he had unlimited mobility.

Welch decided to use the basic skills he learned from his father and went to work at a local plumbing shop. This legitimate job allowed him to improve his plumbing skills to the degree that he was making a living at it by his early twenties, but it also allowed him to hone his preferred craft of burglary. The plumbing job bought him legitimate entrance into the homes of middle- and upper-class neighborhoods. What better way to ascertain the information needed to successfully pull off a burglary?

Welch knew he could not appear too interested in what went on in a residence, as this might cause suspicion later. He learned not to stare directly at what interested him most. He never appeared to listen to conversations that he wasn't part of. Look and listen, but do not appear to be looking or listening. Take in everything, but seem disinterested. Be nondescript and fade into the wallpaper, but be able to chat glibly on most any subject without getting into specifics. It was an added bonus if the homeowner wanted to chat with him. At the plumber's hourly rate, he'd be happy to oblige. Be charming, be nice, and act like a game show host with a pipe wrench.

Sometimes a major plumbing job could take hours or days to complete, and Welch used that time to soak up all the pertinent details about the household. As he was doing his repair job, he could map the location of a house's mechanical areas, which would later be his access point to shut down power, phones, and alarm systems. He could scout the location of loot, learn schedules, establish escape routes, investigate brush cover around the home, and calculate the distance from the street and the neighbors. In the burglary business, neighbors were to be avoided as much as the occupants of the targeted home. Neighbors could call the cops and be potential witnesses.

Building on the shoplifting experience of his youth, Welch was developing an intuitive sense for reading places and situations as targets of opportunity. He was exceptionally observant, with an uncanny ability to read people. Though he abhorred his father's poker habit, he learned a lot from his father's card playing. Once Welch became an accomplished card player, he prided himself on being able to use language, facial expressions, tics, and repetitive motions to sniff out the opponent's hand without actually seeing it. Welch became the guy who was the best at predicting what someone would do next, not only in a card game, but in any situation.

Welch continued working as a plumber and had enough experience by the early sixties that his dad was able to get him work at Eastman Kodak as a steamfitters apprentice and plumber. The Kodak job wasn't full-time, and Welch picked up some part-time jobs on occasion. It was at one of these part-time jobs, cutting down non-producing trees in an apple orchard, where he learned about Anne Marie Hulbert through a friend. He called her up that very night and asked her out on a date. She accepted, and she eventually married Welch in 1963.

Welch did not hide his criminal activities from Anne Marie. In fact, he figured she would be the perfect partner because, as his wife, Welch thought she couldn't be forced to testify against him in a court of law. And Anne Marie, as shocked as she was, found herself swayed by Welch's easy charm and agreed to go with him on his nightly outings. She would drop him off near the house he had targeted for robbery. Then, she would kill some time at the local laundromat, while Welch turned the house inside out looking for valuables. After the allotted time, Anne Marie would drive to their designated meeting spot and pick him up. Even after their first daughter was born, Anne Marie kept on as wheelman.

With a new partner and several years' experience behind him, Welch developed criteria to discern the best items to steal for maximum profit. He was a planner. He knew he could only make one trip back to the rendezvous, which was usually about three blocks away, and he knew exactly how much he could carry inconspicuously.

These factors presented him with an intriguing puzzle to solve. How could he get the most stuff in the least amount of time and sell it at the highest price with the smallest chance of getting caught?

Using these criteria, he eliminated the usual pawnshop staples—TVs, stereos, furniture, and power tools—from his shopping list. Items with serial numbers or an unusual design were nixed. Items had to have a high resale value compared to size, and they should be mundane enough that they wouldn't stick in someone's mind if they were listed on a stolen goods sheet circulated by the police. He didn't want to attract unwanted attention with easily identified rare items.

Instead, Welch aimed for small scores—jewelry, watches, silver, gold, handguns, and smaller antiques. These items could fetch high prices, and they could be found in most homes without a great deal of searching. Another appealing factor was that these items were easy to unload. And Welch was active enough now that he had to find a way to cash out on the merchandise he was collecting.

Welch didn't yet have a plan in place to dispose of the stolen goods quickly and at a good return. He wouldn't deal with fences. They only gave about 10 to 20 percent of the value of the goods. And if the fencing operation got busted, the trail of the stolen property could lead right back to his doorstep. For the time being, he and Anne Marie sold items at flea markets, to antique dealers, and even out of their own house.

While Welch was getting more calculating in his approach to both the theft and disposal of the merchandise, he realized he was getting a little too careless with the selection of his victims. He was relying too much on the part-time plumbing business to generate leads, which meant his targets were too close to home. Welch took the next logical step: he took his burglary business on the road.

On weekends, he traveled far and stayed at a cheap motel, cased the wealthy neighborhoods, and hit a number of homes in the area. He then loaded up a rental trailer with the stolen goods for the trip back to a storage locker he had at home in Naples.

Welch also began disposing of his stolen goods farther away from home. In 1964, he attended a flea market in Penn Yan, New York, a resort village on the north end of one of the Finger Lakes. After taking a look at the impressive merchandise for sale there, Welch decided he had to have some of it for himself. He burglarized the flea market. This brief lack of self-control taught Welch a tough lesson. Not long after returning from Penn Yan, the police paid him a visit and questioned him about this theft. He denied everything, but the cops weren't satisfied. They wanted Welch to submit to a lie detector test, but he politely declined. He bid the police farewell from the porch, turned to Anne Marie, and told her to start packing. They were leaving that night.

Welch drove the convertible into town and came back with a U-Haul trailer on a bumper hitch. He and Anne Marie grabbed the stolen merchandise and all the things they would need to set up a new household. After driving half the night, they ended up in Berkeley Springs, West Virginia, a mineral springs tourist town known for having the first spa in the United States.

The Welch family found it easy to settle into life in the small West Virginia town. Their family was growing, with Anne Marie giving birth to another daughter. Welch also indulged his entrepreneurial spirit and found a prime location for an antique store. Owning an antique store would give him his best outlet yet for disposing of his stolen goods. The startup merchandise stocking the shelves was all stolen property from New York.

Welch personally ran the shop and tried to be friendly with the folks in town. He wanted the shop to be successful so he could move his stolen merchandise quickly. And the modest antique shop did do well, benefiting from very reasonable prices.

But the reasonable prices drew suspicion from local law enforcement. Berkeley Springs Chief of Police Lloyd Williams thought perhaps the prices were a little too reasonable. He had also seen Welch restocking merchandise in the middle of the night from his red convertible.

One day, a local resident showed up at the police station and complained that she spotted some of her sterling silver serving set for sale in Welch's antique shop. It had been stolen from her house the previous week. The chief of police knew the break-ins and theft in his jurisdiction had increased since that antique store had opened up in town. The burglaries always involved jewelry, sterling silver, and other small, valuable items. Silver plate, costume jewelry, and other cheap items were left behind.

Chief Williams asked the West Virginia state police to do a background check on the newly settled Bernard C. Welch Jr. and family. The report came back stating that Welch was wanted in New York for burglaries committed in and around Rochester and for passing bad checks.

Welch was picked up in Berkeley Springs and turned over to the New York state police in early January 1966. He was charged with burglary and grand larceny on the New York offenses. He was sentenced to five years in prison and began his sentence in April 1966 at Auburn Correctional Facility in Auburn, New York. His wife, Anne Marie, was given five years probation as an accomplice to burglary.

Prison turned out to be a very positive experience for Welch, both physically and mentally. The New York penal system took care of Welch's deteriorating dental problems, extracting all of his teeth and fitting him with a complete set of upper and lower dentures. The prison sentence also gave him ample time to further his meager education. Welch used some of his time in jail to complete his GED, but more importantly, he studied the art of burglary as though it were an academic subject.

Welch figured the key to success in a burglary operation was the proper handling and selling of precious metals. His own recent experience showed that sterling serving sets and other silver or gold items could fetch a high price, but they could often be easily identified and traced because of maker's marks, owner's initials, or distinctive styling. The reason he was in jail was because a victim was able to identify her silver tea set in his antique shop. Jewelry could also pay big but was easily identifiable. Sterling jewelry pieces could almost always be sold for their metal content, as they seldom fetched more than the value of the silver anyway. Collectible coins, excepting the very rarest, were virtually untraceable but always worth more than their metal content or face value. They could be sold to collectors almost without question.

Welch spent most of his free time poring over every book and magazine the prison had about antiques and collectibles, jewelry, gems, coin collections, and precious metals. He wanted to have in his head the value and marketability of any object he might come across in a dark house. The subscription service of the prison library allowed Welch to check out the *Wall Street Journal* and other publications on a daily basis. These newspapers were useful for checking spot prices of precious metals, as well as introducing him to the investment opportunities that were available for those with the money. Welch knew that having this financial knowledge, and knowing how to use it, was the mark of a savvy and sophisticated investor. He saw himself as that kind of man and needed to be able to discuss these matters intelligently with the well-heeled crowd he so desperately wanted to be a part of.

In December 1967, after serving only a year and a half of his sentence, Welch was paroled and forced to return to West Virginia to face trial for the Berkeley Springs burglaries. Once again reunited with Anne Marie and his daughters, he played the out-of-work-father card, poured on all the charm he could muster, and received a suspended sentence with three years' probation.

Welch returned to New York, and through his father's connections, he was again able to find work as a steamfitter at the Eastman Kodak plant in Rochester. This job suited him, and it was the kind of work that he had earlier aspired to, but he just couldn't keep his mind off the easy money that burglary offered. His felonious part-time hobby started to creep back into his life again, and with the newly acquired knowledge of precious metals and collectibles he had gained in prison, he watched his burglary profits shoot up from hundreds of dollars per month to thousands.

Welch was a dreamer. He had always wanted to be able to spend large amounts of money without worries, have great toys, and be a big tipper. His deprived childhood in the post-war veterans projects left him with a desire to go first-class and be treated like a "somebody." With a few refinements in the acquisition and disposal of the goods, Welch knew he could easily increase his profits to tens of thousands of dollars per month. Then it would be nothing but the best for him.

It was time to think big. The first thing he needed was storage space and privacy, so Welch paid cash for a nice little house on Brick Schoolhouse Road in Hamlin, New York. Next he had to devise a complete set of rules of engagement for the higher-end burglary he was now pursuing. He needed to limit the exposure he had with the theft and possession of the stolen merchandise. Since he had been caught because of property being identified, he needed to unload all the merchandise far away from where it was stolen. Targeted homes had to be at least an hour's drive away. Merchandise should be disposed of at least two or three counties away. Transactions at this distance were safer. And if he sold directly to dealers at flea markets, he could get 33 to 75 percent of the retail value instead of the paltry amount fences offered. Flea markets had the added bonuses of no receipts or records of the sales and all transactions were in cash. But the best place to unload the merchandise was through newspaper classifieds. As long as he remembered to avoid the hometown papers of where the items were procured, Welch could get nearly full market value for the goods. And to cap off his new commitment to his life of crime, Welch established a second identity, Bernard Miles. This alias, complete with forged ID cards, was the name he used with flea market managers, antique dealers, motel registers, and storage space rentals.

Welch's decision to place distance between his home, his burglaries, and his subsequent sales was a wise one. In addition to ensuring that owners would almost never run into their stolen items, the police would also be stymied in this pre-Internet era. At the time, the various police jurisdictions rarely communicated or cooperated with each other. As long as Welch resided a few counties away from where he was practicing his trade and sold the stolen goods even further away, he could remain undetected.

With these newly considered plans, Welch began breaking and entering again with a vengeance. He would stay in a motel for a few days and pull off a slew of burglaries before driving back home. He would sort the loot and take most of it to rented storage facilities to build up a good supply of stolen merchandise.

The next step in Welch's criminal enterprise was for him to start posing as the rightful owner of the property and dispose of it through legitimate channels. After a suitable length of time, allowing for the hot goods to cool down a bit, he would hitch up a rented U-Haul trailer and pick up the wares. He'd head east, west, or south to area flea markets. To the north was Canada with its border inspections. He dared not go there. Eventually he bought his own trailer and started hauling his stolen merchandise in broad daylight, as he thought it attracted less attention. His instincts were correct, and he never got stopped by the police while transporting the goods.

In the continuing effort to get the most profit out of the items he stole, Welch started taking apart some of the precious metal objects to sell to refiners as raw gold or silver. This was an easy task for someone with a plumbing background. The bases of sterling candlestick holders were plaster, covered with silver leaf. In a set of sterling silverware, the blades of the table knives were made of stainless steel for strength, and the handles were hollow; the rest of the tableware is solid silver. Welch broke the steel and plaster away from the silver by force with a hammer, pliers, and vise. After melting it down, it was off to the refiner.

Although Welch's criminal life was booming, his personal life didn't fare so well. Anne Marie was not as accommodating this go-round. Her first brush with the law, resulting in a suspended sentence and the threat of jail time over her head, was enough for her. The stolen merchandise Welch accumulated, along with the buyers coming to the house to look at the goods listed in the classifieds, spooked her. She felt they were being watched by local law enforcement. Welch accused her of imagining things. Unable to deal with it any longer, she took their two girls and moved out. Welch would say later that Anne Marie was happy to help him spend all the money they took in with his burglary, but she didn't like the downside of the endeavor. Her moving out quickly evolved into a formal separation. It couldn't have been timed better.

Near the end of 1970, Welch burglarized the home of a gun collector southwest of Rochester and took the stolen guns and other antiques down to Florida. On this trip, he stayed away from the flea markets and sold mainly to dealers. A few of the stolen guns ended up in a pawnshop in St. Petersburg, Florida. There, they attracted the attention of a local police officer walking his beat. He copied down the serial numbers of the rifles and checked them against the National Crime Information Center, a new national FBI database of stolen goods. The serial numbers of stolen items, especially guns, were logged on to a mainframe computer in Washington, DC, then made available for local law enforcement agencies around the country. The rifles were listed as stolen from Allegany County, New York, and the pawnshop owner identified Bernard C. Welch as the seller. This would be Welch's first introduction to computerized crime fighting.

In January 1971, New York state police paid a visit to the plumber's home in Hamlin, New York. They found $120,000 worth of stolen goods; the retail value of the loot recovered from Welch's storage lockers totaled $500,000. Caught once again, Bernard C. Welch was convicted in connection with 52 burglaries in the upstate New York area. Police officials thought the take was from nearly a hundred break-ins and burglaries. Untold thousands of dollars worth of stolen property had already found its way into the hands of the general public, never to be recovered. The merchandise hidden and discovered in the Welch household and storage lockers probably would have disappeared within weeks, what with the constant stream of the disposal and liquidation operation.

It was hard to miss the show in Hamlin. When the New York State Police arrested Welch, they needed a semi to load up the pile of riches that he had acquired.

Anne Marie did well in choosing to steer clear of Welch. In June 1971, she filed for divorce in civil court, and the divorce was granted on September 9. Welch didn't get much sympathy in the criminal court system either. This time there was no leniency, no suspended sentence. Welch had gone too far, too many times. They had him for more than one hundred burglaries committed in more than twenty-five towns spanning six New York counties. All of these burglaries were committed in fewer than nine months.

Welch pleaded guilty to the Allegany County burglaries and, in early 1971, was sentenced to ten years at the state correctional facility in Attica, New York. Bernard C. Welch Jr., already well schooled in the art of burglary, had just graduated to the college of criminal knowledge.

The Attica Correctional Facility sits on fifty-five acres of land on the out-skirts of Attica, New York. Built in 1930, this maximum-security penitentiary houses up to 2,500 inmates. In 1971, approximately one third of the inmates had been convicted of murder, rape, or other violent crimes. Another third were in for grand larceny or drug dealing. Bernard Welch fit into the last third of the inmate population—those incarcerated for robbery and burglary.

When Welch arrived at Attica in early 1971, the prison was a powder keg waiting for a match. Welch found himself among hardened criminals with life sentences; violent antiwar, antiestablishment youth with intimate knowledge of urban guerilla warfare, anarchist tactics, and bomb-building techniques; and charismatic college-educated leaders with a revolutionary bent. This volatile brew of inmates posed a real problem for correctional employees.

Once Welch, now 31 years old, was in Attica long enough to get indoctri-nated, inoculated, and acclimated, he realized he wasn't in the casual atmos-phere of New York State's "country club" correctional facilities. The tension level and violence was escalating throughout the prison system. Assaults against prison guards were on the increase. Tensions between rival gangs ratcheted up, even as talk of prisoners organizing increased. Welch, always the lone wolf, tried to keep a low profile, but prison life could be hard on a loner.

One of the newer gangs Welch came across was the skinheads known as the Aryan Brotherhood. As the new group on the prison block, they had to establish their credibility with the other gangs. To do this, the Aryan Brother-hood became the most violent gang around, and they were especially good at retaliation murder. To mess with the Aryan Brotherhood was to court a violent death. Welch shared their racist leanings, but ever the loner, he wasn't much into joining this fraternal organization. On the other hand, he knew that without an affiliation, he was an easy target for the other gangs.

Attica was too intense to survive his sentence safely as a loner, so he paid the Aryan Brotherhood for protection. During his criminal career, Welch saw a lot of money run through his hands. He never wanted a bank account in his name, or even in one of his aliases, because they were too easy to trace. Whenever possible, he tried to divert some of his money to his one trusted confidant—his sister, Marilyn—for safekeeping. Welch thought the authorities would never look as closely at his sister as they would his wife, so that's where he stashed his money for a rainy day.

Welch couldn't have known how important that protection would one day be. On Thursday, September 9, 1971, a few hundred radical prisoners took over the Attica correctional facility and seized forty-nine guards and civilian employees. What developed over the next four days was the most violent and bloody prison uprising in the history of the United States. After the New York state police took control of the prison on Monday, September 13, forty-three inmates and guards had been killed.

The riot started badly with the killing of a prison guard in the first moments. The guard's death meant that complete amnesty for the uprising, as demanded by the prisoners, would never be on the negotiating table. The stakes and the tension on both sides became extremely high, and the unreasonable demands of the implacable inmate leaders led to the final bloodbath. The vast majority of inmates, including Welch, did not actively participate in the riot.

When things settled down inside Attica and the ones responsible for the riot were sorted out, there was a reshuffling of many of the prisoners to other facilities. In 1974, Welch was transferred to Adirondack Correctional Treatment and Evaluation Center in Dannemora, New York. He not only survived his stint in Attica unscathed, but the radical movement's antiestablishment concepts gave him a way to justify his hatred of the upper class, the corporate world, and their wealth. Welch now considered himself one of the have-nots and would feel no guilt stealing from the haves.

The move to Dannemora was a pleasant change from the battlefield of Attica's prison yard. The relatively bucolic setting at Dannemora took some of the sting out of a long incarceration, but this prison was meant for persistent offenders. It was now apparent to authorities that Bernard Welch fit this category.

Welch continued to use his prison time wisely, researching everything available in the library to polish up his act for when he was back on the street. He had a wealth of new information on the economy and changes in laws.

Always the student of precious metals, Welch read that back in 1967, the South African government started minting one troy ounce gold coins called Krugerrands. South Africa was the world's largest supplier of gold, and the coins were sold at a low, five percent premium over the market price of $35 per ounce. Krugerrands became popular worldwide as an investment, but possession of investment gold, sold by the ounce, was still banned in the United States by the Gold Confiscation Act of 1933.

President Gerald Ford rescinded the Gold Confiscation Act on August 14, 1974. Private citizens were once again allowed to own investment gold bullion in the form of bars and ingots. Bernard Welch, keen observer that he was, knew that the wealthy people he preyed upon would now have a new prize for him to seek out. And here he was, stuck in prison with at least another year to serve before any possible release. He was frustrated.

He had to prepare himself for his next one-man crime spree, and he had to formulate a plan of escape. He first thought to assume the mantle of model prisoner and earn furlough privileges, but never come back. If that failed, he might behave himself long enough get liberal privileges as a trustee and disappear when the timing was right. There had never been a successful escape from Dannemora.

Even while Welch was planning his escape, he was working on ways to improve his chances of staying a free man. Welch finally figured out that small town and rural America were dangerous to his chosen profession. He had to move near a large urban area where he could be anonymous and unwatched. Welch felt he needed to fit in better with the upper middle class. He postulated that the police seldom stopped rich people. Therefore, it was better to act well-to-do and live in a good area rather than live in a poor one frequented by police. He read voraciously and tried to perfect his speaking and presentation skills.

To that end, he started hanging out with Paul David Marturano, a Dannemora inmate who had already served two years of a first-degree manslaughter charge. Marturano had been convicted of killing his girlfriend, whom

Marturano claimed had accidentally drowned in his bathtub.

Marturano, from Oswego, New York, was of Italian and Native American descent. To Welch's benefit, he was educated and well spoken. Welch felt comfortable practicing his conversational skills with him. Marturano was never bashful about tutoring him, letting him know when he sounded like a con artist.

Welch was up for a parole review hearing in 1975, but Marturano's release was a much more distant ship on the horizon. He had more than a decade left to serve. When Welch told Marturano about wanting to escape, he found a willing partner.

They began lifting weights to build up their bodies as they developed a strategy. It took three months. Their plan was straightforward. On September 2, 1974, during an evening intramural softball game, they stayed just out of sight of two guards that were stationed at the top of a three-flight stairway that led up to the softball field. There was a third guard there taking passes, but he moved in and out of the doorway, occasionally blocking his own line of sight. At the right moment, Welch and Marturano went down the stairs and jumped up onto an eighteen-foot-high chain-link fence to the left of the stairs. Hidden from the guards, they climbed over and made their escape.

Once they were in the clear and away from the prison grounds, Welch's old camping and orienteering skills suited them well. Dannemora is in the northeast corner of Adirondack Park, part of the New York State Park System. The park has six million acres, roughly the size of the entire state of Vermont. It covers such a large and diverse area, containing so many roads, towns, and cities that there are no gates and no admission charge. Because of the three years he spent trapping there as a teenager, Welch was familiar with this park and its terrain, and Marturano grew up fifty miles west of the park. The two men moved eastward, slowly on foot, successfully keeping their trail untraceable. The escaped felons' goal was to get to Interstate 87, which parallels Lake Champlain, and find a car to transport them south. Beyond that, they had no plans.

After the second day of slogging in streams and hiding in the forest, the two escapees agreed they had had enough of traveling on foot. They came upon an empty house near Plattsburgh, about twelve miles from the prison. A 1970 Pontiac Tempest was parked outside. The two fugitives broke into the home and ransacked it. Welch searched madly for the keys to the car, while Marturano rounded up some blankets and pillows and bagged a bunch of food. Marturano had finished, but Welch was still looking for the keys.

"He found them at last," Marturano recalled, "and that's when we got the first start with money. It was a twenty dollar bill." Welch found the cash while rifling for the keys. They piled into the Tempest and made their way southwest, through the gigantic state park.

The edge of the park boundary was still in the rearview mirror as the men neared Utica, New York, a hundred and fifty miles from the prison. Just ahead, the New York state police had set up a roadblock for the escapees. Welch and Marturano decided to drive around it, bypassing the state patrol cars by using the shoulder of the road. As they zipped past the roadblock, they purposely crashed the car in the woods. They rushed to get out of the car and took off on foot before the state police could scramble after them. Marturano said later they just couldn't see attempting a high-speed chase and evading the state police while driving the underpowered six-cylinder Tempest. They had enough of a lead and the element of surprise to disappear into the woods again.

Making their way toward Utica on foot, the two temporarily split up, with Welch heading into the city to steal another car. This time it was a tan 1967 V-8 Chevrolet Malibu. Welch also shoplifted some merchandise to sell for cash. Marturano killed time outside of town until the tan Chevy rolled into sight. From Utica, New York, they proceeded on into Pennsylvania. There, Welch burgled another residence, where he obtained a compact .380 caliber automatic pistol and other firearms, some of them antique. Marturano described the scene, which would be repeated many times in the future.

"I don't know the name of the town, all I know is that it was in the country somewhere and he didn't know exactly where he was going when he went there. I think we were near Harrisburg [Pennsylvania] and later we got on the turnpike to 81. We just happened to drive by and happened to see a neighborhood that he liked and we stopped. The house was on the corner of a main street. There was a little college in that town, because there were college hangouts, and you could see the room and board signs and college students.... But I never saw the house he hit; I was at the end of the road. I took the car down in the town and waited for him to come back. Then he came down about an hour later, and we took the car back to the house and picked up the stuff, but it wasn't at the house he hit. He had the guns and stuff on the corner lot, and there was another house set back forty or fifty yards from the road, but he said that wasn't the house he had hit. So, I don't know which one of the houses he robbed."

As the duo headed south towards Virginia on Highway 81, Marturano told Welch he knew a guy in Charlottesville, Virginia, by the name of Hank Snow, who owed him a favor. Once they arrived in Charlottesville, it took Marturano most of the day to find Snow, as he had no phone. Marturano finally got an address and went to talk to Snow. Marturano told Snow that he had just escaped from prison with another con who was using the name of Jerry Lloyd. Jerry Lloyd was, in reality, a grade school classmate of Marturano's from Oswego, New York, with no police record.

After the meeting with Hank Snow, Marturano and Welch checked into a motel, got cleaned up, and went to a neighborhood bar to meet Snow and his brother. Marturano later told police, "I asked if I could use his driver's license, and Hank said I could use it for whatever means I needed it, but it wouldn't do me any good because it had his picture on it, which when I saw it, it did. So he gave me his Social Security number, present age, date of birth, address, and the names of a couple of his relatives in case somebody should ask. He was under the impression that it was for me, but I didn't have the nerve to go in (the Virginia Motor Vehicle Department) to get it. Bernard Welch went in there, and he did it. He got the license under the pretense of having lost it." Now Welch had a valid Virginia driver's license.

Welch liked to conduct a lot of his business through the want ads in the newspapers. The next day he found an ad in the Charlottesville paper stating, "I buy and sell antiques." Welch and Marturano went to the gentleman's log cabin home, and Welch sold the guy two antique firearms from the Pennsylvania burglary. This antique buyer was a retired bank executive, according to Marturano, and Welch told him the guns were his, he had just gotten out of the service, and that his name was Myron Snow. They got $700 for the guns.

Welch and Marturano spent two more days in Charlottesville then packed up and headed for the much bigger metropolitan area of Richmond, Virginia. They moved into the Chester Maisonette Apartments on Jefferson Davis Highway, and Marturano signed the lease using the name Angelo Santini.

Once Marturano and Welch were settled in their Richmond apartment, Welch began to work in earnest to perfect his chosen craft of burglary. He would go out three or four nights a week and pull off as many as three burglaries per night. He usually went alone. Even if Marturano went along as driver, Welch wouldn't share any information, such as which houses he hit, what he stole, or what might have happened during the burglary. Welch would occasionally give him some cash or a few pieces of jewelry, but Marturano said he never pawned or sold any of the stuff because he was afraid of being caught. Welch would never tell Marturano how much cash he actually found, and he would always find a reason for Marturano to leave the apartment while he was sorting his loot. He would, however, have Marturano help him with cover letters he needed written when he was shipping out gold and silver and getting paid by the ounce. Marturano was a better writer.

After about three or four particularly profitable burglaries in Richmond, Welch had accumulated enough material to sell off for its precious metal content. Welch started dealing with a smelter and assayer in Houston, Texas. He was also selling some of the antiques to a dealer located just down the street. She would make the checks out to Myron Henry Snow.

Welch soon opened a savings account at a local bank under the Snow alias and began depositing the checks. In a four-month period, he deposited and withdrew $50,000. Marturano never knew how much money Welch made off the stolen goods. He told Marturano, "I'll do the burglaries; you take care of whatever you want at home. You can help me, you can drive with me, but I go in the house myself."

Every time Welch was presenting merchandise for sale, he delivered a different story for why he was selling it: it had been in his family for years; he bought it at a rummage sale out of state; due to a death in the family, he had inherited it; he had just moved into town and didn't have room for it; he just got out of the service; or he just got divorced and needed the money. He always had a story and alias to avoid tracing the stolen goods back to him. The dealers and buyers always heard a pleasant story that seemed legitimate, which sped the deal along to the proper conclusion—cash for Welch.

Welch and Marturano knew that their stolen car was a liability. It was time to get rid of the Malibu with the New York license plates and replace it with something legitimate. Welch went just down the road to the nearby Morton Auto Sales and put down a deposit on a used car. The next day, Welch, accompanied by Marturano, paid cash for and picked up the car, a 1971 Chevy Monte Carlo. They got the plates and the insurance right there at the dealership. According to Marturano, Welch gave the old stolen car to the maintenance man at their apartment complex after Welch removed the plates and a tape player.

Now that they had a clean, legal car, listed in the name of Myron Snow, they took their legitimate wheels out to celebrate. That night they met two girls, Judy Ebersol and Mary Boone, and soon began to date them regularly. Marturano was seeing Judy, who worked at a credit bureau, and Welch romanced Mary, a schoolteacher. Both men successfully kept their past, their escape from prison, and what they were doing now from the women.

The thing that Welch and Marturano had going for them was neither used drugs or drank excessively, unusual for hardened criminals. Their quiet behavior saved them a lot of trouble and unwanted attention. There was no drunken boasting and no slips of the tongue; no neighbor complaints about noisy parties; nor were there unsavory types hanging around the area. These two escaped convicts were able to keep the lowest of profiles and drew no official attention.

Once Welch became familiar with the Virginia area he seriously concentrated on his burglary operation. He got up early in the morning, got ready for "work," and left the apartment before nine in the morning. This sort of self-discipline was unheard of in a criminal. He drove a considerable distance out of Richmond—sometimes as far as Washington, DC, which was two hours away—to an area he thought would be profitable. Then he spent the day driving around, choosing potential targets, and learning the area. As the sun went down, he hit the houses he had cased. He might spend an hour in each home, picking through the belongings for the type of items he desired and looking in the secret hiding places that the owners thought no one would ever think to look in—the refrigerator, inside pantries, bottoms of drawers, behind vents, inside light fixtures. He would hit two to four houses a night and take away pillowcases or suitcases from the homes full of stolen goods and cash.

Around this time, Welch began fine-tuning his tools of operation: the cheap brown cotton gloves that left no fingerprints and could be bought at any hardware store; an oversized slotted screwdriver that could be used as a pry bar; a penlight small enough to hold in the mouth, leaving both hands free, and a large navy blue cotton bandana, folded and tied behind the head to cover the face, like an old-time stagecoach bandit. Welch also began developing what would become his signature rules for burglaries: he never stole credit cards or checks that could be traced when used; and he worked alone. By working alone, there was no one to snitch on him. These tools and rules, and the ability to dispose of the stolen merchandise without using a fence or pawnshops, minimized Welch's exposure to arrest. Unless he was caught inside the home, he was like the invisible man, undetectable.

Because he put in so much effort to scout and pick his targets, Welch didn't want to get caught on his way out. He always had some way of slipping away from a burglary that prevented neighbors and other potential witnesses from observing him leave the home and go directly to his car. Police later questioned Paul Marturano about Welch's MO, because they knew that "they used the car in the driveway when the keys were hanging up in the kitchen and loaded that car and drove maybe two or three blocks and transferred all of the articles out of the car into another car." Marturano replied, "See, Welch never knew exactly what he was going to find in a house. This is something he always told me, he said, 'So if there is a car there, I'm going to fill it up and move it to wherever I've got my car. I'll never leave my car too close to a job.' This wasn't because he didn't want to be able to get to his car, but he didn't want it to be too obvious that he was in the area."

Just before the end of October 1974, Welch took a long trip to Roanoke, Virginia, where he scored big. He returned to the apartment with four full suitcases and lots of firearms. The items from this trip kept Welch busy for a week with the sales of merchandise and precious metals shipments and ended up generating a goodly income for Welch.

With Welch's pace picking up and Marturano's pace stagnating, they were starting to get on each other's nerves. Welch had effectively shut Marturano out of the action. Marturano had no money, no ID, and no car, and he was trapped in their small apartment each day. Add to that, he had a falling out with Judy, exchanging harsh words on Halloween night and breaking off their relationship. Now that Marturano had split with his girlfriend, there was no reason for him to stay. Marturano decided he wanted to end his partnership with Welch and informed him of such.

But the truth was Bernard Welch ran a relationship only as far as it suited him. He had kept Marturano around for less than two months, just until he had accumulated enough cash and sellable merchandise to take this new enterprise to the next level. After getting him the ID and sometimes serving as a getaway driver, Marturano was no longer of value to Welch. In fact, Marturano could now be a liability. If pressed, Marturano might be all too willing to share with the cops what he knew about Welch's past and many false identities. Welch wanted to operate entirely on his own, keeping anyone he was associated with or living with totally in the dark about his past or what he did to generate income.

Bernard Welch and Paul Marturano parted company on November 5, 1974, when Welch drove Marturano to the home of Dorothy, Marturano's new girlfriend, in Scottsville, Virginia. Even though Welch promised to look Marturano up around Thanksgiving, he never showed up again, not even at Christmas. Welch had also promised to send some money, but according to Marturano, he never called or made any further contact.

With Marturano gone, Welch figured it was time to try living with a woman again. Mary Boone was a divorced schoolteacher who couldn't have kids. She owned a nice little brick home on a corner lot, with a freestanding garage in the rear. As far as Mary knew, the man living with her was Henry Snow, who sometimes went by the nickname Hank. She enjoyed his company and didn't ask any prying questions; Welch thought it would be fairly easy to persuade her into letting him move in with her, and it was. As Paul Marturano later observed, "It was a perfect setup for Bernie." And set up he did, in her garage. He used it for sorting and storing his stolen goods before liquidating them.

Welch had a very busy and lucrative winter. He was so flush that he actually spent some money frivolously. In early February 1975, Welch paid for a trip to Bermuda with Mary to break the monotony of winter. While they were gone, still-pining Paul Marturano stopped by Mary's house to drop off a Valentine card for his old flame, Judy Ebersol. When Mary and Welch got back to the United States, they attended Judy's wedding—to her longtime boyfriend, not Paul Marturano. Welch paid the bill for the entire reception.

Welch kept his inventory of antiques and art goods he had stolen in Mary's garage. In broad daylight, he would load a rental trailer and drive north. He frequented the Conestoga Auction Company, a country antique market in Lancaster, Pennsylvania. Welch posed as Hank Snow, antique dealer, and he made many of these trips with his closed-in trailer fully loaded with a fairly classy selection of antiques, etchings, fine ceramics, Oriental rugs, and Chippendale furniture. These regular trips used up a lot of time and gas, but the proceeds from the sales were huge and got better every month. Best of all, these sales took place in another state and were far removed from the sites of his burglaries.

Near the end of summer, the Conestoga's owner, Walt Bomberger, got suspicious about the seller who drove almost three hundred miles up from Chesterfield County, Virginia, with goods he claimed were acquired at estate sales. Bomberger told police investigators that Myron Snow never seemed to know that much about the items he was leaving on consignment, saying instead that his expertise was in jewelry, coins, and precious metals. With this information, the Pennsylvania Crime Commission got in touch with the Virginia State Police, who provided this fact: the real Myron H. Snow actually lived in Charlottesville, Virginia, and worked in a local factory.

The Pennsylvania Crime Commission, involved in fighting organized crime, suspected that Snow may be part of an interstate theft ring. They shared this suspicion with the Virginia State Police, and the two law enforcement bodies formulated a plan. The Pennsylvania investigators would trail Snow from the Conestoga, across their state, and continue to follow him until the surveillance was taken over by the Virginia state police as they approached Snow's house. A state police airplane would also trail Snow back to his home outside of Richmond, Virginia.

The plan almost failed before it began when the Virginia state police plane couldn't take off because the airport was socked in by fog. The ground tracking by unmarked Pennsylvania police cars went fine until they got near Richmond, and then the two squads lost him. Luckily a Virginia state police helicopter was in the area and picked up Snow's car. The tracking was then handed over to the state police, and they followed Snow right to the doorstep of Mary Boone's suburban brick rambler.

It was an edgy trip for Welch. He thought something was fishy at the Conestoga when he was dropping off his goods. There were a couple of new faces on the staff, and he thought he detected a bit of nervous behavior from the owner. Welch suspected he was being followed on the way home. He never exceeded the speed limit, but two nondescript cars were always in his vicinity for at least two hundred miles. Over that distance, he should have eventually passed the dark sedan way ahead of him or that four-door sedan in his rearview mirror should have eventually passed him.

Immediately after arriving home Welch packed up some clothes, grabbed his money and some of his goods, loaded up his car, and prepared to drive off or walk away on foot. He checked the streets to see if those two cars, or anything similar, were on the street. It looked clear, so he curtly told Mary Boone everything was over between them, and he was leaving for the West Coast. Bernard Welch then headed north towards Washington, DC.

Earlier, the surveillance team had watched the man posing as Hank Snow stop at a Safeway store in Chesterfield to buy groceries, go to his house, pick up the newspaper, and head inside. They had no idea who they were tailing or what a sixth sense Welch had about traps, surveillance, and being tailed. Some would say he could smell unmarked police cars. The Virginia state police team didn't have enough suspicion or budget to post an around-the-clock watch on the house, so when it looked as though Snow had gone into his home for the night, they left the area and would pick the surveillance up again in the morning. That was the last they saw of him.

The investigation team realized later that they were dealing with a serial house burglar when Richmond area victims came forward to identify their stolen property using photographs taken at the Conestoga Auction Company.

Now, Bernard Welch was headed to the city and area that was his destiny. He liked Washington, DC, especially Georgetown. He loved the power and money that oozed from this area. The three richest counties in the country were bedroom communities for this center of wealth, politics, and power.

For Welch, the real money was in the houses of the people who commuted between the high-paying jobs in the city during the day and their half-million dollar homes at night. He had to figure out how to get close to this source of income, how to stay anonymous, and how to avoid observation and detection. He knew what he really wanted was to live in one of those expensive homes but not be saddled with that demanding job in the city. He had to find a way to be acceptable to the upper class, so he could prey upon them and, at the same time, pretend he was one of them.

In the fall of 1975, Bernard Welch was hunting for an unattached female in the Washington area who would allow him to live with her and use her name. He was still pursuing his main source of income, burglary, but he wanted living quarters a little more spacious than the neon sign motels he was staying in.

Duluth, Minnesota, is a rail and shipping city on the westernmost tip of Lake Superior, the largest of the Great Lakes. Duluth is located some 2,300 miles by ship from the Atlantic Ocean, about 1,100 miles as the crow flies. It is the world's largest freshwater port and the busiest on the Great Lakes. In

the early 1900s, the port of Duluth surpassed New York and Chicago in gross
tonnage, making it the leading port in the United States. At that time, Duluth
had more millionaires per capita than any other city in the country.

With shipping being so important to the local economy, companies such as
US Steel were major employers in the area. Russ Hamilton had worked for US
Steel as a crane operator in the shipyards until retiring in 1968. Hamilton and
his wife, Francis, had four children—John, Rodney, Carolyn, and Linda.

Linda was shy, quiet, and hardly noticed in high school. She was a little
overweight and a bit bookish. Linda was a Library Cadet and that made her
a natural for the work she did on the high school yearbook. Linda worked
after school at Bridgeman's, an ice cream shop, and graduated from Denfield
High School in 1967.

Around that time, her father suggested she take a civil service exam for
government employment. Linda did well on the test. Unfortunately, the exam
she scored highly on was for federal employment. State or local civil service
would have kept her in the area with her family, but US government employment in Duluth was a pretty narrow field.

Linda moved to Washington, DC, in September 1968. Unable to afford her
own apartment, she stayed for a period of time at a women's hotel on 14th
Street in Washington. Her first job was as a statistical typist for the Department
of Defense. She stayed at the Department of Defense for two-and-a-half years
before moving on to the Corporation for Public Broadcasting. After cruising
along at this job for a while, she switched between government agencies again
in 1974. Her next employer was the National Academy of Sciences, where
she worked as a production specialist and compositor.

Once she was away from Duluth, Linda had little contact with her family,
save letters and an occasional phone call. Although she lost her virginity her
first year in Washington, Linda was still bashful and shy around men; she had
never had a serious relationship with a man nor spent an entire night with one.

In the fall of 1975, Linda was living alone with two cats in the Southern
Manor Apartments in Alexandria. The balcony of her one-bedroom apartment
faced the small hotel where Bernard Welch was currently residing. Welch had
spotted Linda's pets on the balcony and, having always been around cats while
growing up, decided he and their owner had something in common.

When Linda arrived home from work one evening in October, Welch
walked over to the fence between the apartment complex and the motel and
called her over. He introduced himself as Norm Heiman and made small talk

with Linda about her cats. He told Linda he had just moved into DC from Richmond, Virginia, and his line of work was investments: jewelry stores, liquor stores, apartment complexes, antiques, and art. He explained that he mostly bought merchandise from lawyers handling estates and then resold the items.

Welch asked Linda if she could join him for dinner that evening, but she told him she had other plans. So Welch asked her to go out for a meal and a movie the next night. She agreed on one condition. She wanted to double date with her girlfriend Gerry and Gerry's boyfriend, John.

The dinner at the Ranch House went well. Linda was bowled over by this well-mannered, good-looking man. She noticed that Norm could effortlessly talk about almost anything with three people he'd never met before. He even had a beautiful new silver Chevrolet Monte Carlo.

The only hitch in the evening came as they were leaving the restaurant. Linda spotted a pistol in Norm's jacket pocket. She let him know that seeing this handgun really upset her. Welch explained that he needed it because his antique and coin sales required him to transport precious metals and large amounts of cash. Linda was adamant that she did not like guns, and that was the last time she ever saw Norm with one.

After dinner, the four of them went to Tyson's Corner and window-shopped through the mall. Norm stopped them at different shops and pointed out expensive glassware and porcelain and explained where it all came from. He identified the different gems in displayed jewelry and gave Linda a brief description of gold purity and what carats meant. She liked learning about such things. The only jewelry she had ever owned was her high school class ring.

Next they all made it to the movie theater to catch a prophetic double feature—*The Sting* with Redford and Newman followed by *Hard Times* starring Charles Bronson. Toward the end of the show, for a special touch, Norm even held her hand. Linda couldn't believe she was on a date with such a gentleman.

After the movies, they stopped for a couple of drinks with Gerry and John. Linda was excited. He was so good looking and had such pleasant manners. She couldn't believe her luck. At the end of the evening, the two couples went their separate ways, and Norm ended up at Linda's place.

A mere twenty days later, the tall, dark stranger with the nice car, mysterious profession, and little else, moved into Linda's apartment and started paying half the rent.

While dating Linda, Welch continued working at his craft and started amassing ever-increasing amounts of cash and stolen goods. Linda was impressed with how easy it was for Norm to acquire all these antiques and jewelry at such reasonable prices. Soon, Welch became comfortable enough with Linda that he shared some of the techniques he used to clean, restore, or otherwise prepare the antiques and other merchandise for sale.

Even as they were getting closer, the secretive Welch needed to cook up a cover story that was impossible for Linda to check on. And now that they were living together, it wouldn't be a bad thing if they shared a last name.

The consummate con man, Welch was an expert at proposing something outrageous or preposterous and adding just enough fact to make the suggestion seem plausible to the listener. Linda Hamilton listened as Bernard Welch, posing as Norm Heiman, elaborated on the hard time he was having with his estranged wife. He told Linda that he and his wife ran an antique shop together, and they rented a storage building about an hour outside of Washington, DC. He would sneak in there at night and take merchandise he said was rightfully his and liquidate it so his wretched wife couldn't claim her half. This explained his nightly trips to places unknown and triumphant return hours later with a car full of valuable merchandise. He maintained that this shrew was making life impossible because of all the lawyers she was sending after him even though she made plenty of money from the antiques business. He told Linda that he had evaded his ex's phone calls and searches for eight months but needed to throw her off his trail permanently.

As soon as he suggested it, Linda quickly agreed that it would be best for Norm to use Linda's last name. In addition to getting Linda's last name, Welch's story about his vindictive spouse worked on many levels. The sob story about the ex-wife endeared him to Linda even more, and the edgy, illicit quality of his activities and her giving away her last name prevented her from pursuing the matter further or mentioning this to any friends or neighbors. Linda was told the rocky relationship was also the reason he had no desire to return to his family home. This kept the idea of contacting or visiting his family at bay.

Bernard Welch had successfully transformed into Norm Hamilton.

Welch knew they had to get out of Linda's apartment and into a rented single family home so he could more easily ply his trade. In March 1976, they moved into a three-bedroom split-level house at 3445 Rose Lane in Falls Church, Virginia. This home was in a nice neighborhood, and while Linda was proud to be living in a house nicer than the Duluth home she grew up in, Welch was excited to have more room and privacy.

Montgomery County Detectives Mike Tihila and Jim King sat near the back of the roll call room of the rural Virginia police station. The morning sun attempted to shine through the dirty windows and dusty venetian blinds. Detectives Tihila and King had come from Montgomery County, Maryland, to attend the briefing. King sat back in his chair and lit another Winston cigarette to go along with the bad coffee and stale donut. He slowly exhaled a lungful of smoke and stared at the room. He nervously tapped his fingers on the tabletop waiting for the meeting to start.

The room's walls were covered with old FBI wanted posters, some dating back to the early fifties. The faded papers pinned to the wall were tinted a yellowish brown, the result of years of fuming tobacco smoke, sunlight, and fly specks. Several tired, old oak tables, the product of state prison labor, were arranged in phalanx order, facing front. Their worn tops recorded the passing of police officers who had used them three times a day, seven days a week for the past thirty years. Cigarette burns, coffee stains, and prisoner handcuffs had all left a history. The slanting sunbeams highlighted each incident in the life of the tables.

The brown spindrift of grit on the worn linoleum floor, carried in from nearby farms, softly grated as people walked by. At the front of the room, a thin man with slicked-back black hair, wearing a black out-of-date suit and a black, clip-on tie, stood up. His long jaw, wrinkled face, thin nose, and large lobed ears indicated his Appalachian ancestry. His smile revealed brownish teeth indicative of his chewing tobacco habit. He attempted to gain attention.

"Gentlemen? Ladies?"

No one took notice. He raised his voice slightly. "Gentlemen...um, brothers and sisters." He lifted up his right hand as if to give a benediction and raised his voice even higher. "Folks, let's all come to order. Time's wasting. We got lots to talk about here, so let's get 'er going."

His nasal, Blue Ridge Mountain accent finally pierced the murmuring din of conversation. The several uniformed and plainclothes officers moved reluctantly away from their small groups to find seats amongst the varied, no-two-alike chairs.

As the officers found places, the wrinkle-faced host continued speaking. "Thank you all for coming to our little meeting here. We are gathered today...."

It occurred to King that the speaker was probably a deacon in some little whitewashed, clapboard church perched in a field along a Virginia back road. King would bet that he had a King James Bible on his desk.

The deacon-police officer continued. "So we have up first here, Detective Sergeant Buddy Baker from Henrico County, down Richmond way. He wants to tell us about a little ol' burglar they've been chasing. He thinks this burglar fellow might be operating up this way. So I'd like to call up Detective Sergeant Buddy Baker."

Detective Baker stood up and replaced the wrinkle-faced host at the front of the room. Baker was a big man with thinning, grayish hair. You could tell he was a veteran cop. There was that command presence about him that old timers who know their business get. His eyes were creased at the corners from seeing too much evil and staring across the sun-glared hoods of too many police cars. His face had the tanned leather look that outdoor people get and keep until they go into a nursing home. Buddy Baker spoke in the soft accent of Tidewater Virginia.

"Folks, I'm here to tell y'all about a fellow we've been following around, but he's up and disappeared. We think he's moved up here, near DC."

The room was silent. Unlike when the wrinkle-faced host was up front, everyone paid attention when Detective Baker spoke.

"Last year, we started getting lots of B and E's around Richmond, mostly in the well-to-do areas of Henrico County. Later, we connected B and E's from Petersburg, Colonial Heights, and Williamsburg to ours. What connected them all was the MO. They all occurred just after dark in the early evening, not during the daytime, as is usual. Another connection was what was taken.

Not the normal stuff like TVs and stereos that most burglars steal and sell on the street. In these jobs, the burglar took sterling silver, coin collections, cash, good jewelry, antique guns, old dolls, Hummel figurines, old Chinese vases, old oil paintings, and small valuable Oriental rugs. Not your run-of-the-mill thief." Baker paused, took a sip of cold coffee, grimaced, and continued.

"Here's another thing about this guy, he doesn't fence his loot locally. He hauls it to out-of-state auction houses. We know that because the owner of a big auction place in Pennsylvania got suspicious of a customer. On several occasions, this guy pulled up in a Chevy sedan with a U-Haul trailer. He unloaded high quality antiques to be auctioned off. According to the owner, this man just didn't seem right. He was too young, too far from home and had too many good antiques, too often. This person used the name Myron Henry Snow and had a Virginia driver's license with an address in Richmond. The owner of the auction house was concerned that something illegal was going on and got in contact with the Pennsylvania state police who called us."

King fidgeted a little more in his chair. It didn't sound like anything at this meeting was going to pertain to him and his cases.

"Of course, we followed up on the lead. We discovered there was a real Myron Henry Snow in Charlottesville, but it wasn't the guy who went to Pennsylvania. This Myron Snow had had a few run-ins with the law, but the face was wrong. Mr. Snow said he lost his wallet in a bar somewhere. We kind of think there's more to it than that but nothing we can prove. Our investigation revealed that the man with the antiques in Pennsylvania went to a Virginia DMV and got a duplicate license in Myron Snow's name but with his photo on it. So this fella is real slick and as bold as brass.

"Pennsylvania state police got copies of the canceled checks that the auction house wrote to the fake Mr. Snow. We followed up on that information. We eventually got his home address. A local schoolteacher owns the house, and he was living with her there. So we started watching the place. One day he leads us to a U-Haul place and rents a trailer. Then he goes back home to a garage and loads up the trailer. We can't see what he's putting in it. He then proceeds north up I-95. We followed him with the help of Virginia state unmarked units.

"This fellow drives a couple hundred miles, all the way to Lancaster, Pennsylvania, where he unloads his cargo at a big auction place. We contact Pennsylvania State, and they send a couple of unmarked units to follow him back. When he gets to Virginia, we pick up the tail. He returns the trailer to where he rented it and goes home. At that time we're real suspicious, but we got nothing on the guy except a fake driver's license. If we had busted him then it would have just been a traffic violation. He'd have signed the ticket and skipped town."

Detective Baker's voice speeded up, conveying the intensity of the investigation. "We hustled around over the next few days gathering information. We go to the bank where he cashed the auction checks. Guess what? He's got a savings account there and has deposited over $50,000 from January to July 1975. The times match up to when our big burglaries began. So we get some recent burglary victims to hike up to Lancaster, and they ID some of their stolen property."

Detective Baker's voice went from serious to jocular. He rubbed his hands together and smiled. "Well, boys, now we got him. We get a warrant and round up some troops and go over to his, or rather, the schoolteacher's house to arrest him. Guess what? The day after we followed him to Lancaster he squirted out of that house like shit through a goose."

All the officers chuckled, including the deacon-detective.

Detective Baker ruefully continued. "I guess he tagged us when we tailed him. The teacher lady says she didn't know anything about Myron Snow's evening activities, and he was only renting a room." Baker winked as he emphasized "renting." "We can't prove any different."

A few titters of laughter rose in the room.

"According to everyone who's dealt with this guy, he's a smooth, convincing talker. So maybe the schoolteacher's telling us the truth. I hope so. But she also told us that this fella, Snow, once took her to Georgetown in Washington, DC. To quote her, he said, 'Georgetown was a really nice place to visit and work.' And we know what type of work Mr. Snow does, don't we?"

Again, all the investigators chuckled.

"By the way, for what it's worth, she also said this fella had a Yankee accent, which may mean something or nothing." Detective Baker continued on, more serious now.

"So folks, I'm here to alert you all that you may have this fella, whatever his name is, working up here in northern Virginia and maybe DC. From what he's done down our way, we calculate he's a pro. He's smart and he's slick. This is not his first time at bat. He's got to have a history somewhere and probably a prison record. So if you catch him, please let us know. We got a big interest in him. I've brought along some handouts with his Virginia DMV photo. Take one please. And thanks for listening, folks."

Detective Baker sat down. There were some murmurs from the assembled police officers as they speculated on the connection of Detective Baker's information to their jurisdictions.

Tihila looked at King and quietly said, "Doesn't fit anything I know of." King shook his head in negative affirmation. There was nothing in Montgomery County, Maryland, that fit this guy's MO.

The meeting droned on as other officers relayed information on crimes and suspects in their areas. None of it applied to Maryland. King and Tihila knew that that would most likely be the case. There was little cross-river crime traffic. The Potomac River was a natural barrier that thieves traditionally respected due to the few escape routes. But it was always interesting to hear what other jurisdictions were experiencing in the way of crime. One never knew when such information might come in handy.

A few days after Thanksgiving, Detective King was working the four-to-twelve shift. He was in the Bethesda District of Montgomery County, heading to the Bethesda Police Station on Wisconsin Avenue. At about ten o'clock that night, he received a radio call to respond to a burglary that had just been reported.

Within ten minutes, he arrived in the wealthy neighborhood near Kenwood Country Club, about one mile from the Washington, DC, border. King found the house quickly and parked behind the police ID van. He could see a uniformed officer talking to a man and a woman under the front porch light. The officer took notes on his clipboard. As King neared the porch, Officer Howard Tippens turned and smiled in greeting. Tippens was a tall, fair-haired, Pennsylvania boy with an easy grin. He and King had worked together in the Bethesda Traffic Division.

"What do you have, Howard?" King asked.

Tippens gave a quick nod, and he turned back to the couple. "Mr. and Mrs. Connelly, this is Detective King, Crimes Against Property Division." King nodded to the Connellys, who said nothing.

Tippens continued, "Mr. and Mrs. Connelly arrived home," he looked down at his notes and read, "about 2150 hours. They found the rear door open and some silver missing from the dining room. They went next door and called. I received the burglary dispatch and arrived code three with backup. We searched the house, negative. I called for ID and a detective. ID is in there now processing the place. I had the Connellys wait out here until ID is finished."

"Thanks," King nodded. He turned his attention to Mr. and Mrs. Connelly. "Can you tell me what happened?"

Mr. Connelly was in his mid-fifties, and his face was beginning to get jowly. He was wearing a dark, pin-striped suit and a well-fitted, camel-colored, wool overcoat. His wing tips were shiny. Mr. Connelly's sprayed and dyed hair did not move in cool, autumn the wind. Whatever he did for a living, stolid executive or corporate lawyer, it paid well enough to live in this neighborhood and drive the Mercedes Benz 380SL parked in the drive.

Mr. Connelly spoke with a well-educated, yet aggravated, tone. "As we told this person," he said, indicating Officer Tippens, "my wife left home at about five o'clock and took a cab downtown to meet me. We had a dinner engagement with friends. We returned home just before ten. We parked the car," Mr. Connelly pointed to the silver Mercedes sedan in the drive, "and came in through the kitchen door. We found the back door standing open. I assumed the wind had blown it open. That happens sometimes if it isn't closed tight. After we came inside we discovered someone had taken some silver from the dining room. We didn't know if the culprit might still be inside, so we quickly left and went to our neighbors to call the police."

"That was probably for the best." King shivered. The wind was picking up. It had been a mild fall, and he had not yet put in the liner of his London Fog raincoat. He buttoned his coat and stuffed his hands into the pockets. "Was the kitchen warm or cold when you first entered?"

Mr. Connelly seemed confused by the question. "What do you mean?" he asked.

King tried not to be pedantic, but it was a simple question. "Let me explain, if the kitchen was warm, the burglar had just left. If the kitchen was cold, the door had been open for a while, meaning the burglar had been gone for some time. So, was the kitchen warm or cold?"

Mr. Connelly looked to his wife to answer. Mrs. Connelly looked at King and said, "It was freezing in the kitchen."

King looked at Mrs. Connelly closely for the first time. She was pretty and several years younger than her husband—probably a second marriage for him and maybe for her. The coat collar of her full-length mink was pulled up around her face. Her hands were deep in her pockets. She was wearing only a dress and high heels; she had to be as cold as King was.

"Howard, would you go inside and check with the ID officer and see if we can come in yet?" King requested. "It's cold out here."

Tippens went into the house to check on the progress of the ID officer and returned quickly. "Come in, but stay downstairs. He'll be finished soon."

The Connellys, followed by King, entered the foyer of the large house. They peered around the house, as if seeing the place for the first time. Mrs. Connelly looked down and pointed.

"John, look, that little Persian rug is gone. I'm sure the maid would have said something if she had moved it."

Mr. Connelly stared at the bare area of the foyer's shiny, wood floor. "I'll be damned. Well, it was only worth a few hundred," he said dismissively.

King leaned towards Tippens and murmured sotto voce, "Put it on your list." Tippens nodded and added the rug, with a value of $500, to his notepad.

The couple walked into the dining room, followed by the two officers. There, the Hepplewhite sideboard drawers were pulled out, and its lower doors were standing open. Mrs. Connelly looked into the open drawers and turned to her husband. "Look, oh God, look. It's all gone, even Momma's silver. Oh God, he got it all, even Momma's old silver!"

Mr. Connelly's haughty composure began to melt. He put his arm around his wife's shoulder. She turned into his chest and began to cry.

King and Tippens stood in the dining room doorway. Watching people discover that their family heirlooms were gone was always difficult. It wasn't the value of the items that was important. It was what they represented to the owners that mattered. Links to the past had been broken, never to be mended. Even if an exact copy could be obtained, it would not be the same. In situations like this, police officers are helpless.

"Howard, stay with them," King instructed. "Get an estimated value of the stolen stuff." Tippens nodded and flipped to a clean page on his clipboard, resigned to being at the crime scene for some time. The Connellys would have to go through their entire residence to discover which possessions were missing.

King first went to the basement. Nothing seemed to have been disturbed there. Next, he went to the living room where, again, nothing seemed out of place. He did notice vague shoe prints on the recently vacuumed, plush carpet. These prints indicated that someone—thief, cop, or maid—had circled the area one time, as if checking out the room.

King could tell a lot about thieves by their MOs—how they made entry, what they did or didn't take, what they did once inside; did they eat, drink, vandalize? There were a hundred different signs left behind. He enjoyed this part of his job, the figuring out what happened using only the meager hints. He had always like solving the unknown.

The average burglar was a junkie looking for quick money for the next fix. Junkies usually stole color TVs, stereos, cameras, and liquor. These items brought ready cash on the street. These items were all still present in the Connelly household.

Junkies usually operated as a two-man team. The items they stole were usually bulky, so it was quicker to have two people to carry off the goods. King surmised that this was a one-man operation. This burglar was different. He was deliberate. This guy knew what he wanted and rejected everything else. In this case, what he didn't steal was just as important as what he did steal. Something for King to think about.

In the kitchen, King found the ID officer, Ron Clemens, packing away his camera and getting ready to leave. Clemens was good at his job. If there was a clue to be found, Ron would find it, print it, photograph it, and save it.

"Hey Ron, what did you find?"

Clemens looked up and shook his head. "Not much, Jim. The bad guy wore gloves. I got lots of fiber prints, looks like those brown cotton work gloves."

King already knew that would be the case. The only people who left fingerprints were drunks and kids. Everybody else wore gloves.

"No foot prints outside, dry ground," Clemens continued. "Master bedroom was a toss-and-throw. The popped back door over there is the point of entry." Clemens indicated the kitchen door that opened to the rear porch. "Looks like a pry with a half-inch screw driver and a shim of the lock."

King went to the door and inspected the latch area. When he knelt down and opened the door, he observed two half-inch indentations just above the bolt on the edge of the door. He stepped outside into the windy evening and looked at the exterior molding around the doorframe. Taking a small flashlight from his coat pocket, he shone it at an oblique angle up the frame. There were two round dents in the wood made by the screwdriver shaft matching the location of the blade marks on the edge of the door. The slivers of paint sticking out around the indentations indicated the marks were fresh.

He closed the door and saw a quarter-inch gap between the white painted door and its frame. The door was probably original to the house twenty-five years ago. It was shrunken in the dry, cold weather. The key-in-knob lock was cheap; a Harry Homeowner special sold by every hardware store. Once a screwdriver was inserted into the gap between the door and jamb, the culprit could apply pressure with one hand while inserting a thin piece of metal or plastic with the other hand. That would allow the shim to force the latch bolt back and unlock the door.

The two pry marks were precise. The burglar knew what he was doing. The first pry was to start the process. The second pry was just below the first and enabled a better angle and a little more leverage to make shimming the lock easier. The whole process took less than thirty seconds, made almost no noise, and created little damage. It was easily overlooked. To King, this confirmed it wasn't an amateur. This burglary was committed by someone with experience.

King went back inside, closing the door behind him. "Cheap lock and no dead bolt."

"And no alarm system," noted Clemens. "But the bad guy didn't know that."

"What?" King asked. He noticed a sneaky little smile on Clemens's lips. He knew Clemens liked to kid around.

Clemens chuckled. "Check out the upstairs hallway. There's one of those new smoke detectors in the ceiling that's been knocked down. The guy probably thought it was a motion alarm. Kind of looks like one with its little flashing red light. First time I've ever had somebody beat up a smoke detector in a burglary." Then Clemens became more serious. "After that, the jerk ransacked the master bedroom."

King absorbed the information, but put it aside for the moment. "Ron, did you make a mold of the pry marks?"

Clemens shook his head. "No, it's too cold outside. The latex would have froze before it set up. Anyway, not much of a mark there; he didn't have to use much force to pop that old door."

Clemens picked up his two battered cases and walked towards the front of the house. "See you at the next one," he called over his shoulder.

King followed Clemens out of the kitchen but peeled off into the dining room. Mr. and Mrs. Connelly were still there with Officer Tippens. Tippens turned to King as he entered. "ID get anything?"

"Nope, fiber glove prints and a screwdriver used on the kitchen door."

Mrs. Connelly was now looking into her china cabinet. Mr. Connelly asked, "No fingerprints?"

"No, sir, the thief wore gloves," King explained. "Have you found anything else missing, other than the silverware?"

Mr. Connelly looked over at his wife, who had turned around to face them. Her mascara had run down her cheeks. The backs of both index fingers were dark from wiping her tears away. Given her present emotional state, King felt compassion for the lady.

"Yes, of course there are other things missing," Mr. Connelly answered, not bothering to hide his annoyance any longer. "They are, or rather were, in the china cabinet. The missing items are four antique, English toby mugs, three lusterware pitchers, and two old porcelain figurines. Do you know what those things are?"

Mr. Connelly looked at his wife, who had stopped crying but was still wiping her eyes with the back of her hands. "Can we go upstairs now?" Mr. Connelly must have figured out that things were missing from the second floor as well.

The four of them walked up the carpeted stairs. At the top of the landing, King saw a round, white plastic smoke detector hanging by one wire from the ceiling. He ducked slightly so his 6'4" frame could pass under it. The Connellys stopped to stare at the broken, hanging unit.

"Mr. Connelly, when did you have the smoke detector installed?" King asked.

"We had the house rewired when we moved in last year. It was installed then."

Smoke detectors for homes were fairly new on the market. They had to be hardwired into the house electrical system. Just the previous year, Montgomery County required installation of smoke detectors in all new and renovated construction. King realized this thief didn't recognize the smoke detector for what it was. That might indicate he was new to the county. A professional thief who made a mistake. Good, thought King, maybe he isn't so smart.

The Connellys continued on, looking into each bedroom. Since they lived alone, the rooms contained nothing of value. The mirrored medicine chest in the bathroom had not been touched. No search for prescription drugs by the bad guy. Interesting, thought King. No drugs, no booze, and he didn't touch the illegal Havana cigars in the humidor downstairs. This was an unusual burglar.

When they reached the master bedroom, it was a mess. Clemens had been right; it was a toss-and-throw ransack. All the dresser drawers had been pulled out. The culprit had taken each drawer and tossed its contents into the air, over the queen-size bed, so he could not only see if something was taped to the drawer bottom, but also quickly discern what was inside. The heavier jewelry would separate from the clothing, which fluttered down. There were sweaters, nylons, bras, socks, and male and female underwear in great piles on the bed and floor. In the large walk-in closet clothes and boxes were strewn on the floor.

"Goddamn," muttered Mr. Connelly.

Mrs. Connelly stood still, wrapped in her mink with her hands clenched into small, tight, white fists. "Jesus, Mary, and Joseph, look at the mess."

This burglar was fast and thorough. In the house for ten, maybe twenty, minutes at most. He knew what he wanted and where it would be—in the living room, dining room, and master bedroom. King also took note of the missing pillowcases from the bed pillows. Most likely the thief had used these to carry out the stolen goods. If he needed two, King thought, he must have gotten a lot. The guy was good, and King felt certain this would not be the last time he'd see his handiwork.

King and Tippens exchanged a knowing look. Any and all valuables that had been in that room were now gone.

King spoke up. "Did you folks have any cash, valuables or jewelry in this room?"

Mrs. Connelly turned a sad, freshly tear-stained face to King and Tippens. "Oh yes, all my good things were here. I hope he missed them." King knew otherwise but said nothing.

Mr. Connelly looked at the boxer shorts and socks at his feet. "I had a few hundred dollars in cash, but I guess it's gone now."

"Okay, it's going to take you awhile to figure out everything that's missing," King began. "Here's my card. I want you to contact me as soon as you have some sort of list. What I suggest is when you find something gone, write it down. If you find it later, scratch it off. Include detailed descriptions, brand names, styles, and value. I'll write a supplemental report to Officer Tippens's original report. I'll have your case number that you'll need for the insurance company."

King turned to Tippens. "You got enough details to do the original?"

"Sure do," Tippens replied.

"We'll be going now," King explained to the Connellys. There was nothing further that either officer could do for them. "You have a long night ahead of you. I'm sorry this happened."

As King and Tippens began to leave, Mrs. Connelly turned to her husband, her voice pleading, "John, don't let them go. What if…?" Her face, which had been pale, was now mottled red. Her eyes widened as her mouth moved but made no sound. Looking down at her expensive clothing tangled together in mounds on the floor, she searched for the right words to describe her ultimate fear. "What if this fucking, no good son-of-a-bitch returns?" Mrs. Connelly, pushed beyond her emotional limits, finally blurted out.

Mr. Connelly's face colored in embarrassment. "Officers, please excuse my wife. She's very upset now."

He reached for his wife's shoulder, but she turned her back on him and sobbed loudly. Mr. Connelly, truly embarrassed, averted his eyes from the officers. His studied demeanor was of no use to him in this situation.

Mr. Connelly had been more stunned by his wife's outburst than either officer. Ten years on the force had inured King and Tippens to just about anything that they heard, saw, or smelled. But they were not hardened enough to ignore a victim's pain. A home invasion constituted an unauthorized entry into their most private space.

"I'll secure the back door up for tonight," offered Tippens, "but tomorrow you should get a locksmith to put dead bolt locks on all your doors. And you should think about getting a burglar alarm system. I'll also notify the beat car to keep checking through the neighborhood."

King saw it was time to make their exit. He nudged Tippens out the door as he said good night for both of them. He could tell that Tippens really felt bad for Mrs. Connelly, but there was little they could do for them now. Their real help would come later, when the asshole who did this was caught.

At the bottom of the stairs, Tippens and King went into the kitchen. Tippens wedged a kitchen chair under the knob of the broken door before both officers exited out the front of the home.

Outside the wind was still blowing. King cupped his Zippo lighter from the wind and lit a cigarette as they neared their cars.

"That woman can cuss like a sailor, huh?" King said.

"Yeah, she was real upset. That bedroom was a mess."

"Yeah, it was. What did they say was the value of the silver?"

Tippens thought for a moment. "About ten grand, but that was a guess. Don't know about the other stuff, except the little rug was five hundred."

King fumbled in his coat pocket and finally fished out his notebook. He made a note of the value under the dim streetlight. When he finished, he looked up and smiled at Tippens.

"Hey, we got to get together soon."

"Sure, Jim. Next time our shifts match up."

They parted, Tippens to the Bethesda station to write his report and King to headquarters. It was after eleven and both of their shifts ended at midnight.

As he drove north, King couldn't stop thinking about the Connelly case. Thoughts of silver, jewelry, and antiques danced in his head. What kind of person steals antiques from homes? Unusual. When you steal them, where do you fence them? This guy worked alone on the inside. He took time to ransack the bedroom after knocking down the smoke detector. So he was confident about not getting caught. Did he use a police radio? Not unheard of. Did he have a partner outside watching in a getaway car? Possible. But inside had all the earmarks of a pro. No drugs, no booze, none of the usual things a drug user steals. He only took items from the dining room and master bedroom, and he might have taken a walk through the living room. He only took small, high-value portable items. What did he wrap the ceramics in? Note, call victims to check on missing towels.

A surprising thought suddenly occurred to King—this guy was shopping! This was a first.

Now some thoughts were coming together for King. Something about a burglar in Richmond, Virginia, stealing antiques. He tried to remember the information from the meeting he attended in Richmond with Mike Tihila. Maybe Tihila could jog his memory.

King pulled his unmarked, maroon Ford into the station at quarter to midnight. He almost ran inside. He found Tihila and George Neville talking next to Neville's desk.

"Hey, Mike," King interrupted as soon as he was close, "remember that meeting we went to a few months back down in Virginia?"

Tihila's face showed some surprise at this random query, and he responded with a drawn out, "Yeah?"

"Remember that Richmond detective talking about that burglar who got away?" King continued.

Tihila offered another mystified, "Yeah?"

"What was his name?"

Tihila smiled at Neville to let him know that a zinger was coming. "Which one, Jim, the detective or the burglar?"

King frowned at the two grinning detectives. He was not in the mood for Tihila's humor. "Shit, either one. I don't care."

Tihila could see King was serious. "Okay, okay. I still got that handout somewhere. Wait a minute."

He went to his desk and rifled through some folders in his desk drawer. It took more than a minute, but he finally produced the handout that the Richmond detective had brought to the meeting. He read it to King. "Myron Henry Snow was the name of the suspect."

He handed King the paper with the lousy photocopied picture on it.

King grabbed the paper. "That's the one. Thanks."

King read over the paper as he walked back to his desk. He hadn't even unbuttoned his raincoat yet. But he did notice Tihila and Neville look at each other and shake their heads.

Neville lowered his voice to a stage whisper, loud enough to be heard by King. "I told you he was a strange dude. Listens to that classical music stuff, rots your brain. What can you expect from a guy like that?"

Tihila and Neville laughed. King heard but ignored them. He was thinking about Myron Henry Snow and what the Richmond detective had said.

Falls Church, Virginia
Boundary Waters Canoe Area, Minnesota
March to November 1976

With a new woman, a new name, and new home, Welch was now making enough money from burglaries to do two things. First, he went to a dentist. The set of false teeth he was issued by the New York state prison system was giving him trouble. For $750, he was able to order a whole new set, uppers and lowers. Second, he requested that Linda quit working at the National Academy of Sciences and help him out in his business enterprise. Welch figured the skills Linda had gained from her eight years of government employment could be put to use selling and shipping his ill-gotten gains. On June 6, 1976, Linda resigned from the National Academy of Sciences. She gave up her career as a civil servant for the man she thought she could grow to love.

A deal seemed to have been struck between them, but no official papers were ever signed. However, Linda began to take the lead socially, introducing themselves by telling new neighbors, "I'm Linda Hamilton, and this is Norm." There were two assumptions to be made from these statements: 1. This guy's name is Norm Hamilton and 2. They are married.

Linda told Norm about her family in Minnesota, the beauty of the North-woods, and the friendliness of the people. It sounded idyllic to him. It also sounded like a great business opportunity. With the days getting longer and burglary opportunities slowing down, it was time to take a break from getting more goods and time to start unloading what he had. Linda talked Norm into taking a road trip to Duluth at the end of June.

The Hamiltons started their laid-back vacation on Mackinac Island, an island between Upper and Lower Michigan. They stayed in the fabled Grand Hotel, and with no cars allowed on the island, Welch was able to relax after so many months of hard work. From there, they traveled through Michigan's Upper Peninsula, across northern Wisconsin, directly to Duluth to meet Linda's family. They planned to spend three weeks with Linda's parents and then do some camping in the area.

Russ and Francis Hamilton accepted Norm into their home right from the start. They enjoyed the easy company of the very polite and considerate man their daughter had brought home.

Linda then took Norm on a grand tour of Duluth, including the waterfront, her high school and hangouts, and the different neighborhoods throughout the city. Linda explained how treacherous the steep hillside roads became with a winter coat of ice supplied by winds off Lake Superior. They trekked up steep hills to get an elevated look at the Duluth skyline with over three hundred miles of Lake Superior behind it.

Welch was immediately impressed. He thought unassuming Duluth would be the perfect hideaway during the summer months when the days were too long and the nights too short for effective burgling in Washington, DC. Once daylight savings time was over in November, it would be back to work on the East Coast. And taking into consideration the other benefits—Lake Superior, the natural air conditioner, made the summer days in Duluth very livable, and they were surrounded by woods and lakes for fishing, camping, and hunting—Welch quickly made up his mind. He and Linda started their hunt for a summer home in Duluth.

If Welch was going to summer in Duluth, he had to be sure there were ample outlets for unloading his merchandise. He researched the local coin and precious metals action. Linda was sent to make her first contact with Stan Sunde, a local coin dealer. She brought along some rather unremarkable silver dollars to sell to Sunde to get some cash to finance the Minnesota visit. Welch also investigated antique dealers, art brokers, auction houses, assayer's offices, and furriers. Duluth was a bustling port city, but it wasn't really large enough to support some of the services he was seeking. However, he didn't have to look far to find them. He was directed to Minneapolis, about three hours south of Duluth, to find what he was looking for. With such a large geographic distance between Washington, DC, and Minnesota, Welch knew that selling his goods in Duluth and the larger Twin Cities market to the south gave him extra security against his goods being identified as stolen.

Before the Hamiltons headed back east, they drove north out of Duluth on Highway 61 to Grand Marais, where they turned onto the Gunflint Trail. They followed the Gunflint Trail all the way up to Hungry Jack Lake, where they stayed at the Hungry Jack Lodge. The lodge was located at the gateway to the Boundary Waters Canoe Area, over one million acres in northeastern Minnesota dedicated to canoeing, camping, fishing, and hiking. Norm and Linda stayed in one of the log cabins at the Hungry Jack Lodge, and he was so taken with this place that they stayed there almost two weeks. Norm enjoyed having talks with the owner, Jerry Parson, also a Duluth native. When asked, Parsons told Norm that it would take around $150,000 to get him to part with his rustic lodge.

The Hamiltons had been away from the East Coast for four months. The days were starting to get shorter, and although he enjoyed being on vacation, Welch was itching to get back to Washington, DC. He and Linda finally packed up and headed back to their rental home in Falls Church, Virginia.

In late 1976, Washington, DC, area police departments were noticing something unusual. Apparently, a very cunning group of thieves was operating regularly in the wealthy suburban Washington neighborhoods, and they had a special fondness for precious metals, especially items made of sterling silver. The price of silver was skyrocketing thanks to the infamous Hunt brothers of Texas, and all things silver appeared to be the motive behind the gang's operation.

The authorities attributed the latest rash of burglaries to a "Silver Gang" and suspected these guys of being responsible for break-ins and thefts that blanketed the northeastern United States during 1976. Police were willing to credit this gang with burglaries totaling in the millions of dollars throughout the year. The police also noticed something else was odd. The stolen goods didn't seem to be going through the normal fencing system for liquidation. None of the valuable and identifiable stolen merchandise was showing up at any antique stores, flea markets, pawnshops, or other outlets they canvassed. They figured the crooks were selling the goods in an area far removed from where they were stolen.

Late in the afternoon on February 25, 1977, Bernard Welch left Falls Church and cruised up toward Potomac, Maryland. He had just made a great haul over the weekend at Bethesda and Silver Spring, so he thought he would try his luck a little farther out. He leisurely motored into Potomac Falls, a subdivision of nice upper-class homes situated on two- to four-acre lots where the evergreen shrubbery provided good separation from the neighbors.

Welch was very focused this afternoon. He spotted a classic ranch house made of brick with a split-rail fence and a sixteen-foot runabout on a trailer in the driveway. The house lighting and lack of car in the drive indicated that the homeowners were gone.

Welch parked three blocks away from the home. He made his way to the back of the house and proceeded to the window of the master bedroom. With his hands protected by brown cotton work gloves, he broke the window with the handle of his screwdriver. Once inside, he immediately noticed the orderliness of the bedroom, from the arrangement of the furniture to the personal items. Welch thought this organized home could belong to a military family. His suspicion was confirmed when he spotted the "Semper Fi" coffee mug. "Jarhead," thought Welch. Looking around some more, Welch found an engraved saber on the wall, indicating this marine was an officer. The glitter of gold flight wings caught Welch's eye, and now he knew he was burglarizing the home of a Marine pilot.

The pilot's wife had a bountiful jewelry box, and Welch dumped it unceremoniously into a pillowcase he'd stripped off the bed. He'd take all of it and sort it later.

Displayed on the wall was quite a collection of medals this pilot had earned, many of them still in the presentation boxes, and more than half of them were solid silver or gold. Welch found more presentation boxes in drawers and stacked them. He carried them to the dining room to lay them out on the table for a better look.

Bernard Welch had spent plenty of time in prison, but he always tried to keep a handle on current events. As he walked from the dining room to the living room in search of more items, Welch saw a few striking pictures in the hallway and a startling revelation came over him. This guy is an astronaut!

Welch went back to the dining room and opened the medal box with "CCCP" on the front. He stared at the huge .999 fine gold medallion awarded by the Russian cosmonauts for an epic space flight in 1962. This guy is THE astronaut! Bernard Welch was robbing John Glenn's house.

The shock of this situation stopped Welch in his tracks for all of five seconds. Welch quickly got back on task, finished the house ransacking, and headed back to the living room carrying a large, flat carved ivory Oriental countryside scene. He set down the framed ivory and continued sorting the precious metal, bagging them in the pillowcase with the wife's jewelry.

Welch caught a glimpse of the headlights turning into the opening in the split-rail fence and heading up the drive. Time to get out the way he came in and with only what he had gathered up to now. Welch, with the pillowcase full of loot, headed out the bedroom window into the backyard and backtracked the three blocks to where his car was parked. Just as he slipped away, John Glenn arrived home with his wife, Annie. While Annie parked the car in the garage, Glenn walked in the front door. John Glenn's medals, or what few remained, were still lined up on the dining room table. Welch had taken only those that were solid gold or silver.

Welch arrived home and immediately started sorting out the loot from the Glenn burglary, which amounted to $30,000 worth of irreplaceable mementos, jewelry, silver service pieces, and medallions. A great looking diamond ring from Mrs. Glenn's jewelry box jumped out at him from the pile of loot. It was a brilliant-cut diamond in a solitaire setting. Welch also had literally pounds of precious gold and silver that, because of the markings and where they came from, needed to be melted down.

The robbery of John Glenn's house was added to the tally of "Silver Gang" burglaries, which now totaled more than 110 homes in Montgomery, Arlington, and Fairfax Counties in Virginia. It was noted that "in all the burglaries they demonstrated an ability to distinguish between sterling silver and silver plate, between real gold and costume jewelry, and between real gems and imitation stones." News reports described the gang as very elusive, having a high degree of discipline and organization within the group. For crooks, they were very tight-lipped, and they seemed to be acting in concert, as though they were one individual.

As the days got longer, the burglaries slowed down for Bernard Welch. He was settling into the Falls Church neighborhood, and he would tell neighbors, or anyone else who asked, that he had made a bunch of money working as a plumber. The story continued that he invested in apartment buildings in the DC area now and also dabbled successfully in the stock market. He began studying the real estate prices in the Washington, DC, area, and his subscription to the *Wall Street Journal* helped him monitor precious metal prices as well as keep up his successful facade with the neighbors.

In the spring of 1977, the Hamiltons had a little more vacation money in their stash, so they traveled to the Caribbean. On April 27, they left for a resort on Pineapple Beach in St. Thomas, Virgin Islands. After a twelve-day dose of fun and sun, the next trip was to head back to Minnesota to liquidate merchandise and make some legitimate investments. Linda also had a ten-year high school reunion to attend. She was excited to show off Norm to her classmates at Denfield High School in Duluth.

But before Welch could head back to Minnesota, he needed Linda's help again. As they were preparing for their trip, Welch sat Linda down and explained he had a huge favor to ask of her. He informed her that he needed to make his identity as Norm Hamilton more legitimate and permanent. Welch proposed that on their next visit to Minnesota, Linda should borrow her brother Rodney's birth certificate, which he could then use to get a driver's license from the Virginia DMV. Even Welch was a little surprised at the big smile that spread across Linda's face. She loved the idea of being included in this intriguing collusion and said she didn't see any harm in using Rodney's birth certificate.

When they finally arrived back in Minnesota, Linda's family was glad to see Norm again. They were still of the opinion that he was quiet, reserved, courteous, and moderately good-looking. They agreed that Norm was quite a catch for Linda.

Linda happily whisked Norm off to the ten-year reunion of the Denfield High School Class of 1967. There she introduced her boyfriend simply as "Norm" and flashed the big diamond ring he had given her before they left Virginia. Little did Linda or her classmates know that the expensive bauble she was sporting once graced the slender fingers of Mrs. John Glenn, astronaut and US senator's wife.

The Hamiltons also looked at more houses for sale. There was a large, gorgeous house at 700 Valley Drive, in Duluth's posh Hidden Valley neighborhood, that caught Welch's eye as a potential Midwestern base of operations. It was a split-level on a large corner lot with a good setback from the street, and the backyard was heavily wooded. The home featured four bedrooms, three bathrooms, a family room, a library, and a huge living room fireplace. But what really sold Welch on the house was the indoor swimming pool, a rarity in the 1970s. In Welch's mind, if you owned a home with a large indoor pool, you had arrived. An interesting social statement for a guy who didn't know how to swim.

There was only one more item that needed attention in Duluth, and Linda did not disappoint. Just before she said all her good-byes to family and friends, she went to the desk where her parents kept the important family papers and took her brother's birth certificate. As she pulled the document from the desk, Linda didn't feel the least twinge of guilt about helping Norm hide from his badgering wife.

Welch was formulating new plans on the long drive back from Minnesota. He knew from previous experience how to get a legitimate driver's license with Rodney Norman Hamilton's stolen birth certificate. He could fully assume the identity of Norm Hamilton and solidify his stature in the community. He was on his way to obtaining the previously unattainable dream of a beautiful house in a nice neighborhood in Duluth, and once they got back to Virginia, they would move into a house in South Down Farm, a trendy home development northwest of Washington, DC. He had been studying that area and thought the rental prices were very reasonable for the type of property that was available there.

Their standard of living was rising rapidly, because Welch was hitting at least three houses a night, four nights a week. He stopped selling at flea markets and to antique dealers out East, where he had repeatedly gotten caught selling stolen articles. Duluth and Minneapolis had opened up a whole new avenue for sales of his stolen goods, and thousands of dollars were already pouring in.

Welch had promised they would create retirement funds for Linda and put away plenty of money when she quit her government job. She could expect this regular income, because she was doing all the paperwork for Norm's ersatz antique and collectible merchandise sales. Linda tracked the sales and shipment of the precious metals and the collectibles. She packed and shipped them, and she was keeping official books on the proceeds of this endeavor. She claimed that Norm gave her figures as to how much was spent on the purchased items and how much was taken in by the sale. From this, she was able to mock up profit and loss sheets. She also handled all the letters of transmittal that accompanied the precious metals shipments to the assayers and refiners, keeping track of the payments that came in. With Linda handling all of these administrative duties in his enterprise, Welch could spend more time robbing people's homes.

Welch decided to ship the broken down gold and silver in a more compact form to the precious metals refineries he dealt with around the country. He bought two propane-fired metal smelting furnaces with ceramic crucibles, one furnace for silver and the other for gold. He set these units up in the garage, and every other weekend he would break down the jewelry settings and sterling silver he couldn't sell on the used market. For the time being, the precious and semi-precious gemstones that were removed from the jewelry settings before smelting went into storage.

Sterling silver is 92.5 percent silver and 7.5 percent copper. The mixture of the two metals gives the sterling silver better wearing qualities and toughness. This alloy also makes sterling more malleable, easier to mold or beat into shapes. Pure silver would be too soft and wear easily; silverware, jewelry, and tea settings would bend, dent, and even break quickly if made of pure silver. Welch still came across silver coins in collections, and if he couldn't sell them for the collector's value, they would also be relegated to the smelter. Coin silver is 90 percent silver and 10 percent copper. This higher alloy content made silver coins tougher and more resistant to the handling they were subjected to every day.

The gold he smelted came from jewelry settings that were too distinctive to sell without being noticed or broken settings homeowners had kept for repair. Welch would carefully remove the gemstones from the settings, and the gold would be ready to melt in the smelting equipment. All gold jewelry, watches, and accessories are stamped with the carat rating of the gold they are made from. Twenty-four carat gold is 99.9 percent pure and very soft; usually only bullion and ingots have this rating. Twelve-carat gold is 50 percent pure gold; fourteen carat is 58 percent pure; eighteen carat is 75 percent pure; and twenty-two-carat gold is 92 percent pure. Ten-carat gold is only 42 percent pure but pretty tough. Welch mixed the different purities of gold together, knowing the refineries would test a small sample boring of each of the ingots he sent them to assay the purity.

The mold he used for ingots was a simple, divided, stainless steel cafeteria tray, like those used in state institutions, prison dining rooms, or military mess halls. Each tray compartment would yield a convenient size ingot when the molten metal cooled down.

On Monday mornings, Linda collected the silver or gold ingots, separated and wrapped them in four or five pages of newspaper, layered them in a small box between sheets of cardboard, and sealed up the boxes. Then, she shipped them off to precious metals refineries in Texas and California. About two weeks later, a check would arrive for the proceeds based on the current spot price quoted in New York by the Commodities Exchange. This smelting routine became a source of regular, bankable income for the Hamiltons.

In January 1978, the Hamiltons decided they should take a road trip to Minnesota. He wanted to make some more business contacts and make a down payment on that house in Hidden Valley they both loved. They decided to drive again. Linda was late in her first pregnancy and expecting to deliver in a couple of months. Driving also offered the added benefit of allowing Welch to haul the goods he needed to unload. The car was packed to the headliner with sterling silver tea sets, collector coins, framed artwork, collectible ceramics, and a shoebox full of hundred-dollar bills. High-end mink and ermine coats, newly acquired from the walk-in closets of trendy houses in the nicer suburbs of Washington, DC, acted as expensive packing blankets.

The weather got progressively colder as they swung around Chicago and turned north toward Madison then St. Paul. Once they arrived in Duluth, they picked up some coffee before making their way to the real estate office. At the real estate office, they submitted a $24,900 down payment for the house, in cash. Linda contributed some funds she had saved from her former government job, but Welch paid the lion's share.

Welch always had a number of stolen coins he needed to dispose of, but he wanted to get top dollar out of every transaction. When he ended up at Duluth Coin and Stamp run by Stan Sunde, he showed Sunde a few of the more commonplace coins to see what he would offer. Welch was satisfied with the initial transaction, so he took out some coins that made Sunde's jaw drop. He showed Sunde a collection of forty-five different three-dollar gold pieces. These exceptional coins were minted for thirty-five years starting in 1854, and they were tied in with the US postal system's three-cent stamp. This gold coin would buy one hundred stamps. They were never very popular with the public and all but disappeared from circulation (as did most gold coins) with the outbreak of the Civil War in 1861. This unusual gold piece was about the same diameter as a nickel but extremely thin. For some reason it survived the Coinage Act of 1873 that killed off the two-cent piece, the half dime, and the three-cent piece. It was minted until 1889.

Stan Sunde was taken aback at the rarity and high quality of these coins and asked Welch where he got them. Welch explained that he was invited to a private estate sale back east and bought out the whole inventory. Sunde commented that he wished he were lucky enough to run into such high-class merchandise at the occasional estate he was invited to liquidate. He informed Welch the coins were too high-test for the local market and had them shipped to Sotheby's in New York and sold at auction.

Sunde struck up an agreement with Norm Hamilton to sell his lesser coins locally out of his shop. Rarer coins that demanded a well-heeled clientele would be shipped out to high-end auction houses that specialized in selling rare individual coins and collections.

Stan Sunde believed Norm Hamilton to be an accomplished businessman and a shrewd investor. He obviously knew his way around coins, antiques, and precious metals. Norm didn't elaborate much about acquiring the estates on the East Coast, but Sunde chalked that up to discretion. Anyone who had thousands of dollars worth of coins and antiques around the house had to be cautious about security.

Linda's pregnancy was rapidly approaching full term, which signaled two things. Linda needed to return to the East Coast, and Welch wanted some variety in his sex life. During the short time the Hamiltons spent setting up the Duluth house in the winter of 1978, Linda's teenage niece, Susan Swanson, made a couple of appearances to visit and help out. Welch instantly sized up the provocative way Susan dressed and figured she knew the score. The opportunity for sex, no strings attached, was too hard to pass up.

With the down payment made on the Hidden Valley house and merchandise unloaded, the Hamiltons headed back east. Linda Hamilton gave birth to their first son on March 16, 1978. She had a difficult delivery and was essentially bedridden after the baby was born. Welch busied himself packing and boxing up all their household items and furniture for the move to their new home in Duluth. Given Linda's condition, he figured that they needed and could afford the help, so he contacted a professional moving company.

Once Linda's health improved, they planned to drive to Duluth on April 10 and have Neptune Movers haul their furniture and possessions up on April 25. They had already given notice to their landlord, and all that was left was to transport their possessions to Minnesota. The Hamiltons knew this would be a most difficult trip—another marathon drive, and now tending to the needs of an infant. The car was fully packed again with stolen merchandise to sell in Duluth and Minneapolis. There were silver serving platters, an ornate mantel clock, small, original oil paintings in ornate frames, fine porcelain bowls, vases, delicate cameos, and gold and silver jewelry with settings of precious and semi-precious stones. The usual assortment of pricey fur coats and stoles provided the padding so items didn't get jostled. He also brought along another pile of money. Welch wasn't able to bring as much as he wanted, as he also had to leave room for the baby and necessities.

Planning ahead, Welch decided to pack up his metal smelting equipment so he could continue that operation in Duluth. He shipped the smelting equipment and some other boxed and sealed stolen merchandise with the movers, which they could unpack later in the month.

They arrived back in Duluth safely, and on April 14, the Hamiltons closed on their new home at 700 Valley Drive. The furniture and smelting equipment arrived a couple weeks later. The furniture fit perfectly into their first attempt at homeownership. These furnishings weren't too pricey or showy for modest Duluth.

The Hamiltons comfortably settled into their new neighborhood in Duluth and began meeting the others living around them by attending the occasional barbeque or cocktail party. Hidden Valley was a typical upper-middle-class neighborhood that housed local business owners, politicians, corporate officers, attorneys, and even law enforcement officials. They immediately got acquainted with Stuart Seiler, the owner of Security Jewelers, because he and his wife, Robin, lived right across the street. Welch bought a lot of jewelry from Seiler, which was better than having Linda wear the stolen stuff. Alan Mitchell, St. Louis County Attorney, lived nearby, as did the Postmaster of Duluth, Frank Blatnik. The Hamiltons were adapting very well to this affluent suburban lifestyle. Little did these welcoming and friendly folks know who they had living in their midst.

Even while he was getting to know his neighbors, Welch wasted no time securing his new home. He busted up and removed a sidewalk and trimmed the brush and trees near the back and sides of the house. He wanted to make sure the two surveillance cameras he planned to install had a clear line of sight.

Since Linda stayed up in the house taking care of the baby most of time, Welch would take the opportunity to go out for a short run some mornings. The jogging was not only to keep in shape, but also served as an extension of his security cameras. Ever vigilant, he wanted to keep an eye on this little corner of Duluth. The jogs also gave him more chances to talk to the neighbors, meet some of the movers and shakers of the community, and enjoy his little slice of northern Minnesota heaven, so different from Washington's pretension and one-upsmanship.

So far the pieces of Bernard Welch's master plan, which originated back in the veterans housing in Rochester, were falling into place nicely. He was good at his "profession," he had a helpful significant other, and he now owned his own home. But he needed one other item to complete his "Norm Hamilton" persona—a nice car. He needed a high-end car like the ones driven by the people whose houses he robbed. Welch knew this was an important step toward blending in with the moneyed crowd. It would be a lot easier to drive into, and out of, those neighborhoods with an expensive car. He thought of a Mercedes Benz immediately, because he'd seen so many doctors, lawyers, and CEOs driving them. Also, European cars didn't change their styling every year like American cars did. That would make it easier for the occasional witness to confuse or forget what they saw. He started to set aside some cash for the purchase of that nice car later in the year.

Welch also knew that he couldn't stay in Duluth full-time. He needed to buy a home near Washington, DC, soon. He wanted a place near the beltway, with the flexible storage area and privacy that a large house in the country afforded. He needed to be removed from neighbors' prying eyes and the overhanging threat of unannounced visits from a landlord. He needed multiple garage bays and doors that were motorized so he would be able to drive in and out of the garage with no one seeing what he loaded or unloaded. Even to a casual observer, most of what Welch had in the garage and what he did in the garage would look suspicious. That house close to DC would be the new base of operations for his lucrative career. They had been looking in the Great Falls area and narrowed the possibilities down to a few properties. Welch was especially intrigued by a house he drove past that had a large lot and plenty of room for expansion of the floor plan. They had almost enough money now to make a sizeable down payment, but he wanted to be able to pay off at least 75 percent of the value of the home up front if he could.

To finance these impending purchases, Welch had to get down to business in Duluth. With all the new contacts Welch had made, it proved fairly easy to sell the goods through legitimate channels again. Coins and stamps went to Stan Sunde; furs and collectibles were listed in the classified ads in the *Duluth News Tribune.* Until now, the precious and semi-precious gemstones removed from the jewelry settings before smelting went into storage. Welch had been collecting loose gemstones for a while and had a large supply of unmounted cut stones, many of high quality. He made contact with Jerry Kaufhold, owner of Rose Galleries of Minneapolis, to handle the sale of the gems, as well as some antiques and Oriental rugs. Rose Galleries also occasionally auctioned off some of Welch's artwork. The relationship with Rose Galleries became very lucrative for the Hamiltons, netting them hundreds of thousands of dollars. Kaufhold thought Norm Hamilton was very smooth—reserved, well spoken, and seemingly educated.

Welch wasted no time in setting up the smelting furnace. He spent every Sunday smelting precious metals in the garage. He started pouring the molten metal into a cast iron frying pan, making larger, ten-inch disc ingots. Linda would wrap and box the gold ingots and ship them during the week. The silver ingots were being stockpiled, waiting for shipment. In August, the smelting operation got some unwanted attention. Welch left the garage for a few minutes to move the yard sprinklers, and his propane-fired smelter got out of control and started the garage on fire. A neighbor called the fire department, and a couple of Duluth fire rigs showed up, sirens blaring. So much for his low-key operation; it was time to get all that silver out of the garage.

Welch was getting tired of paying the high postage to get the silver ingots to the Texas and California assayers and refineries. Even if he had to do the driving, he wanted to find an assaying and refinery operation close enough that he could transport the silver on the ground.

He invited Stan Sunde, the Duluth coin dealer, to come up to the house and help him with the silver liquidation. Sunde set up a deal with a precious metals refiner in Illinois to handle what looked to be almost two tons of smelted coin and sterling silver. Welch knew that silver prices had been steadily on the rise because of the Hunt Brothers activities in trying to corner the silver market.

He figured this shipment should bring a return well into six figures.

Sunde rented a truck. He went back to Welch's house, and together they threw a few hundred ten-pound discs of silver onto the truck bed. Sunde arranged to spend the night at a friend's house in Minneapolis, before swinging east towards Chicago. When he arrived, his buddy wanted to see the cargo he was carrying in the back. Sunde swung open the back door of the truck box, and his friend took in this huge pile of silver.

"Do you think it might be stolen?"

"Oh no!" Sunde countered. "This guy's totally legit. He's an antique dealer and coin collector. This is just his junker stuff that's only worth its weight, so he smelts it into bullion."

After an early departure from Minneapolis, Sunde arrived at the Englehardt assayer's office in Chicago early on the afternoon of November 20. The tally from the truck was about 52,500 troy ounces of silver (almost 4,000 pounds). Sunde started the long drive home to Duluth the next morning with a check for $315,000.

The Hamiltons were doing well for themselves in Duluth. The sale of merchandise in Minnesota was steady. The antiques and artwork they couldn't sell were left in the house for decor. At worst, they could try to get a better price next summer when they returned to Duluth. The checks from the gold and silver refineries came in steadily. Linda deposited the money in a local bank account, and they also invested a few thousand dollars in her name with Bruce Howe, a stockbroker with Dain Bosworth.

Welch relished his status in Duluth, but he wasn't ready to quit the burglary game yet. He was anxious to get back east so he could pick up his trade where he left off, hitting three to five houses a night. When he returned, Welch resumed his burglaries, and he was becoming more arrogant. There were more close calls, and occasionally a homeowner was unlucky enough to come in on him during the break-in. More than once, the career felon had gotten the drop on a female victim and raped her. Welch was always armed with a stolen .380 automatic pistol and two pair of handcuffs.

Police in the Washington, DC, area were building their own profile of the meticulous, well-armed silver thief who was not averse to pistol-whipping and rape. Interviews with unfortunate victims revealed chilling encounters with this increasingly aggressive criminal. One rape victim revealed in her police report that she was told, "Keep your mouth shut. Don't scream. If you don't cooperate, I will beat you into the bed," before the attacker accused, "Maybe if there was more money around, I wouldn't have to do this." Another rape victim was threatened, "Keep your mouth shut and don't say one word or I'll smash your face in." The suspect bragged to one robbery victim, "I usually tie people up. I've shot some [people], raped a few people."

Police bulletins were sent out describing the suspect as "a very smart criminal who is armed and very dangerous." Through victim interviews and evidence evaluation, police also compiled a comprehensive MO of the suspect. He "walks in behind houses and looks in to see if they are occupied. He does not break into occupied houses intentionally." The suspect forces his way into the rear of the house, "cuts phone wires," and "gives the house a complete ransacking if he has time." The police know he uses drawstring bags to carry the stolen items, but he's also put items in "bowling bags, suitcases, and pillowcases" he finds around the home. In his burglaries, he has stolen eleven cars, using the vehicles to transport the stolen goods before abandoning them in a "public lot near the house."

Law enforcement officials agreed; this was a predatory, violent character in a dangerous profession. They knew it was just a matter of time before a physical confrontation would result in either a homeowner or the burglar headed for the emergency room. The police could only hope it would be the Ghost Burglar.

Detective Jim King left the office at ten in the morning, after the rush hour traffic was over. He was heading to the incorporated village of Chevy Chase.

Chevy Chase Village was an exclusive residential area of turn of the century houses. It was the child of the District's urban expansion, which had started in the 1880s. Downtown Washington, DC, is in a marshy hole in a river valley. The prevailing winds on the East Coast are from the north and west, blowing over, rather than through, the city. Surrounding land to the west and north is much higher, therefore cooler and cleaner, as any warm air and pollutants blow off the higher land into the city below.

Land developers in the nineteenth century began to buy up the farmlands of northern Washington, DC, subdividing the area into building lots for those who could afford it. When all of the available land within the boundary of Washington was exhausted, the developers bought up the farms in Maryland, just across the dividing line of Western Avenue. A trolley system extended along Connecticut Avenue to a resort lake just north of the District in Maryland. Two country clubs were also established along Connecticut Avenue to service the affluent homeowners.

The well-to-do Chevy Chase area, thus, straddled the boundary of Washington and Maryland. It was, for many years, quiet, isolated, and wealthy. After World War II, things changed when automobiles became more commonplace. This rich area of the District and Montgomery County, Maryland, became a hunting ground for thieves. Detective King headed to this area of old money to follow up a possible lead for some burglaries he was investigating.

The burglar who had plagued lower Montgomery County, northern Virginia, and northwest DC for three years had been dubbed the "Standard Time Silver Burglar" by Montgomery County Detective Mike Shawn. Shawn was on King's shift in the Crimes Against Property Unit. Shawn was one of the first to notice the particular burglary pattern, which coincided with the inception of early sunset around the beginning of standard time in late October. This unique criminal pattern would continue through the winter until the sun began to set later, about when daylight saving time began. Then, these particular types of burglaries would stop for the summer, only to begin again the next fall. Because of the rising value of silver, there were many burglaries in which silver was stolen. To differentiate the common silver thieves from the unusual methods employed by this one criminal, Mike had coined the term "Standard Time Silver Burglar."

The media loved it. It had that certain ring, like "Jack the Ripper." It gave the reporters something to lead their stories with and provided a good tagline for the six o'clock news. Local reporters kept dossiers and stock film footage about this type of crime. They put detectives' names and numbers in their Rolodexes for later reference. The police accepted this practice as much as they complained about the sensationalism it engendered. At least it alerted the public about the problem. In many cases, alert citizens were often a valuable resource for solving crimes.

As King drove toward Chevy Chase, he thought about how he was going to speak to the female victim. She had been raped by a man inside her own home when she was there alone. The entry had all the earmarks of the Standard Time Silver Burglar. There was another burglary in the same area on the same evening. It was similar—telephone wires cut, rear window pried, silver, jewelry, and a few small antique items removed. There was little doubt in King's mind that the rapist and the Standard Time Silver Burglar were one in the same.

King had no desire to hear the details of the rape from the victim; he had read the police report. He did not like to work rapes. After interviewing the victims, he came away feeling violated himself. The only person to whom he had been able to describe his feelings was his wife. Once, when he had drunk a little too much wine and they were sitting alone together, he told her that it felt like putting on someone else's sweaty, dirty underwear. King thought she would laugh at him, but she had understood.

King knew he had too much empathy with victims. He identified with their pain too closely. That's why he did not try to transfer to the Homicide and Rape Unit. Detectives there were considered the best of the best. They had to be. Burglary was a much cleaner crime. Only things were stolen, not lives. At the end of the day, a burglary investigator could go home and not worry about victims, not think about brutality, violence, and injury. King often wished he were made of sterner stuff.

No, he did not want the intimate details of the sexual assault. What he wanted were the details of the rapist himself. Two other victims who had met this same criminal had been unable to provide any useful information. One had been an old man in his seventies who had been pistol-whipped when he resisted. The other had been a bedridden woman unable to converse intelligently. The Crimes Against Persons detective who was assigned this new rape case said this woman was a good witness. She had not been hysterical, and she had the ability to distance herself from the act as it was happening and observe details. She was a survivor type. King wanted to hear what she had seen, heard, felt, and thought about her assailant.

King turned off Connecticut Avenue into Chevy Chase Village. The narrow street, lined by giant oak trees, had been built for Model Ts. Parking was allowed only on one side. Large homes of various vintages were set well back from the curb on expansive lots. King knew the area well, having patrolled it when he was in uniform in the Bethesda District. It was 10:30 a.m. when he parked in front of the victim's home.

The house was a big, three-story foursquare, white clapboard building. It had a massive chimney in the exact center on its high peaked roof. This style had been popular in the 1920s. A wide porch ran around three sides of the home. Elaborate wood columns held up the roof that covered the porch. White wicker furniture decorated the front porch. The yard had piles of brown leaves that had fallen from the several huge oaks that dotted the half-acre lot. There were ancient azalea and boxwood bushes around the property. This overgrown landscaping, one of the charms of the area, was also one of its weaknesses. It gave perfect cover for a night prowler.

King walked up the old concrete sidewalk to the four broad wooden steps that led to the porch. The ornate front door was original to the house. It had stained glass in the top half and an old brass doorknob. King noticed the newly installed dead bolt lock just above the doorknob. In the center of the door, just below the stained glass, was a brass knob, set in a matching escutcheon. This was an old, mechanical doorbell. King turned the knob to the right and a bell on the other side of the door rang like a windup alarm clock.

He waited a minute. There was no sound from inside. He had noted a car in the driveway, parked in front of the freestanding garage, so he believed someone was at home. He reached for the brass doorbell knob again. As he was about to turn it, a female voice from inside questioned, "Who is it?"

"Mrs. Smith? It's Detective King, Montgomery County Police. We had an appointment this morning."

"Could you slide your identification through the mail slot, please?" the voice responded from the other side.

King reached into his inside suit coat pocket and removed his police ID wallet. It contained a gold badge on one side and his photo ID card on the other. He pushed it through the scrolled brass mail slot just below the doorbell. He did not hear it hit the floor, so the woman on the other side must have grabbed it as it came through. After a few seconds, the locks turned and the door opened.

The woman standing in the open door appeared much younger than her forty-nine years. She was about five foot, five inches tall, well proportioned, and quite pretty. Her long, dark brown hair was tightly pulled back into a ponytail. She wore a red cashmere sweater and black, wool pants. Her lipstick matched her red sweater. Having no wrinkles or lint, her clothes appeared to have just come from the dry cleaners. King surmised that this woman paid attention to details.

Mrs. Smith handed King back his ID case. "I'm sorry. I'm just a lot more careful now than I was before the...." She let the sentence hang, trying to think of an appropriate word that could encompass her sexual assault and all its consequences on her life.

"I understand, ma'am," King said.

Mrs. Smith gave a weak smile and led King into the home's interior. The house was decorated in Arts and Crafts, a popular motif in the early twentieth century. Everything was clean and neat. Even the large books on the coffee table were arranged in artful disorder. There was a casual elegance to the furnishing.

The two walked through the large center hall foyer. Oriental carpets were spread along the center hall's length, which ran from the front door to the rear of the home. The ceilings were ten feet high with Tiffany-style stained glass hanging lamps. A long stairway to the left of the hall led to the second floor. The living room was on the right and the dining room on the left. Each room had its own bay window. Immediately behind the dining room was an expansive kitchen. It was into this room that Mrs. Smith led Detective King.

She indicated a round oak table with ball and claw feet. King sat down on an oak pressed-back chair with a cushion atop its caned seat. Mrs. Smith stood on the other side of the table. A coffee pot was steaming on the counter. "Would you like some coffee?" she asked.

"That would be fine. Cream and sugar if you have it."

As Mrs. Smith poured the coffee, King looked around the room. It was a good kitchen, designed to be efficient and comfortable. He noticed the appliances. There was a commercial Viking six-burner stove, normally found in small restaurants, and a commercial stainless steel Sub-Zero refrigerator. Copper and stainless steel cooking pots hung from a rack over the counter.

"I feel like I'm in a restaurant, " King commented as Mrs. Smith delivered the coffee.

"My husband's in the restaurant equipment business," she replied with a slight smile. "He insisted that everything be the best."

King shook his head in admiration. "My wife loves to cook. She would really like your kitchen."

"My husband loves to cook also. He does most of it here at home."

"I burn water," said King glumly.

Mrs. Smith actually smiled enough to display a pair of dimples. "I'm not so good at it either."

Mrs. Smith sat down at the table across from King. He sipped his coffee and opened his black vinyl notepad folder. On the first page, he had jotted some notes about the crime at Mrs. Smith's home.

"Mrs. Smith, let me explain why I wanted to speak to you. I'm a burglary detective. I don't investigate sexual assaults. But in your case, I believe your attacker is primarily a burglar. There was a similar burglary a couple of blocks away on the same night as your assault. I believe that your attacker did that first, before coming here. What happened to you is what the police call a crime of opportunity. You may have heard about this guy in the news. He's been called the Standard Time Silver Burglar."

Mrs. Smith shook her head no. She had lost her smile. Her lips were now drawn thin; her nostrils were pinched in and had turned white.

"To make a long story short, I'm trying to figure out who this guy is. He leaves nothing behind except his method of operation. My only hope of pinning this guy down is to interview people who have had contact with him. I'm trying to build a profile, a description that may help identify him."

Mrs. Smith listened but did not move. She's waiting, thought King, to see if this is just a waste of time.

"To that end, I spoke to Hutchinson, the Crimes Against Persons detective who is handling your case. He was impressed by your description of the event. I was hoping that I could glean some bit of information about your attacker that might help me."

Mrs. Smith nodded that she understood. Her eyes were half lidded, and her brow furrowed in thought. She still said nothing, requiring King to sustain his monologue. He wetted his lips with a sip of coffee. This would not be easy for either of them. He would have to ask questions requiring her to revisit a terrible incident. But he had drawn blanks everywhere else. This had to be done.

"Now, I don't want to know the details of the attack. You gave those already. What I want to know is what you can remember about the man himself."

Mrs. Smith's face relaxed slightly as she understood that she would not have to retell the intimate details.

Referring to his notes, King said, "I know he was wearing a mask, a kerchief, but at one point you saw his face briefly. You said he had dark hair and dark eyes."

Mrs. Smith nodded again without speaking.

"So, let me start off. Did he have any body odor?"

She drew her head back slightly and raised her eyebrows. Her eyes widened in surprise. It was obvious that she had not expected this question. She thought for a moment, eyes closed and her forehead creased in concentration. "No, no body odor."

"Any aftershave?"

"No, none. No smells at all. I would have noticed. He was on top of me, you know." This snapped out, like she was flicking an annoying bug off of her arm.

"Yes, I understand," King mumbled. He knew that this impatience was not directed at him, but rather at her rapist.

King looked at his notes again. "Did he talk to you?"

No pause before her answer; she expected this question. "Yes, he came in and said, 'Don't move.' Then he ordered me upstairs to the bedroom. He told me to take off my clothes. I had to strip in front of him. He had a gun." She began to tremble slightly and clasped her hands together. King grimaced slightly in sympathy.

"Okay, could you tell if he had any kind of accent, like northern or southern?"

"Well, it was definitely not southern. It was northern, but not like New York City. It was maybe like Pennsylvania or upstate New York, but not New England."

"Good," King nodded and quickly recorded her response. "You said in your statement he was of medium build and height. How was his physical condition? How old do you think he was?"

"I think he was thirty-five or forty. He was in good shape but not really muscular, just average. He didn't seem heavy when he laid on me." She had said this last sentence without thinking and drew her breath in quickly.

King knew he could not let her think too long about that statement. She was getting comfortable with the interview process, and it was becoming an intellectual exercise and not an emotional one. He asked the next question quickly. "What about his breath? Was he a smoker?"

"No cigarette smell. I don't smoke, so I would have noticed," she replied. After thinking a bit longer she offered, "Oh yes, there is one thing I do remember. That made me think of it."

"What's that?"

"You mentioned his breath. He did kiss me." She quietly continued, "He kissed me, and I felt his teeth move."

"Teeth move?" It was King's turn to be surprised.

"Yes, like he had dentures."

"False teeth? I see. Uppers or lowers?"

"No, both. Uppers and lowers. They both moved."

King's eyes widened and his head cocked to the right. He was stopped in his questioning. He had not expected this. A full set of false teeth in a fairly young man, that was rare. He knew in the service when a new recruit had multiple dental problems, military dentists would just pull every tooth and issue dentures. This had happened to a friend of his in the Navy. King knew that prison dentists would do the same thing. All he could think to say was, "Well, that is significant. That's maybe something I can check out." He scribbled "full false teeth" in his notes.

King plowed on. "Anything about his clothes?"

Mrs. Smith closed her eyes again, remembering. "Black jogging suit, zipped up. Black athletic shoes."

"Anything about the clothes—smells, like laundry, dry cleaning, texture, quality?"

"No, just a clean smell. Smooth, good material. Not cheap fabric."

"Did he take anything?"

"No, not that I've found. All my good jewelry is in the safety deposit box. We don't like silver. You have to keep polishing it. There's really nothing of value to steal."

That would explain the lack of a burglary report, thought King.

"Was there anything that he said or did—mannerisms, movements, anything—that stood out as unusual, not normal? I'm sorry, I know that's a far-reaching question, but you are very observant."

Mrs. Smith's face was now passive, showing little emotion. "No, nothing. He was right-handed. At least he held his gun in his right hand. He didn't use any curse words. His voice was cold and authoritative, but normal. Nothing stood out. Just an average, normal white man. Well, maybe not normal. I mean, normal men don't break into houses and rape women, do they?" Mrs. Smith's voice rose slightly at the end of sentence, indicating to King how close to the surface her emotions were.

King responded to her rhetorical question as best he could. "No, ma'am, they don't, and this guy is not normal. Most burglars aren't violent, unless cornered. They go out of their way to avoid people. This guy doesn't. He's got a gun, and he's not afraid of people. Someday he's going to hurt somebody bad."

Mrs. Smith eyes had begun to tear up. He knew he had wrung as much information as possible from this witness. He didn't want to push her too hard. She was still very fragile.

"Ma'am, unless you have anything else, I'll be going. You've given me a couple of new avenues to investigate. Here's my card. Call if you think of anything else."

Mrs. Smith took the proffered card, looked at it briefly, and laid it on the table. She looked into King's eyes and, with her lips stretched tightly over clenched teeth, responded in almost a hiss. "I hope you get that bastard. I can't sleep at night thinking he'll return. I've got new locks on the doors and a burglar alarm now. I've had to change my whole life because of him."

Good, King thought, she was mad. Anger was better than despair.

"I know, ma'am. What you're experiencing is normal. If it's any comfort, this guy doesn't hit homes with alarm systems. So always use it, even if you're home, okay?"

Mrs. Smith seemed to have calmed slightly. She nodded. "I hope I've helped."

"Yes, ma'am, you have. And thank you for your time. I know this wasn't easy for you."

Mrs. Smith led him out of the kitchen to the front door. As she opened the door, she stepped partially behind it so that her right hand was still on the doorknob. King believed he knew why. She did not want to shake hands with a strange man. She had been deeply affected by her attack. She was insecure, suspicious, and afraid. This was not unusual for a rape victim. She had been violated sexually, that was bad enough. But being attacked in her own home was even worse. If it had happened in an alley or a parking lot, she could avoid those locations. But her own home…that she could not avoid. In King's experience, women more than men felt personally violated when their homes were broken into. To also be raped there had to compound that feeling. He knew the Smith residence would probably be for sale by next spring, along with the bed she was attacked in. That was also not unusual. He hoped her husband was an understanding man.

King did not offer his hand. He merely said good-bye when he exited. As he walked away from the home, he heard the dead bolt lock click. He drove away slowly. As he looked back at the victim's residence, he saw a window curtain flutter closed. Mrs. Smith had been watching to make sure he left. It would be a long time before she would be trusting again. Still, she was alive and functioning almost normally. He knew of some rape victims who had been so psychologically shattered they never fully recovered.

Detective King turned right and headed north on Connecticut Avenue, back toward the station. The next question was where to go from there.

The Standard Time Silver Burglaries continued. There were several each week; each one a major hit, thousands of dollars in silver, jewelry, antiques, and collectibles taken. Not a clue, not a rumor as to who was responsible.

King knew that traditional police methods were not going to catch this guy. He was different from any thief they had ever confronted before. And he was getting bolder with time.

King's first hint to the thief's identity had started with that small, regional crime information meeting down in Virginia when Detective Baker described a suspect who committed the same type of burglaries.

When similar crimes began occurring in Montgomery County, Maryland, King had contacted Detective Sergeant Baker in Richmond. It took awhile, but when Detective Baker sent King what he had on the suspect, it was a lot. There were many photocopied reports and interviews. King read everything, twice.

The photocopied pages detailed the investigative efforts of the state police departments of Virginia, West Virginia, and Pennsylvania, and local Richmond area departments. They had apprehended Paul D. Marturano in Charleston, West Virginia. Marturano had been serving twenty years for first-degree manslaughter at Dannemora prison in upstate New York. He escaped from that prison in September 1974, accompanied by Bernard C. Welch, Jr., who was serving a twenty-one-year sentence for numerous burglaries.

The two escapees had broken into houses and stolen cars after their escape.

They ended up in Richmond, Virginia. There, they moved into a cheap apartment, assumed fictitious names, and supported themselves by committing house burglaries. Welch took the lead, as he was a professional burglar by trade. At first, Marturano was the wheelman, but after the first few burglaries, he was left behind at the apartment.

Not long after the pair arrived in Richmond, they broke up. Marturano went first to Charlottesville, Virginia, and then to Charleston, West Virginia, where, through an informant, he was arrested. In West Virginia, Paul Marturano was interrogated by state police from Pennsylvania, West Virginia, and Virginia. He gave an extensive interview before being returned to Dannemora. In that interview, Marturano told everything he knew of Bernard Welch's habits, crimes, and methods of operation. King read this interview several times.

Reading between the lines of the interview, King came to believe that, had Marturano not left when he did, he would have been found dead in a ditch along some back road. Marturano was not a hard case, like Welch. Welch kept Marturano around only until he was no longer useful.

It all fit. The Richmond pattern was happening again in Montgomery County, Fairfax, Arlington, Alexandria, and Washington, DC. Criminals are like any other human. Once they establish a successful pattern, they stick with it. That's why burglars' methods of operation are so important; it was all they left behind. The Richmond pattern had reappeared in Montgomery County several months after Welch had eluded police in Richmond in September 1975. He must have gone somewhere and cooled it for a while or, possibly, to scope out the area and establish a new identity and residence.

It took time for King to put it together. The burglaries were spread out across the DC metro area. Not every day, never in the same neighborhood twice in a row. These crimes blended in with the hundreds of other burglaries that constantly occurred. When mixed in with the scores of crimes that were assigned to dozens of different investigators in several different jurisdictions each month, they were undistinguishable.

But the Standard Time Silver Burglaries were really identifiable because of the antiques. No one broke into private houses to steal antiques. The theft of antiques is a two-part crime that involves knowledge of what to steal and knowledge of where to fence them. The thief had to be able to discern what was valuable; there were a lot of reproduction antiques used as decorator items that had almost no value. And antiques are just too hard to get rid of. It's pretty difficult to sell a mid-eighteenth-century Chinese porcelain vase out of the trunk of a car. Few, if any thieves, had this information. If his history in Richmond was any guide, Bernard Welch possessed this knowledge, and it made him one of a kind. He was like John Dillinger, the master criminal from the thirties who had his fingerprints erased with acid. Dillinger became the only man in America with no prints, which actually made him all the easier to identify. Welch possessed knowledge of antiques that no other common burglar would have.

The final piece that fit everything together was the false teeth. King had recently received confirmation from Dannemora that an escaped prisoner by the name of Bernard Welch had a full set of fake choppers, upper and lower. The rape victim in Chevy Chase had confirmed it. With that, and her description of her attacker, there was no doubt in King's mind that Bernard Welch was the perpetrator of the Standard Time Silver Burglaries.

The scariest part was that this guy was getting bolder. He was becoming more aggressive and less afraid of running into people inside a home. There were two more rapes in other jurisdictions that might be him. In the rape in Chevy Chase, he had produced a pistol. According to Marturano, Welch would kill if necessary.

Over the last year, the burglary investigators in the Washington area slowly came to the realization that some of their assigned cases were connected. Police in neighboring jurisdictions had always kept in loose, informal contact with each other, sharing information on suspects, crimes, and informants. There were two basic geographical groups of police forces in the metro area— one north of the Potomac River and one south of it.

South of the Potomac were Fairfax, Arlington, and Alexandria, comprising the area of northern Virginia. North of the Potomac were Washington, Montgomery, and Prince Georges Counties in Maryland. Each group experienced, within its region, lots of cross-border crime. The road system allowed criminals to move freely within the geographic areas. There was some cross-river criminal movement, but that was mainly to the District of Columbia to sell stolen goods and purchase drugs. Washington was the pivot spot, the center around which the entire region rotated. Its crime rate was the highest; its criminals the worst; its drug scene the nastiest. The District's mix of drug markets, pawnshops, and buyers of stolen property was like an open sewer drawing flies.

Washington's Second Police District bordered on the Bethesda District of Montgomery County. Early in his detective career, King had made contact with Detective Dave Roberts of DC's Second District. Roberts was a veteran cop who knew almost everything about the District and its crime. King found him a wealth of information. Through Roberts King found out that, not only were DC's wealthiest areas experiencing the Richmond pattern burglaries, but so was Fairfax County, Virginia.

Casually and individually, the various investigators of the two geographic groups came together and shared information. As the burglaries increased, they met in person and in groups. These informal contacts coalesced into a working group, an unofficial task force.

All these investigators were drawing blanks on the Standard Time Silver Burglaries. Traditional methods of crime sleuthing had failed. Normally, what solved burglary cases was either a mistake by the criminal, a trace-back of stolen property, or an informant. Informants were a primary source of criminal information. Someone would get nabbed on a "beef" and would "drop a dime" on somebody else's crime in order to get a sentence reduction for their infraction. It was an old police practice to trade prison time for good information. Only the FBI had the budget for paid informants.

Sometimes, a thief would get identified because he sold his stolen goods to a legitimate pawnshop and not on the street. This had been a recent experience of King's. An antique grandfather clock had been stolen from a vacant home in Kensington, Maryland. The clock was valued at about two thousand dollars, and the owner had a good description of it. King had made the rounds of clock shops and antique stores and found it. He traced back the seller and discovered that a couple of weeks earlier, the seller had been a hired painter in the house the clock was stolen from. When King arrested the painter in his home, he discovered a bunch of marijuana plants growing in the kitchen and basement.

The painter was charged with felony theft and manufacture of narcotics with intent to distribute, also a felony. The two charges were slam-dunk convictions, good for ten years each. The painter was also an ex-con on parole, with several years of prison back-up time to complete if his parole was violated. So, the painter contacted King and offered a deal. He gave King the name of the culprit in two commercial arsons and a murder-for-hire plot to kill an Internal Revenue Service agent investigating a tax fraud. The information was good. The defense attorney worked out the plea with the Maryland States Attorney's Office. The painter served six months in the Montgomery County jail, and his parole was not violated. For this, Montgomery County arrested a guy for two big arsons. The insurance companies saved hundreds of thousands of dollars, and two people went to prison for conspiracy to commit murder. The IRS agent got a chance to die of old age. Not a bad deal all around.

Nothing like that happened in the Standard Time Silver Burglary cases. No prints, no clues, no snitches, no witnesses, except the lady who was raped and the three-year-old statement of Paul Marturano. The lady had given one other bit of usable information, the false teeth. Who would believe false teeth would be the identifier of a serial burglar? King had to convince his supervisor to back him on his next move.

King entered Lieutenant Bill Barry's office. Barry bore a striking resemblance to Lieutenant Barney Miller on the popular TV comedy police show of the same name, down to the full mustache. Lieutenant Barry was an old-timer, wise in the ways of criminals and cops. He came off as a good ol' boy who loved women, booze, and his pipe, but Barry was more, he was smart. He had gotten a law degree by going to night school after work. He hadn't had time to do much with his degree yet, except represent himself in his last divorce.

The lieutenant was lighting his large, briar pipe when King entered. Minute burning tobacco embers cascaded from the pipe as he puffed it to life. The embers floated down onto his tie, white shirt, and dark blue trousers. He casually brushed them off, but not before a couple burned miniscule holes in the fabric of his pants. Most of Lieutenant Barry's clothing had burn holes from his pipe. The joke in the office was that someday, all of the holes would connect and he'd be wearing nothing but his belt, gun, and pants zipper.

At a wave of Barry's hand, King sat down in the chair at the front of his desk. Barry didn't speak for a moment, as he continued to puff on his pipe. Soon, clouds of smoke created rancorous smog around his head and shoulders. He finally moved his eyes from the bowl of the pipe to King's face.

With a smile wrapped around the pipe stem clenched in his teeth, the lieutenant said, "Yes, James, what can I do for you today?" Lieutenant Barry often used a formal mode of speech when he was in a good mood. This was a positive sign.

"Well, Lieutenant, I need your advice and backing," King said seriously.

Barry raised one eyebrow. "Yes, and what is your particular conundrum?"

"Lieutenant, you know about the Standard Time Silver Burglaries. You know how we, DC, Fairfax, Arlington, and Alexandria are getting beaten up almost every night by this guy. We're losing hundreds of thousands of dollars each year. As far as I can tell, this pattern started here in late 1976 and continues to this day. This guy hits us hard during the winter months and lays off during the summer, like he goes on vacation. We all forget about him and go on our merry way. Then, the pattern starts up again the next winter.

"We haven't a clue as to who the thief is, except I believe he answers in all respects to the description of Bernard Welch. I've told you about him. His MO in Richmond was exactly the same as here, and it's a unique MO. He's known to carry a gun and has stated he will kill any witness, so as not to be sent back to prison."

Lieutenant Barry leaned back in his gray, swivel chair, holding his pipe in his right hand. King could see his jovial mood melting away.

"I've also told you about my interview with a rape victim in Chevy Chase. She described her attacker as having a full set of false teeth. I just received confirmation," King held up the letter he had received with the prison letterhead from Dannemora, "that Bernard Welch had a full set of false teeth in prison. Welch answers the description of her attacker, and she said he had a northern accent, similar to New York State. That's where Welch grew up. His entry into her house matches the MO of the Standard Time Silver Burglar. I think this nails it down. Bernard Welch is the Standard Time Silver Burglar."

Lieutenant Barry rubbed his neck with his left hand. His eyes were slits, either from the tobacco smoke or concentration. He removed the big briar from his mouth, spit a small piece of tobacco off his tongue, and replied, "Okay, you've made a good circumstantial case that the bad guy is Welch. What advice do you want?" Lieutenant Barry was now all business; his smile was gone.

King tried to arrange his request in a logical order so that it might be more appealing to the lieutenant. "Well, I know who the thief is; I just don't know where he is. I know he must be stockpiling the stolen loot at some storage site, but I don't know where. I know he must be transporting the stolen antiques out of the area to sell them, but I don't know where. I believe he thinks he has hit on a winning combination, and he's going to stay with the plan."

King continued, quickly, afraid of losing Lieutenant Barry's interest. "One last thing, this guy, Welch, is getting bolder. The rape in Chevy Chase proves it. He's taking more chances because he's been successful. I think he's beginning to believe he can't get caught. I think he's addicted to the thrill. Now, it's not enough just stealing and getting away without being seen. To me, it looks like he wants the excitement of confronting his victims, taking control and fooling the cops."

Lieutenant Barry had leaned back in his chair and stared at the ceiling as King spoke. "Lieutenant, the only way I can think of to flush this guy out is to go to the media with this information and ask for the public's help."

Barry's head came forward quickly, and both of his eyebrows rose together, making his squinty eyes wide at the mention of the media.

King hurried on. "Lieutenant, we've got an FBI wanted poster about him that details his Richmond crimes. We can give that to the media, say he's suspected to be in the area committing crimes, and ask if anyone can tell us anything about him. If he's anywhere around DC, somebody will know him. So I need your permission to contact the press with this information."

Barry rocked back and forth in his chair. He did not speak. His eyes were now closed as he puffed on his pipe. It had gone out, but he sucked on it as if it hadn't. After a long time, he rocked forward, placing his forearms on his desk. He removed his pipe and placed it on the desk in front of him. Using his thumb and index finger, he wiped away the excess saliva from the corners of his lips. He sat very still, looking at King.

He stared directly into King's eyes, a no bullshit expression on his face. "First," he started, raising one finger in the air, "this type of appeal would generate hundreds, maybe thousands, of calls, not only to us, but to every police department for fifty miles. Ninety-nine percent of the calls would be bogus. By the time we figured out which caller gave us the correct information, Welch's scrawny ass would be a thousand miles away."

Barry held up two fingers. "Second, I like my job. It's all day work with no weekends. In five years, I can retire. I hope to stay here, in this office, until I do retire. If I give you permission to go to the media, I'm toast, no matter which way the cookie crumbles. If you are wrong, we—that's you, me, and the entire department—will look like the world's biggest fools. And that's the good news. If you are right, this guy will skip town. So then, we're assholes for letting him get away to start again somewhere else. And if he just happens to shoot somebody while escaping, or runs over a child during a high-speed chase, or takes hostages when he gets cornered, we—you and me—are double-wide assholes. And just guess who'll get sued? It's a no-win situation."

The lieutenant held up three fingers. "You know what the folks upstairs think of the media. Let's just say they would take a dim view of your plan. The less the media knows about us, the better. To put it nicely, the gentlemen of the press are not considered our friends. If I were to allow this to happen, guess what? I'd end up working a permanent Night Hawk shift, with Tuesday and Wednesday off, for the next five years out in East Podunk, Montgomery County, where the cows live." Barry's voice was rising and beginning to sound angry as he continued. "And you know what else? I'll be supervising you, because I'll guarantee that your ass will go through the grinder right beside mine."

King began to get up, knowing his idea had gone down in flames, but Barry waved him back. "No, sit down. I'm not finished." Barry's mood softened and his tone smoothed out, becoming almost apologetic. "Listen, Jim, I appreciate what you're trying to do, to solve a tough one. I know your dedication and efforts on these cases. Believe me, I understand your frustration. I used to be full of piss and vinegar once, until I got older and wiser." Barry smiled at the thought.

The lieutenant stopped for a moment. Then, with a cheerful tone, he said, "How about this? You've got the FBI poster, right?"

King nodded.

"Can't get into trouble sending out an official FBI poster, right?"

Again, King nodded silently.

"Okay, you say he's selling the stolen goods out of state. How about mailing those FBI posters with a cover letter from you to all the antique auction houses within, say, two hundred miles?"

King sat for several seconds considering the proposition. The lieutenant had offered a deal. He knew King could go to the press behind his back and that King was just rash enough to do that if he thought it was the right thing to do. Barry also knew that if the media got wind of this, it wouldn't take long for the old-timers in the administrative offices upstairs to figure out who had leaked the information. One of the many things the old-timers especially did not like was a leak to the media. If that happened, they'd get King for sure, but Barry would also get a black mark against him for not controlling his people. In the next promotion list, he'd be passed over, maybe even transferred back to the uniform division.

King was aware of Barry's motives for offering him a bone. He could almost see the wheels turning inside Barry's brain. Still, everything Barry had said was probably true, if exaggerated. For sure, there was one thing Barry had said that King knew to be absolutely correct; if King went to the media without permission, he would be working a beat in a district as far away from his home as could be found. King's daughter was sick, really sick. He could not afford to exercise his Joan of Arc complex and go to the fire for what he believed to be right. He owed that to his family; they came first.

He took the deal.

"Okay, lieutenant, that'll work. Thanks." King stood up and walked out. He licked his wounds knowing that he hadn't retreated, he was just advancing in another direction. That helped a little.

Lieutenant Bill Barry tamped his pipe, relit it, and rocked back in his chair. He smiled serenely, congratulating himself that he had dodged a bullet that might have wounded him. It most certainly would have hurt Jim King's career. Barry relaxed and puffed on his black briar. A hot ember drifted out of the pipe bowl and settled on his pants, burning a new hole.

Welch hit the Washington, DC, area hard upon his return from Minnesota in January 1979. He amassed enough stolen merchandise to again fill a rental truck, and the Hamiltons looked forward to another summer getaway in Duluth. Welch knew he could easily turn a fifteen-foot truck of antiques and collectibles into cash in the Midwestern markets of Minneapolis and Duluth. The local dealers had been very receptive to the high quality, East Coast antiques and collectibles he'd brought them before.

For two summers in a row, Welch sold more than $100,000 worth of coins through Stan Sunde. Sunde was still selling the semi-rare collector's coins on consignment, while the very rare and exceptional items went to specialty coin houses for auction to the high rollers. Money was also coming in from the antiques and artworks being sold in Minneapolis at Rose Galleries and from the gold and silver ingots being sent to refineries.

Welch also brought a load of fur coats to sell this time. These furs still carried personalized identification tags or maker's marks that could lead police back to the original owners. He knew these tags had to be carefully removed and patched up professionally in order to safely unload them and retain the value of the expensive furs. Welch published an ad in the classifieds of the July 28, 1979, *Duluth News Tribune*: "Wanted: Seamstress for sewing new linings in fur coats plus some embroidery, part-time only, your hours."

Welch hired a local girl who worked on thirty-five fur coats and got paid thirty dollars for each one. Once the fur coats were altered, he sold them through newspaper ads in Duluth and the Twin Cities as high-end used merchandise. Later, the seamstress told police she had no idea the coats were stolen, as Welch had turned on the charm and spun another of his plausible yarns to cover up the source of the goods.

Moving the fur coats and the other goods out of the Duluth house became a methodical process. He retained some of the operating procedures that worked for him early in his career of crime while he was still with Anne Marie in Spencerport, New York. Some folks who glimpsed the goods he stored in the basement compared it to the inventory of a pricey department store. Welch loved hiding in plain sight by dealing directly through the want ads. He also ran ads selling collector's plates and other items.

The money coming in from Bernard Welch's burglary enterprise in 1979 was dazzling. Welch arranged for Linda to open a personal savings account in Duluth with a hefty deposit. The profits of Welch's dealings also allowed him to dabble in the stock market in a big way—in Linda's name, of course. Anytime Welch had a surplus that didn't need to be committed to the fund for the new house they planned to buy back East, he would invest it in Linda's accounts with Bruce Howe. Dealing through Howe, Welch picked up thousands of shares of Pan American Airlines stock, and he started buying the stock of the spice company McCormick. They were building quite a portfolio. More deposits in the stock brokerage account brought the balance in Duluth up to almost $500,000.

He and Linda were pulling in so much cash she even filed income tax returns, as if she were running a legitimate business. Linda Hamilton's reported income for 1978 was $647,569. In 1979, she reported approximately $500,000.

With so much money to play around with, Welch started having a good time entertaining his neighbors. He would frequently invite the gentlemen of this upscale area over to enjoy a few drinks and adult movies. These activities allowed Welch to show off his new Sony Betamax VCR, a piece of high tech equipment that was perfect for a gadget freak like Welch.

Although he rarely drank himself, Welch would go out of his way to find out what his guest's favorite liquor was and made it a point to have a bottle of that brand on hand, either for his movie nights or in case that person decided to drop by. But his thoughtful favors came with a price. If the visitors decided to drink a brand of alcohol other than the one he personally bought for their use, Welch would take this as a huge personal insult and let them know about it in no uncertain terms.

Welch enjoyed letting the more powerful and influential guests at his pornographic film festivals have enough drinks to loosen their tongues. Every once in a while someone would reveal a few dirty little secrets that would usually never see the light of day in a small city like Duluth. He relished getting his neighbors to spill the beans. He liked the power the information gave him, although no one knows what he did with the information.

As the people of the Hidden Valley neighborhood in Duluth spent more time with Welch, they noticed that he could talk a pretty good game of football, the stock market, and surveillance systems, but he wasn't very well versed in culture or the arts, and he didn't seem know much about basic financial principles. A few thought this was unusual for someone who bought and sold antiques for profit and supposedly invested successfully in stocks and real estate.

When Welch wasn't busy filling his coffers or entertaining his neighbors, he liked to spend time outdoors. He went on several fishing expeditions. He fished Lake Superior, went on fishing trips in northern Minnesota and Canada near the Boundary Waters Canoe Area Wilderness, and even entered local fishing contests. His fishing partners included Linda's relatives, neighbors, and business associates, such as Stan Sunde. In 1979, Sunde got on Welch's bad side because he owed thousands of dollars to Welch for the sales of stolen coins. Sunde claimed he was too short on cash to keep up with the brisk turnover of Welch's items. Later, Welch heard Sunde bought a twenty-one-foot fishing boat and trailer, completely outfitted with the latest gear. Welch did not approve.

Welch was getting more comfortable hanging out with the upper-class denizens of Duluth's Hidden Valley neighborhood. Frank P. Blatnik, the Postmaster of Duluth, was also an avid fisherman, and he invited Welch to join a group of neighbors on a Canadian fly-in fishing trip. The Hidden Valley neighbors went to the Lake Manitou Weather Station lodge on Lower Manitou Lake in Ontario, about sixty miles north of International Falls. After a road trip into Canada, the only way to get to the lodge was by plane or boat. Once visitors are there, they are there for the duration.

This particular lodge was also a favorite fishing hole of the then–vice president of the United States, Walter F. Mondale. In 1979, Mondale and his entourage were there at the same time as the Duluth Hidden Valley fishing expedition, including current fugitive from justice, Bernard C. Welch. The Lake Manitou Weather Station was not a busy corner of New York City, nor was it a surging crowd on the campaign trail, but security was necessary. There were enough Secret Service agents to cover the shift changes for keeping a watchful eye on the vice president.

Once Welch caught sight of the Secret Service contingent shadowing the vice president, he became very scarce. He figured his trail was fairly cold after being out of prison a few years, but there were still those wanted posters circulated by the FBI. The Secret Service guys would be sharp, the best of the best, even if their appearance made them easy to pick out at this wilderness fishing lodge.

When they went out fishing for the day, Welch would always take a quick look around to see if the coast was clear before heading to the boat. He ducked out as Mondale's security team approached or turned to face away when cornered. The agents were in the lodge dining room, on the boat pier, and in the woods. Welch's efforts to remain unnoticed were becoming noticeable to the group he was with. Instead of the confident investor they knew, Welch's neighbors saw an extremely nervous and evasive man.

Bernard Welch was truly relieved when the shore of that lake receded behind the de Havilland Otter floatplane that flew them south toward Minnesota. He never went on this particular fishing trip again.

Back at the homestead in Duluth, Linda was pregnant again and pretty far along. The baby was due in late August, and they planned to have this child back East. Welch was again forced into late pregnancy celibacy and not enjoying it one bit. He mentioned to Stan Sunde that he was growing tired of "that big cow" Linda and asked if he knew any loose women that he could "date." Sunde suggested Welch try prospecting on his own in some of the areas around Duluth and neighboring Superior, Wisconsin, where the longshoremen and merchant seamen went for entertainment.

Whether or not Welch succeeded in finding a female companion on his own, fate seemed to smile on him when Linda's niece, Susan Swanson, ended up on their doorstep looking for a place to stay. She had gotten pregnant the previous year, right around the time the Hamiltons were in Duluth buying the new house. Linda worked it out so Susan could stay with and work for them in Duluth through the summer and then travel back to Virginia to live with them and watch the kids. This live-in babysitter job would help Susan avoid the stigma of being an unwed mother in Duluth, and for the astounding pay of two hundred dollars per week.

As the summer ended in 1979, Linda was nearing the end of her pregnancy. They packed up for the long drive back to Virginia with Susan and her infant daughter, Heather, in tow. With an expanding family and Welch's business growing, the Hamiltons needed to get into a larger house and a more prestigious neighborhood in Virginia. They had enough money now to make that move.

When they got back to Virginia, Linda contracted to rent an interim home in Falls Church for three months. She delivered their second son in September, right after they closed the deal on a big house in Great Falls, Virginia, for $235,000, paying $155,000 in cash. They would make payments on the remaining $80,000 and wouldn't start living there until November. Welch got in touch with local contractors to take care of some remodeling projects in the living area before they moved in with the kids. Welch had big plans for this new house. This was going to be the base of his empire, his castle, proof that he had made it once and for all.

The Fairfax County, Virginia, police station was just off the Capital Beltway, near the Potomac River. A meeting was scheduled for ten o'clock, to miss the morning rush hour, but the early morning rain froze on the overpasses, making the commuter crawl even slower.

The cinder block walls in the austere meeting room were painted government green. The room functioned mainly as a place for uniformed police roll call and orders of the day. The dented dark gray tables and chairs were arranged in rows facing the shift sergeant's desk, which was piled high with law books, folders, clipboards, two used coffee cups, an empty Coke bottle, and a large, half-filled green glass ashtray.

The newest addition to the room was an easel with a large December 1979 calendar. The first two weeks of the calendar displayed writing on some of the days.

As the detectives from jurisdictions around Washington, DC, straggled in, they stopped to sign in at a table by the door. They hung up wet coats and put their briefcases and folders on one of the long roll call tables. Greeting people they knew, recent arrivals made their way toward a large, electric coffee urn at the rear of the room. Beside the urn were disposable cups, dry creamer, sugar, and two large boxes of donuts.

Occasionally, a detective would approach the calendar with a piece of paper in hand. The men and women present would pause in their conversations and watch. The first to approach the calendar was Dave Roberts, a detective from Metropolitan Washington, DC's, Second District. The Second District encompassed the wealthy northwest quadrant of the District of Columbia. Roberts picked up a black felt-tipped pen and slowly wrote down two addresses under the date of Monday, December 12. Detective Tom Bailey, Fairfax County, Virginia, Police Department, left a conversation with three other men and walked to the calendar. He wrote two addresses under Wednesday, December 14, and three under Friday, December 16. A few minutes later, Detective James King of the Montgomery County, Maryland, Police Department, Crimes Against Property Unit entered the meeting room. King, still in his raincoat, went directly to the easel and wrote down two addresses under Tuesday, December 13, and two under Thursday, December 15. Saturdays and Sundays were blank.

It was now 10:20 a.m., and the room was half full. Cigarette smoke began to haze the air. Detective Bill Ballard, who was hosting the meeting, walked to the front of the room. He rapped on the sergeant's desk with the empty Coke bottle. In a loud voice, he urged, "Okay, okay. Let's get on with the show. I know traffic held everybody up. I'm sure you all have a busy day scheduled, so let's get going. Dave Roberts from DC, 2-D, you were the first in, so why don't you start off?"

Roberts, in his wrinkled suit, laid down his cigar, took a last sip from his coffee cup, and grimaced. His jowled Irish face looked like a bulldog's. Roberts spoke quickly, with a clipped accent that could have derived from any big city in the northeast. His appearance and speech belied his photographic memory and a sharp mind that took in every detail.

"Well, this guy, like usual, cut the outside phone lines first," Roberts started. "He then popped a rear window and entered an unoccupied house in Chevy Chase, DC. This was up near the Montgomery County line, off Western Avenue. Anyway, he took a couple three old Chinese vases and the good silver. He left the plated stuff. He got a fur coat, a small coin collection, and some good jewelry from the master bedroom. We figure he hit the place between 7:00 p.m. and 9:00 p.m."

Roberts went on to the second burglary. "The second address I wrote up there was a few houses down from the first one and during the same time period. He didn't get in this one. He cut the phone line and was prying on the back door, but there was a big dog inside. I figure the dog's barking scared him off. In both jobs, no prints, no witnesses, no suspects. Nothing's showed up at the pawnshops. As I said, the usual for this guy."

"How did he get the rear window open?" one of the newer group members asked.

"Nothing fancy," Roberts replied. "Just forced up a wood double-hung with a half-inch-blade screwdriver and climbed in. Used the same tool down the street on the back door."

"Any more questions of Dave?" Ballard stood up as Roberts finished. "Okay, if not, we'll go with Jim King from Montgomery County next." King stood up and looked at his notes. His hand trembled slightly as he held the papers.

King's face was drawn, and the bags under his eyes were puffy. He had again spent the night sleeping in a chair beside his daughter's bed at Children's Hospital. She was eight years old and recovering from a second surgery for brain cancer. King's dark, straight hair had streaks of gray. He looked older than his thirty-seven years.

"All of Montgomery's were, as Dave said, the usual," King said in a deep, almost unaccented voice. "Late evening, wire cutters on the outside telephone line first. Avoids occupied houses, burglar alarms, and dogs. Half-inch, flat-blade screwdriver to pry a door or window, whichever is more secluded. On Tuesday evening, he hit the Potomac area along River Road near the Beltway. He went through backyards. On Thursday, he chose Chevy Chase, Maryland, maybe a mile from the ones Dave told us about. At all the places, he took small, valuable, portable antiques, figurines, ceramics, good jewelry, sterling silver flatware, and some fur coats. He got everything from the first floor and master bedrooms. Also missing were some pillowcases and towels, probably to wrap up the breakable stuff. My estimation is he spends maybe ten to twelve minutes inside each house."

King continued. "We had K-9 run tracks at all the scenes looking for anything he may have dropped. The K-9 officers say this guy hides behind bushes and trees, as if he's watching the houses from the rear, probably trying to avoid people and dogs. K-9 tracked him for a mile or more through backyards. The track always ends on a dark street, between houses, where he parks his car. That's where we lose him. I've knocked on every door in the neighborhoods and no one has seen anything. He leaves behind nothing but pry marks."

King looked up from his notes and said slowly, "I made up a poster with the Virginia DMV photo of Bernard Welch." He immediately heard the murmurs from around the room—"Welch again."

"You all know the reasons why I believe our guy is Welch," King continued, his voice growing stronger and faster. "I've started mailing these posters out to antique auction houses on the East Coast. If it is Welch, then he'll be using the same MO as he did in Richmond."

King forged on, ignoring the uttered, "Fixated," from the back of the room. "In Richmond, he stockpiled his loot in a rented storage place. When he got enough to fill a U-Haul trailer, he'd drive to an antique auction gallery in Pennsylvania. He sold nothing locally."

"This guy is not the run-of-the-mill junkie, selling the goods the next day so he can get high," King continued with greater surety. "Welch is smart. He knows that dumping his stuff locally is the one way we can get at him. So, we've got to leapfrog him and find his out-of-state buyer. That's his one soft spot. It's a long shot, but it's all we've got."

King waited for the crowd to settle down, waited for the final "Needs a vacation" to die out before he went on. In a softer tone, he stated, "I've got copies of the poster with me here on the table. Please take some and hand them out to anyone you can think of. Give some to the patrol cars in the target areas. We've got to get lucky sometime."

King sat down and sipped his cold coffee. He slipped a couple of Tums into his mouth, his stomach on fire again.

Ballard stood up. "Any questions of Jim? No? Okay, let's hear from Tom Bailey of Fairfax County."

Bailey was a big man with a ruddy face and infectious grin. He looked like a school principal who had once been a college football lineman. Everybody liked him. He spoke with a soft, northern Virginia accent.

"Well, as you can see, we got hit hard on two nights," Bailey started. "Same MO as always—cut phone wires, just after dark, rear door or window. Stolen were small antiques, old watches, sterling silver, coin collections, fur coats, old dolls, and small works of art. This past week was probably over $100,000 in all, and we're still counting. We thought he'd hit us here in Virginia on Wednesday, because he hit DC on Monday and Montgomery on Tuesday. Figuring he's using the Beltway to get around, we had unmarked cars at the exits to the areas that this guy likes. They wrote down the tag numbers of every car getting off the Beltway and moving towards the target areas. We ran all the tags and came up empty on known felons. We used K-9 to track him after the break-ins were discovered. K-9 went through a lot of backyards and lost the track where he parked his car, just like Montgomery. But there was one thing we did find."

Bailey paused and shuffled through his folders. There was no sound in the room except for the drone of a police radio from a nearby office. Bailey produced a black-and-white photograph.

"This is a footprint our guy left under a window he pried in Potomac Falls," Tom explained, holding it so everyone could see. "It appears to be a man's size 10 athletic shoe."

Bailey turned toward King and, with a small smile, asked, "Jim, what size shoe does this Welch guy wear?" All the detectives laughed except King.

King tried to respond lightly to Bailey's little joke, but he only managed a creasing of his thin lips. He understood Bailey was just teasing. He and Bailey had a close working relationship. Bailey thought King's research into Welch's background had developed a possible suspect, but he was not as committed to Welch as King was.

King looked up at Bailey and said quietly, "I don't know. That sounds about right for his build. I'll find out." The same people behind him let out a few more snickers.

Ballard, noting the strained look on King's face, stood again. "Okay, okay. Any questions for Tom? No? Anything from Alexandria, Arlington?" The officers from those jurisdictions shook their heads.

"No? You guys got off easy this time," Ballard said. "Well, next week is Christmas and then it's New Year's, so we'll skip those. Let's hope this guy eases off over the holidays and goes to visit relatives. In three weeks, we'll meet again. It'll be Montgomery's turn, okay, Jim?"

King nodded as he slipped on his coat.

"Then that wraps it up," Ballard announced. "Don't forget the handouts up here. Thanks for coming."

The detectives gathered their folders, reached for their coats, and started out in small groups, talking as they went. Most ignored King's stack of Welch posters.

It was almost eleven o'clock. Another meeting of the unofficial Standard Time Silver Burglar Task Force was over. The detectives hurried through the cold rain to their cars. There were many other cases to work, cases that had some hope of closure. Every detective knew that, to keep his job, he had to produce results. Useless meetings did not produce results.

King walked to his unmarked police car, the umbrella in his hand unopened and forgotten. The comments he overheard earlier and Bailey's remark stung. Couldn't they see he was right? He had done his research. All the little things they knew about the Standard Time Silver Burglar fit into place. It could be no one else, and yet they thought he was chasing a chimera.

But King was adamant that Welch was the guy they were after. Now, who could he call to find out what size shoe Bernard Welch wore?

The brand new silver Mercedes Benz sedan slipped slowly through the dark northwest Washington neighborhood. Here, streetlights were rare, one per block at best. The DC government was not good at repairing potholes or at replacing burned out streetlights. Except for the occasional porch light blocked by trees and bushes three generations old, there was little to lighten the India ink darkness. The new Mercedes engine made almost no noise as it idled slowly through the quiet, cold January evening, like a silver shark patrolling a lagoon, hungry.

Bernard Welch knew the area. He had visited here many times in the past four years. He was seeking his prey for the night. He determined which houses he would invade by looking at their lights. The outside porch light didn't much matter; people left those on all the time. The inside lights were the tell he was looking for, the signal that shouted no one was home. Occupied homes had interior lights on when it got dark, unoccupied homes did not. It was a half hour after the sunset, just past five-thirty, and dark houses were his objectives.

Finally! Three dark houses in the same block. Perfect. The sedan picked up speed and turned the corner searching for a place to park. The parking location was critical. It had to be dark. It had to be between homes. It had to be a place that allowed access to the rear yards without being easily seen. It had to be close to the intended target, but not too close. It also had to provide cover for him from witnesses when he came back with the goods. He was most vulnerable when returning to the car carrying a load.

Caution was the first commandment in his business. And while caution was important, so was time. He could not afford to waste time. There was a short, three-hour window in which to work. The more time that passed after sunset, the higher the risk that someone would come home. He was what the business world described as "risk averse."

He had just pulled over to park when headlights approached him from the front. This was not unusual. Residents came and went, even in quiet neighborhoods, but he was always on guard. He had to know where the oncoming car was going, possibly to one of the dark homes he had chosen. He waited by the curb with the motor running, waiting for the other vehicle to pass.

"Son of a bitch!" Welch mumbled. It was a DC police cruiser, moving slowly, patrolling. As the police car passed, the cop looked into Welch's window without recognition. He waved at the officer and smiled. The cruiser kept going. Cops were stupid.

Welch slowly let out his breath as the cruiser's taillights turned in the direction of the dark houses. Bernie turned on his headlights and pulled away from the curb. He could not stay here now, too risky. He made a few turns to get out of the area but was careful not to speed. He didn't want to draw attention to himself.

He drove on, making turns, watching his rearview mirror. No one followed. He was in the clear, probably just a random cop driving by. He stopped at an intersection. It was Western Avenue, the borderline. He only had to cross the two-lane street and he'd leave Washington behind. In Maryland, a hundred feet away, the houses were a continuation of the rich, northwest area of DC.

There were a few differences between Washington, DC, and Montgomery County. In Maryland, the houses were a little newer, a little bigger. The streets were in better condition, and most of the streetlights worked. It was a quiet, high-dollar place with lots of big old trees and big old bushes; his favorite type of hunting ground.

The DC area was a great playground for Welch. There were a dozen different jurisdictions in Washington, DC, Virginia, and Maryland, each with their own police department. In prison, it was common knowledge that the cops never traded information among jurisdictions. If the cops weren't comparing notes, Welch knew he was harder to catch.

There was not enough time to drive back home to Virginia if he still wanted to hit a couple houses tonight. After all, in his profession time was money. It was almost 6:00 p.m. now. The cops would still be dealing with rush-hour traffic. There would be no neighborhood patrols at this hour. Welch waited for a break in traffic and pulled across Western Avenue into Montgomery County, Maryland.

Welch rolled along the dark streets crowded with expensive cars—Cadillacs, Lincolns, BMWs, Mercedes, Saabs, Porsches, and the occasional Volkswagen. VW Bugs meant teenagers or college students, who were often home at odd hours. Young people were unpredictable. If surprised in their home, they might try to jump him even if he pointed a gun at them. Then he'd have to shoot the idiot kid. The cops and the press would go crazy. There would be police patrols in the area for months, cutting into his territory and decreasing his profits. That kind of downturn in business meant he'd have to go back on the road. He did not want to do that; things were just fine the way they were. So, he avoided houses with VWs parked in front and kept moving. Something would turn up. It always did. Rich people were stupid, too.

He wound through the twisting streets. The luminous compass on his dash swirled as he rounded corners but always settled back to point north, the direction he wanted to go. North provided his best escape route. In that direction lay Route 495, the Capitol Beltway, the fastest way back to his home in Virginia. It was also traveled by thousands of vehicles each day, making it a route in which he could easily blend. That's why he drove the Mercedes, to blend into the neighborhoods where he worked and lived. It was his stalking horse. He used it like hunters of old, hiding behind it as he sneaked into the lair of the big game he sought.

No one suspected a Mercedes Benz owner of being a burglar, especially not the cops. In fact, a month ago he returned to his car after hitting two houses. Welch had loaded everything into the trunk and turned on the ignition. Nothing, a dead battery. He got out, opened the hood, and probed around to see if he could find the problem, when a Montgomery County patrol car pulled up. He told the cop he was visiting friends and his battery went dead. The officer actually gave him a jump start with the police car. He thanked the cop and drove home. It was just more proof for Welch that the police really were stupid.

After several minutes of reconnoitering, he found what he wanted; several dark houses all within a couple of blocks of each other. He could smell the wealth inside them. He didn't try to analyze his instinct that these houses were loaded. He just trusted his years of experience.

He turned left at the next corner and parked under a tree. The tree was leafless, but there was a large azalea bush near the curb marking the boundary between properties. He parked so his rear door was beside the bush. He turned out his lights and killed the engine. Located between the streetlights that lined the road, the Mercedes became a dark blob on the street, just like the other dark blobs parked there.

He sat for a moment in the dark, letting his eyes adjust to the night. He reached over to the passenger seat and found some of his equipment. First, the big, navy blue bandana. He folded it into a vee and tied the ends in a knot around his neck. To a casual observer, it looked like a neck scarf for the cold night, but it was also a mask that could quickly be pulled into place. Then came the black knit wool cap. It was pulled down over his ears and low across his forehead, covering as much of his face as possible.

From the glove box he removed the black rubber-handled screwdriver, side-cutting pliers, and a penlight. The penlight was clipped into his shirt pocket under his soft navy blue, zip-up jogging-style jacket. The other items went into his right coat pocket. He groped under the driver's seat and located the .38-caliber, six-shot, Smith and Wesson. This blued-steel, two-inch-barrel revolver went into the left inside pocket of the coat. A pair of Peerless hand-cuffs, also under the front seat, went into his hip pocket. His wallet, change, and extra keys went into the glove compartment, which was closed and locked. A pair of ordinary, brown cotton work gloves was in the center console compartment. He placed them in his lap.

Finally, he stretched his arm between the seats and into the back of the ve-hicle. By feel, he found the four rolled-up, drawstring sacks. They were made of double-stitched, heavy-duty nylon. They were strong but folded nicely into a small package. These went into his left coat pocket. It took less than two minutes to don his uniform and assemble his tools.

He opened the Mercedes door. The interior light did not come on. Welch had loosened the bulb to keep it dark inside. He left the car and stood beside it listening and looking. No one was in sight and nothing sounded abnormal. There was only the dull roar of traffic on Connecticut Avenue a few blocks away. He shook his head slightly in disbelief at the sound. He was amazed that people would live in a place where traffic was so bad. If it were not for the nature of his work, he would never venture out into the crush of after-work traffic. Of course, the traffic did cause people to get home late, making his "shopping" easier.

He closed the car door quietly, using his butt to push it shut. There was no noise, other than a metallic click as the door locked. He appreciated the precise German engineering. Then he moved around the car and stood on the grass where it met the curb. There were few sidewalks in suburbia and that made things a little easier, as both cars and pedestrians had to use the same road. Welch stood in the shadow between the streetlights. It was colder now that the sun had set. The humid air was condensing on horizontal surfaces, making them damp. It created a misty, fog-like aurora around the streetlight a hundred feet away.

He was tense but not nervous. He had done this a thousand times before in many places. He was good at what he did—better than the cops; better than the homeowners; better than anybody in the world. He was a true professional. The best ever, not one of those amateur junkies who get caught all the time. He'd never be caught. His system was perfect. It had taken years of study, sweat, and pain to get here, but he was here now and nothing could stop him. He smiled inwardly, confident as his eyes flicked up and down the street.

He put his gloved hands in his pockets and shook them a bit to make sure there was no clanking or clunking as he walked. He moved to the old azalea bush and looked behind him again to ensure there were no witnesses. Welch slipped into the darkness between the houses and slowly threaded his way through the shrubbery. He began his cautious, stalking maneuver across the backyards of the housing block.

Although his night vision was good, it was not perfect. It was very dark and he moved ahead as much by feel as by sight. He heard a sound and froze in place like a startled deer. It had been a crunch noise. The sound was not repeated. A human or animal would have moved again by now. He analyzed the noise and identified it as a branch falling from a tree. In the distance to his left, a dog barked. It sounded big, like a German shepherd. Shepherds were very territorial and could be vicious. He did not like them. He would stay to the right, away from that dog.

He slowly made his way through the yards. Piles of leaves crunched under his feet as he moved along, so he shuffled his black leather running shoes to make less noise. In the dim glow of an outside light ahead, he could make out a fence. It was a chain-link fence that met the one from the other yard behind it, so he was forced to go over. He easily vaulted the fence, making almost no noise. In this yard, the house was well lit at the back. Most people in big homes lived in the back, where the kitchen and family room were. The lights from inside glowed out into the backyard, making it like a flood-lit football field, delineating everything out back in a black and white contrast. He passed quickly through the darkest part of the yard and jumped the next fence. The next home was also lit up, and there were people moving around inside. He passed on.

He finally found what he was looking for. Another row of houses that were dark. He passed the first dark house—it seemed shabby—and selected the second. Just what Welch needed, no one home on either side to see anything. He moved up close. There was a light on, but only one. He peered through the windows. It was a hall light apparently left on all day. The light provided enough illumination to reveal what appeared to be a lot of stuff inside. The house seemed well kept, inside and out; a millionaire's home he'd bet.

In Welch's worldview, the owner did not need all that crap. It wasn't doing any good sitting on shelves and in drawers. But he, Bernard Welch, could use it. All these millionaires had insurance to pay for any loss. This guy would be pissed off, but he'd have a good story to tell at the country club, and his wife could go shopping with the big, fat insurance check. Not to mention this guy was probably crooked anyway. Welch believed most rich people were. They may have legit jobs, but they were still skimming off the top. He knew all about dishonest lawyers, judges, cops, accountants, stockbrokers, politicians, and business owners. They were all crooked. At least, he was honest being a thief. These rich, pompous bastards were not. They deserved to get ripped off to balance things out, and Welch was just the man to do it.

Welch prowled slowly around the building. No car in the driveway and none in front, a sure sign no one was home. No alarm company sign, another positive. He did not walk across the front, which was asking for a witness to see him. He retraced his steps back to the rear, went around to the other side. He was looking for the telephone line running from the street pole to the house and down the wall to the first floor. There, the cable would enter the basement. By feel, he found the phone wire, near the electric power meter. He knew what it was without using his flashlight. He removed the wire cutters from his coat pocket and cut the cable with only a slight "snick" sound. That was insurance. If anyone was home, they would have to run to a neighbor's house to call the cops. If there was an alarm system, it would take the alarm company half an hour to call the local police. He'd be gone by then.

The rear kitchen door had a dead bolt lock, which seemed to be in use. He bypassed it—too much prying. Breaking the door glass would make noise. There may be an easier way, he thought. He moved back to the low rear window he had passed earlier. It was an old, double hung, wood window with a screen. He removed a clasp knife from his pants pocket and cut the metal mesh screen around three sides. The knife easily slit through the woven metal fabric. He lifted up the flap he had made and pushed his flat-blade screwdriver between the halves of the window and pried. This created a space that his knife blade could fit through to reach the window lock. A few swipes of the blade caused the old C-shaped clasp to unlock. He pushed up on the lower portion of the wooden paned window, but it was stiff and resisted his efforts. The screwdriver was wedged under the window's edge and pried upward with force, its steel shaft indenting the wood windowsill as he did so. The old window popped up an inch under the pressure.

He paused and listened, his ear near the one-inch gap. He detected no sounds from inside. That was good. He was sure there were no humans home, but there might be a dog. He did not like dogs. He was vulnerable to them when he climbed inside headfirst, when they could bite his hands or face. He had his hands bitten once early in his career. He was off work for two weeks, a lesson he never forgot.

Assured that no one was home and there was no dog present, he muscled up the window enough to crawl in. Fortunately, there was no table or chair directly under the window, and he was able to slide inside almost noiselessly. Once inside, he crouched under the opened window and listened again. Extreme caution in his business was a necessity. Unlike other businessmen who got caught stealing, he could not pay a fine and walk away. His ass would be in the slammer for years.

He was in the dark family room. The hall light cast some light through the doorway but not enough to see any details. He unclipped the pen light from his shirt pocket, and probed the area where the ceiling and walls met, especially in corners. That's where alarm sensors would be located. There were none. He grinned slightly and stood up. The flashlight beam was lowered to scan the walls, shelves, tables, and floors. He only found family pictures; nothing he wanted in here. Quietly, he moved out of the family room and into the lit hall.

The hall led to the foyer and front door, with other doorways that led to the left and right. He turned left into the living room. He first went to the front window. The venetian blinds were closed, making the room very dark. He opened the slats enough to let some street lighting inside. Now he could see the headlights of any car pulling up in the front of the house.

Quickly, he walked around the room's perimeter. The items he'd be interested in would be found there— art on walls or items on tables, bookshelves, or the fireplace mantel. There were a couple of Oriental rugs on the floor, but they were new. No market for those. The art on the walls was not valuable, just the usual suburban decorator junk. Nothing on the sidepieces was of interest. He was disappointed. This guy was not a collector, he thought. Welch reached the mantel and, surprisingly, found a pair of nineteenth century Staffordshire dog figurines from England. They had some value and were untraceable. He stuck the thin flashlight between his teeth and grabbed them, one in each hand, and looked about the room fruitlessly for something to cushion the fragile ceramic statues. If they banged together, they would break and be useless to him.

With a statuette in each hand and the flashlight in his mouth, he went back into the foyer to the coat closet. Setting the figurines on the floor, he opened the closet door and flipped through the hangers until he found a fur cape. It looked like mink inside its zippered clear covering. Good; that was good packing material and also saleable. Welch jerked the fur from its hanger and cover. He rolled one figure in the wrap and the second one in the heavy plastic bag. These were both placed in one of the nylon drawstring sacks pulled from his coat pocket. The sack was now stuffed full.

Carrying the bag by its drawstring, Welch turned and entered the dining room. A dining room was always one of his major objectives in a burglary. They were where rich people kept their silver. They did not store it or hide it; they openly displayed it and kept it available for entertaining. Silver could be turned into cash in a couple of weeks. The other stuff, like the dog statuettes and the mink, was a bonus, but he had to store them. He would not see any return from those items until they were sold in Minnesota in June or July. Still, that money would carry him through his long off-season.

When he entered the dining room, the glow from the small flashlight made the polished silver gleam. He dismantled the two candelabras on the sideboard and dumped them into another nylon bag. A five-piece tea set also went into the bag. The silver pieces banged against each other, but the dents and scratches didn't matter to Welch. This stuff would soon be melted into silver ingots and shipped out to the refinery in Colorado. He passed on the large serving tray that the tea set sat on. He saw base metal showing through the wear marks around its edges. "EPNS" was stamped on the tray bottom, indicating it was silver plate over nickel; not worth taking.

Welch pulled the top drawer of the Sheridan sideboard open. Bingo! It was filled with sterling silver flatware and serving pieces. He removed another nylon bag from his coat pocket, held it open with his left hand, and scooped up the silverware with his right. He filled the bag by the time he had cleaned out all the drawers of their silver. The china closet had only china and crystal, all too heavy or breakable. He grabbed the three bags by their drawstrings and carried them through a swinging door into the kitchen.

The two bags of silver weighed over twenty pounds. As he moved the full bags, he quickly figured that at $500 a pound from the refinery, the total value of the metal came to about $11,000. Of course, he'd lose some to the stainless steel knife blades and plaster-filled candleholder bases, but he'd still clear ten grand. Not bad, and he hadn't even gone upstairs yet.

While in the kitchen, he checked the dead bolt lock on the rear door. It had a thumb latch on the inside and not a key. He unlocked the door and cracked it open just in case he had to leave fast. He heard a noise and froze, his hand still on the door. Then, almost instantly, he relaxed. It was the gas furnace kicking on, probably because of the window he left open.

The stairs were in the lit center hall, near the front door. He moved back up the hall quickly; time was important. The second floor was the most dangerous place for him. There was only one way out, and that was the stairs at the front door. He had to be alert while up there. People coming home could enter through the front door and trap him upstairs. If that happened, he'd have to run like hell and hope he did not have to shoot anyone.

He purposely ignored the basement. People did not place valuables in the basement unless they were hiding them. Time was money. He could waste a half hour searching for something that might not be there, or he could move to another treasure house and find something good in five minutes.

"Treasure house" was Welch's name for these wealthy homes. It reminded him of the pirate stories he used to read as a kid. The pirates were always on the lookout for treasure ships filled with jewels, gold, and silver. He used to pretend that he was a pirate when he was little, shooting ships with cannons and stealing their treasure. He really was a pirate now, but his treasure ships were stuck in the dry ground and cannons were not necessary. He wondered if the old pirates would have envied him.

He reached the top of the steps quietly. You could never really tell if someone was at home or not. He had been surprised once by an old woman in bed. She screamed and he beat her brutally.

He walked down the hall with the flashlight still in his mouth. He flashed his light into each room as he passed. Three bedrooms were devoid of any valuables he might be interested in. The fourth room at the end of the hall, the master bedroom, would be the most promising.

The master bedroom would have most of the valuable things—jewelry, furs, and cash. Almost all homeowners stored their good stuff there. Welch had no interest in credit cards, bonds, checks, or cameras. They were too easy to trace.

He entered and went straight to the lady's dresser. That's where most of the jewelry would be. First he surveyed the dresser top. There was a large, antique, brassbound, wooden box. He opened the hinged lid and grinned around the penlight in his mouth. The box was like a small treasure chest full of good stuff—gold, silver, pearls, opals, rubies, and diamonds in the form of earrings, necklaces, bracelets, and rings. Welch removed the last of his nylon bags from his pocket and opened the bag's mouth wide enough to stick the top tray inside and dump it. The jewelry tinkled to the bottom. He dropped the tray on the floor and looked further into the wood box. There was more stuff inside; papers, coins, and more jewelry. He grabbed the papers and threw them aside. He upended the box and poured its contents into his bag. He could sort through all that crap at home, when he had more time.

Next, he methodically pulled out each dresser drawer and tossed its contents into the air. Welch watched the items fall to the floor. Women liked to hide money and good jewelry under their clothes. Tossing the drawer contents into the air made it easy to find hidden stuff in seconds. Articles of female clothing fluttered through his flashlight beam on the way to the floor. Nothing of value until he got to the lowest drawer. As he pulled it out and tossed its contents, he saw a flash of white on the drawer bottom. A large, white envelope was taped there. He smiled again as he ripped the envelope off and threw the drawer aside. Hundred-dollar bills, maybe twenty or thirty of them. The envelope also went into the bag.

He crossed to the man's bureau and conducted the same operation again. Nothing much there, a few gold rings, some silver and gold tie bars, cuff links, and a gold watch with diamonds. These were also bagged. Welch felt under the mattress for cash or a gun. Again, nothing. The closet was crammed full, but there did not seem to be anything he wanted.

Welch had gotten all the easy stuff. He looked at the luminous dial of his Rolex watch. He'd been in the house nine minutes now. Time to get out. He did not like to be inside longer than ten minutes, because that was about how long the police took to respond to a suspicious situation call. He walked over to a front window, stepping over the pile of clothing and dresser drawers on the floor. He took the flashlight from his mouth and eased back a window shade to look out. No spotlights or flashlight beams moving around. Cops always used them to find house numbers. He patted his inside coat pocket making sure his revolver was still in place. He would not want to lose that in the house. The gun was Welch's business insurance.

He drew the drawstring closed on the partially filled blue nylon bag. It had some weight, maybe three or four pounds of good stuff plus the cash. Not bad, he thought. He left the bedroom and walked fast down the hall to the steps. As he did so, he calculated the value of the haul in his head. He had lots of practice judging these things. It'd be close to $20,000 that he had made in ten minutes. Those old pirates would have envied him, and he didn't have to split his booty with the scurvy crew.

At the bottom of the steps, he turned left, walked down the hall, and entered the kitchen. He picked up the three bags by the rear door, and the one with the tea set clanged as the bag moved. He noticed some tea towels by the sink and grabbed them. These were stuffed into the bag around the teapot and sugar bowl to stop the metal-to-metal contact. He shook the bags again, and this time he heard only a dull thunk. That was acceptable.

Welch turned off the penlight and reclipped it inside his shirt pocket. He did not want to lose it jumping fences. He had more work to do tonight.

He opened the rear door and walked out on to the concrete porch where he stopped. He looked right and left and listened. Quiet; no dogs barking. Cops were noisy when they tried to sneak around. With all that gear and their big feet, they always made noise. That noise would cause the neighborhood dogs to bark their heads off. The quiet assured Welch that no one was waiting for him in the dark. He stepped off the porch into the darkness toward his car. In another yard not far away, the German shepherd heard him moving and started barking.

It was just 6:30 p.m. now. He'd dump this stuff in his trunk and skulk around. A judge had once said he had been "skulking." He'd liked that word. Yes, he would skulk around and look for more targets. Welch needed to bag a couple more houses before he called it a night.

He always thought of his activities as "work." The nighttime skulking was the part he liked best. The rest—sorting, breaking down, melting, shipping, storing, moving, and selling—was a pain in the ass. But it had to be done properly to keep his one-man business a going concern. Otherwise, it was just a hobby.

Welch neared his car and paused in the darkness, setting his bags on the ground as quietly as possible behind the big azalea bush. He waited a moment, surveying the street, making sure no one was present. Just as he began to step out into the slightly brighter area near the roadway, he heard a male voice utter, "Come on."

Welch quickly slid back behind the bush. As he crouched down, he eased his hand inside of his jacket and wrapped his fingers around the handgun's grip, pulling up slightly to ensure that the revolver's hammer would not snag on the inside of the pocket if he had to jerk it out. He watched through the bush branches as an old man, muffled against the cold, shuffled by while walking his dog. Motionless, Welch barely breathed as they passed. Even the dog did not detect him in the shadows.

The man and dog reached the corner under the streetlight and crossed the road, turning into a driveway. Welch stood up and went to the rear of his Mercedes. Reaching into his left pants pocket, he found the one key on the ring. Two keys together might have jingled. He put the key into the trunk lock and opened it, holding on the trunk lid so that it did not pop open. The interior trunk light did not come on; he had removed that bulb also.

Welch left the trunk lid ajar and returned to the azalea bush. Again, he surveyed the street and then carried his four bags to the car. He held the bags by their drawstrings in his left hand down along his left leg, and when he reached the trunk, opened it with his right hand. As the lid raised, he lifted the bags up and set them inside the trunk.

The dangerous part was over. If anyone saw him now, he was just a guy looking in his trunk. He felt around to the left corner and found another pile of rolled up nylon bags. He removed four of the sacks and stuffed them into his left coat pocket.

Welch closed the Mercedes trunk lid gingerly, quietly pressing down with both hands so that it made only the faintest of noises as it latched. He crossed the narrow, blacktopped street to the opposite side. He paused on the grass just inside of the dark shadows created by the surrounding trees and shrubbery. Again, he was alert to the street scene. He paused to ensure he was still alone.

There came the sound of a car engine approaching. Lights moved into the intersection. A large, four-door vehicle turned the corner, its headlights sweeping the street edge in an arc, illuminating the space that had been in shadow.

No one was there when the headlights passed.

Great Falls, Virginia
February to December 1980

For decades, Bernard Welch dreamed of being independently wealthy. During the years he spent in prison, he imagined owning a great house in a really nice neighborhood and having plenty of money to spare. Now he had that. Actually he had two nice houses, two live-in girlfriends, and a new Mercedes Benz. But he was on his ninth alias now, still living a double life. He was always looking over his shoulder, like any convict, except he was an *escaped* convict still on the lam. He sometimes wondered just how long he could keep up the charade.

He had a legitimate driver's license with his assumed name of Norm Hamilton, but no useable Social Security number. He had to stay away from financial and legal processes that required absolute proof of identity. He couldn't marry Linda, own a car or a house, possess a credit card, or buy insurance. The qualification and registration steps were too invasive, and Norm Hamilton could be too quickly exposed as Bernard C. Welch Jr. So, Linda had to handle all these official responsibilities, even filing income taxes.

Avoiding probing questions, as well as displaying behavior atypical of a convict, allowed Welch to hide in plain sight, drawing occasional, and then only brief, suspicion. Unlike other convicted criminals, Welch drank very little and never did drugs. His behavior was exemplary when he was being observed or while he was in public. Most of the time.

Neighbors recall that Welch was well mannered and friendly, but he had the occasional unguarded moment when his true personality came through. Mrs. Gene Pisodi, a Great Falls neighbor, recalled that when her mother was visiting from Florida, she commented to Welch that he "sure looked familiar, like someone [she] met who went by a different name." Mrs. Pisodi and her husband remembered that Welch gave her mother "a really strange, evil look with *hard* eyes," until after an embarrassing moment of absolute silence, she remembered and explained that it was her granddaughter's softball coach down in Tampa. Welch remained undiscovered, but these neighbors never forgot his tense and unsettling reaction to their mom's small talk.

Neighbors also noticed other odd little things about Welch that, in hindsight, could have tipped them off about his true identity. Welch, with his odd working hours, rarely made it out of the house before noon. He never drove to work, nor did he ever mention an office. Perhaps most telling of all was Welch's lack of knowledge regarding the inner workings of mortgage banking or Wall Street, which should be an easy conversation for someone who bought and sold stocks and real estate as Welch claimed he did.

But it wasn't only Welch's employment that kept the denizens of this Washington, DC, bedroom community talking. Other oddities that caught the neighbors' eyes were the provocative clothes worn by Susan Swanson, Linda Hamilton's live-in niece. Susan was frequently seen in hot pants and spike heels. Even more scandalous was the fact that she usually accompanied Welch to neighborhood get-togethers or cocktail parties instead of Linda. In the middle of her third pregnancy, Linda preferred to stay back in the huge house alone and care for her two little ones and Susan's daughter. The body language between Welch and Susan strongly suggested there was much more between them than just babysitting. One neighbor in particular would hold large and lavish poolside mixers and Welch and Susan would arrive arm in arm like they were on a date.

When Welch wasn't mingling with the neighbors, he was busy remodeling his house. Some of the home improvements he undertook in Great Falls grabbed the attention of his neighbors. He installed a huge emergency generator that ran off natural gas, which gave it an uninterruptible fuel source from the city gas pipes. This emergency power source was really for his eight-camera security system, which was installed so nobody could approach the house unannounced. Welch graciously invited neighbors to run an extension cord up and use the generator should there be a power failure. This friendly gesture also served as a bribe to buy the neighbors' goodwill, as Welch's security alarms were frequently set off by the smallest trigger and rang for no reason.

But Welch had good reason to take such drastic security measures. He had a large inventory of very valuable metal to protect. Silver prices had gone as high as six to seven times what they were in 1979, and gold had about tripled. Welch knew this couldn't go on forever. The unprecedented all-time-high prices forced him to modify his approach to burglary and concentrate on the theft of these two metals. He sought out homes he figured were more likely to contain sterling silver services, flatware, and gold, in one form or another.

Welch's Sunday smelting routine became very important. He melted down everything made of gold or silver. Anything that was being held for repair or reconditioning was pulled off the shelf and smelted for the metal content. He had to keep this money-maker rolling in high gear and hope that the long nights and short days would stay with him as long as possible.

The checks from the smelters were getting to be immense, in excess of $50,000 per month. The profit Welch made every month from each of the two metals was about equal. The gold averaged twenty times the value of silver per ounce, but on any given night, he could steal twenty times more silver than gold. People were more likely to show off larger silver pieces in glass-fronted hutches and on top of china cabinets and sideboards. The gold pieces—jewelry, coins, or bullion—generally stayed out of sight, more likely to see the inside of a lock box than to be displayed for friends and family.

Because of the profits from his silver and gold sales and because he felt that his continuing affair with Susan Swanson was starting to get some attention from the neighbors and possibly from Linda, Welch rented an apartment in a nearby town so that he and Susan could discretely spend more time together. And Welch tried to take Linda's mind off any suspicions she may have, and assuage any guilt he may have, by buying her a new brown Mercedes 450 SL.

But Linda wasn't interested in a new car at that point, nor was she interested in much else. She learned she was early in her third pregnancy, and she seldom left the house. She still took care of the bookkeeping and the packing duties for the smelting enterprise, but she left the heavy lifting and transporting of the melted ingots to the post office for Welch now.

Against all odds, Bernard Welch was on his way to producing a large family. This is most unusual for a lifelong felon. Career criminals are the worst candidates for family life. Rotten childhoods, broken homes, firsthand observations of a dysfunctional family at work, and spending half your life in penal institutions is usually enough mental and physical pressure to prevent people from procreating.

Silver values started to slide in February, and those prices continued a gradual decrease until mid–March, when silver quotes were down to half their January high. Silver prices plummeted 40 percent in three days with the market coming to a head on "Silver Thursday," March 27, 1980.

These price decreases had a deleterious effect on the stock market. Welch and Bruce Howe, the Duluth stockbroker, had bet heavily in margin accounts on a planned buyout of McCormick Spices by the European drug giant Sandoz. This buyout would have forced the value of the McCormick stock way up. It didn't happen, and they were leveraging their stock purchases with borrowed money. The gamble didn't pay off, so they had to pay up. Bruce Howe was not in a position where he could pay the $25,000 back to Welch, and the Hamiltons lost $300,000 in their stock dealings.

March had been great for gold and silver production. So even if the prices were lower, Welch still had a large stockpile of precious metals to sell. Those high prices at the beginning of the year had made him step up the pace of silver theft and smelting. Even with the price of silver dropping like a rock, he netted $75,000 in April from just one of his assayers alone, J & J Smelters in California.

As the weather warmed up and the days grew longer, Welch began preparing for another trip to northern Minnesota. He kept himself busy with burglary and smelting, anticipated that the next trip to Duluth would reap a bonanza of riches from merchandise and bullion sales. He'd been stockpiling all the right items to pack for the journey, all the small and valuable things that could be easily turned into ready cash at the other end.

He had a stash of antiques, artwork, furs, jewelry, and gems for Rose Galleries. Rose Galleries in Minneapolis was now handling the lion's share of the stones he had pulled out of their settings. Loose gems were not the type of merchandise that could be sold to just anyone. People think that only a jeweler or a goldsmith should have such items. The sight of a handful of diamond, rubies, and emeralds would stop people short, taking their breath away. Also, another Duluth jeweler was still making his regular runs up the North Shore to Ontario. Eventually, these precious stones ended up in a Thunder Bay jewelry operation untraceable to Welch, and Welch ended up with the cash.

Welch rented a U-Haul truck in Falls Church to haul his stolen goods to Minnesota for sale. Linda was now five months pregnant, due to give birth in September, so Welch did most of the packing again. The blue Ford station wagon had plenty of room, and they'd need it. Linda would drive the station wagon with the two boys, as well as Susan and her daughter. The wagon would also hold everyone's luggage and the cats. Welch would bring up the rear with the loaded rental truck. They would do a one-way drop with the truck, using the station wagon to get around in Duluth and haul everyone back to Virginia at the end of the summer.

Remodeling projects on the Great Falls home started just as they were getting ready to leave town. Welch started with a 6,500 square-foot house plus about 3,500 finished square feet in the basement, large by anyone's standards. There was to be a 3,000 square-foot addition that would house a fifty-by-thirty-foot indoor pool. Fourteen skylights would top the pool wing, and it would also contain a sixteen-by-fourteen-foot sauna and exercise room with unique environmental controls. The contractor and the workmen had their plans and work orders and a $100,000 down payment. They were to keep Welch updated by phone, especially if there were any problems.

Welch, Linda, Susan, and the children took off for Minnesota on May 13. Frequent restroom breaks for Linda and the little ones made the already long trip even longer. Welch kept his speed near the 55-mile-per-hour limit in order to avoid any state police patrols on duty between Great Falls and Duluth.

Cool breezes off Lake Superior whistled up the steep streets of Duluth as the Hamiltons settled back into 700 Valley Drive. Welch was eager to get everyone, and everything, unloaded. It was time to start turning goods into money.

More money started rolling in at Duluth. There were big checks—payments for antiques and art from Rose Galleries, coins from Stan Sunde, and gold and silver bullion from J & J Smelting of California, as well as extra cash for the loose gems sold on the local jeweler's runs to Canada. Linda made so many deposits into the Duluth brokerage accounts that they made up most of the stock market losses. It seemed to Welch that everything was going just great. What more could he possibly want? More of the same and bigger helpings, of course.

That summer, in an unusual gesture, Welch suggested that the men in the Hamilton family take a road trip across the border into Canada for fishing. He even volunteered to drive everyone in the Ford Country Squire station wagon north of the border to the Atikokan area. The beer was great, and the fishing was even better, but Welch had an ulterior motive for hosting such a generous outing.

On the way back to Duluth, he asked Linda's dad if he would like to own the Ford station wagon and offered to give him the car outright. It was generating a little more road noise than Welch would have liked, so he was looking to get rid of it.

Russell Hamilton stalled and said he would have to think about it. In private, he told his son David that he didn't want the car. Later, Russell diplomatically told Welch that he had to decline this generous offer because he was satisfied with the car he had now, which got pretty good gas mileage, he explained.

Welch did a bit of a slow burn as it really bothered him when someone wouldn't accept his generosity. Still, he figured he scored high-roller points with the rest of the Hamilton clan just for making the offer to the old man.

Linda's father wasn't the only one growing suspicious of Welch. Some of his Duluth neighbors started wondering what he was up to. One neighbor, who worked for the Drug Enforcement Agency, thought things weren't quite right with this guy. He ran a criminal record check on "Norm Hamilton" and, of course, found nothing. Once this seemingly definitive snooping failed, word got around that Welch had no police record, and no one bothered to delve any deeper into his background.

The Hamiltons had an abbreviated trip that summer. The construction work on the big house back east needed to be checked on. Welch wanted to see firsthand how things were going rather than rely on the word of the workmen. He also wanted to be back in Virginia before the birth of their third child. And most importantly, staying in Minnesota too long would cut into his work schedule, and he needed the money to support his increasingly lavish lifestyle.

Linda was so late in her third pregnancy that she decided to fly back to Virginia instead of taking that long car ride in the mid-August heat. Unlike previous trips, Welch also rented a U-Haul truck for the return trip this time. The furniture company he used to furnish the Duluth home had some bargains that he picked up for the Great Falls house. He was actually going to haul goods back east for a change. On August 13, they drove the two vehicles into Minneapolis, and Linda boarded a plane bound for Washington, DC. Welch continued south toward Chicago and then east to Great Falls, with Susan driving the station wagon following close behind. She had three kids under three and two cats for company.

Welch's concern about the construction progress was well founded.

Enough problems had popped up in his absence to set the schedule back at least three weeks. There were so many projects going on at once it was hard to keep track of the work and completion schedules. The stonemasons couldn't start because the bricklayers weren't finished. The drywall and taping was held up by the plumber's or the electrician's unfinished work inside the walls.

The best Welch could hope for at this point was to get as much done as possible before winter really hit in January. Two new fireplaces were being installed at once, which brought the house total up to four. He especially needed the outside concrete and brickwork completed before the hard freeze. Although the temperature would dip below freezing, the weather would be fairly mild in this area, unlike upstate New York or, worse yet, northern Minnesota.

In addition to the construction setbacks, Welch also had to deal with Linda and another difficult pregnancy. Bedridden and cranky because of a sore back from the trip home, she wasn't pleasant company. On September 4, Linda finally gave birth to their third son.

With the stress of the construction projects and a new baby, Welch unwound by going back to what he did best. The days were getting shorter and the nights longer, and he started gearing up for the autumn time change. Everyone would lose an hour in late October, and he wanted to be busy by then. Welch was investing more and more of his ill-gotten wealth in the Great Falls home. Combining all the projects Welch commissioned, the total would be $750,000 spent to remodel a $250,000 home.

Welch settled into his routine of going out at dusk and burglarizing up to five houses, returning home before ten o'clock. He would sort and store his take for the evening, being sure to separate the items for smelting. He had a huge amount of storage area now and could break his loot down into more specific categories. He had different areas where he kept stolen handguns and handcuffs, antique long guns and sidearms, fur coats, antique china, figurines, Hummels, coins, antique dolls, Oriental rugs, artwork, jewelry, gold Krugerands, and silver and gold to melt into bullion.

In early December, Bernard Welch took a stroll around his two acres in Great Falls. He walked past the garage, now holding three cars, including the new Mercedes Benz sports coupe he bought for Linda. He checked out the new swimming pool annex, its walls constructed of 60,000 hand-chipped bricks. Figuring in the finished part of the basement, this addition brought the total area of the home to just over thirteen thousand square feet. The property taxes in 1981 were $6,300. Welch also owned a large summer home, great furniture, a Brunswick pool table, a jukebox, color TVs, two pinball machines, a Bang & Olufsen stereo system, and a baby grand piano. Add to that $1.5 million in stocks, $500,000 in the bank, money in the mail, money in the basement, and money stashed in New York. Welch completed his tour of the property and walked toward the front door. As he reached the sidewalk, he stopped and viewed his million-dollar residence, the tennis court in the expansive backyard, and his wealthy neighborhood. He smiled. He had made it. All of this was proof that he had made it. And the cops didn't have a clue; they would never catch him.

Bernard C. Welch Jr. was a success. All the cons in all the prisons wanted this life, but only he had it. Welch entered his Great Falls home, the tour completed. He had to get a move on; it was almost time to go to work.

The million-dollar home of Bernard Welch at 411 Chesapeake Drive in Great Falls, Virginia. December 1980. Reprinted with permission of the DC Public Library, Star Collection, © Washington Post.

A large addition to the Welch home was under construction when he was arrested for murder. It housed a huge swimming pool and a climate-controlled sauna room. December 1980. Reprinted with permission of the DC Public Library, Star Collection, © Washington Post.

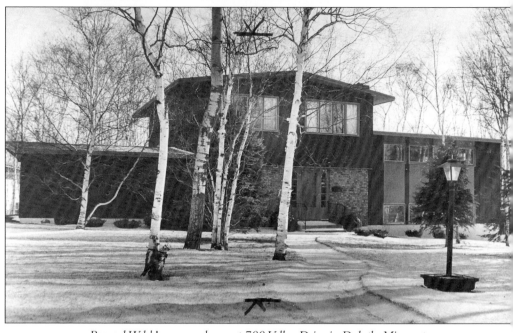

Bernard Welch's summer home at 700 Valley Drive in Duluth, Minnesota.
The right side contains an indoor swimming pool. December 1980.
Reprinted with permission of the DC Public Library, Star Collection, © Washington Post.

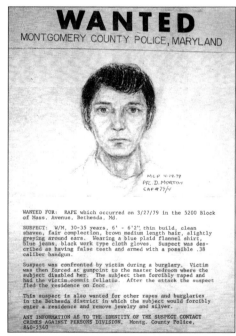

Vienna, Virginia. December 21, 1979.

Montgomery County, Maryland.
March 27, 1979.

WANTED

ROBBERY/BURGLARY   CASE NO. 91086251

DATE OF OFFENSE: 4/18/79 TIME: 2030 HRS.

LOCATION: 7202 ENTERPRISE AVENUE,
           McLEAN, VIRGINIA.

DESCRIPTION OF SUSPECT: WHITE MALE/23-24 YRS.
6'2", 170 LBS., MEDIUM BUILD, DARK BROWN CURLY
HAIR, BLUE EYES, WEARING MAROON JACKET (WIND-
BREAKER), AND BLUE JEANS.

M.O.: SUBJECT ENTERED HOME BY PRYING REAR
DOOR, FOUND COMPLAINANT IN FAMILY ROOM, TOOK
HER TO UPSTAIRS BEDROOM, MADE HER LAY DOWN
ON THE BED, FACE DOWN. JEWELRY TAKEN, AND
SILVER CHECKED BUT NOT TAKEN (IT WAS PLATED).

ANY INFORMATION, CONTACT INVESTIGATOR T. A.
BAILEY, McLEAN DISTRICT STATION, CRIMINAL
INVESTIGATIONS SECTION, TELEPHONE: 703 -
893-0886.

Fairfax County, Virginia.
April 18, 1979.

**IF YOU HAVE ANY INFORMATION AS TO THE WHEREABOUTS
OF THIS PERSON—CALL YOUR LOCAL POLICE OR NOTIFY**
FAIRFAX COUNTY POLICE DEPARTMENT

ADDRESS: 10600 PAGE AVENUE
            FAIRFAX, VIRGINIA 22030

TELEPHONE: DAY - AREA CODE 703 - 893-0886
           NIGHT-AREA CODE 703 - 691-2131

P.D. FORM 121

Known items of appearance on this guy

W-M 6' Atheletic build wears a knit hat, or white golf hat on
occasion, wears blue jean slacks, blue tennis shoes, brown
ripple sole shoes, blue denim jacket, maroon windbreaker
Dark hair,moustache, carries a bag either green or blue,
looks like a laundry bag or book bag with string.

Washington, DC.
February 6, 1979.

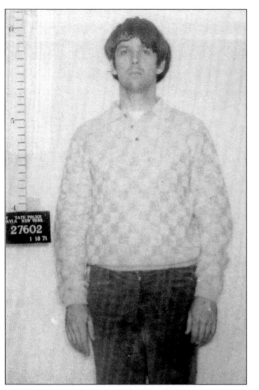

Early in 1971 Welch was again found guilty of burglary and sentenced to ten years in Attica. He was
processed and photographed still wearing his courtroom
suit and tie. Reprinted with permission of the DC Public Library, Star Collection, © Washington Post.

Booking photo of Bernard Welch on suspicion of burglary. January 1971. Taken at State Police Headquarters in Batavia, New York.

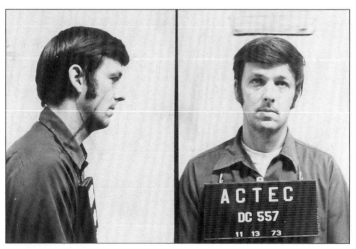

Mug shot of Welch when he was transferred from Attica to the Adirondack Correctional
Treatment and Evaluation Center in Dannemora, New York. November 1973.
Reprinted with permission of the DC Public Library, Star Collection, © Washington Post.

Bernard Welch leaving the Washington, DC, jail on the third day of his first degree murder trial for the shooting of Dr. Michael Halberstam. April 9, 1981. Reprinted with permission of the DC Public Library, Star Collection, © Washington Post.

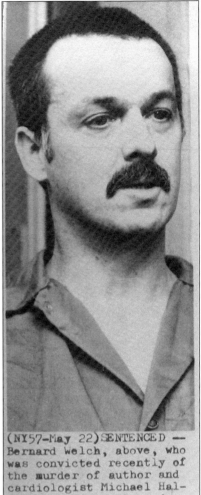

WESTMORELAND
COUNTY PRISON

Name WELCH BERNARD C. JF
Address 545 W. NEWTON ST
GREENSBURG PA.
D.O.B. 4-28-40   Age 45
Race WHITE
Hair BROWN   Eyes HAZEL
Ht. 6'1   Wt. 180
Marks & Scars NONE

Bernard Welch was led away after being sentenced to nine consecutive life terms by Chief Judge H. Carl Moultrie. May 22, 1981. Reprinted with permission of the Associated Press.

Bernard Welch's 1985 prison photo ID card issued after his capture in Greensburg, Pennsylvania. An escaped convict, he was immediately transported to the Supermax federal prison in Marion, Illinois, by US Marshals.

Washington, DC, detective Sally Kirk escorted victims of a recent burglary through stolen goods recovered from Bernard Welch's home. The merchandise was on display at the Fairfax County Police Department Headquarters. December 1980.
Reprinted with permission of the DC Public Library, Star Collection, © Washington Post.

Stolen sterling silver, antiques, and collectibles on display at the Fairfax County Police Headquarters. This merchandise represents only two months of Bernard Welch's burglary enterprise. December 1980.
Reprinted with permission of the DC Public Library, Star Collection, © Washington Post.

Stolen handguns, handcuffs, and ammunition on display at the Fairfax County Police Headquarters in Fairfax, Virginia. The loot was taken from Bernard Welch's house in Great Falls, Virginia. December 1980. Reprinted with permission of the DC Public Library, Star Collection, © Washington Post.

Washington, DC, police officers display stolen goods for the local and national media. These burglarized items were recovered from the Duluth home of Bernard Welch. January 1981. Reprinted with permission of the DC Public Library, Star Collection, © Washington Post.

Linda S. Hamilton. 1967. Duluth, Minnesota.

The Chicago Metropolitan Correctional Center in downtown Chicago. Managed by the Federal Bureau of Prisons. Image by Joe Lekas Photography.

It was Saturday morning, December 6, 1980, a clear, almost warm day. Not much was going on at the Montgomery County Police Headquarters, a modern, brown brick office building at the edge of Rockville, Maryland. The only thing that distinguished it from the other buildings nearby was the brown wooden sign in front and the several police cars parked around it. The building was not originally designed as a police facility but was adapted for that use after the fact. The first floor was filled by the Records Department, Identification Division, and the Central Investigation Division (CID). The CID was comprised of Check and Fraud, Crimes Against Persons, and Crimes Against Property. The centralized Crimes Against Property unit handled all the crimes in Montgomery County that were related to burglary, theft, arson, bombs, or any other incident that was deemed appropriate.

The walls in Crimes Against Property were a light cream color, and the acoustical ceiling tiles were white. Years of dense cigarette smoke stained both a faint yellow. Along the outside wall was a row of windows that could not be opened. This added to the concentration of internal pollution and smells that lingered in the building. The undersized central ventilation system was the sole source of fresh air. It was not very effective in removing odors emanating from the Identification Division next door nor from the homicide office across the hall.

Weekends tended to be quiet in the Crimes Against Property office. The captains, lieutenants, and secretaries were off. There were no interdepartmental mail runs. No new cases would be assigned until Monday. The only thing that might change a quiet weekend was something big, such as a murder. If something did happen, the property detectives would be assigned to assist the homicide investigators working the case. Nothing important had occurred overnight, and so far, it was quiet. It was seven-thirty in the morning, and the phones were not ringing. The two midnight-to-eight detectives had just left the building.

The few men who were working the day shift were drinking their first coffee of the day. For most of them it was hard to get moving after being out late on Friday night. They sat around the long roll call table in the middle of the room. The duty sergeant, Jim Taylor, was at the head of the table, flipping through a clipboard stuffed with teletypes, memos, and notices. He was skimming the reports, only reading aloud if there was something of importance to the unit. Taylor was young to be a sergeant. He was smart, blond, and nice looking.

Taylor finished going through the clipboard and looked up. "So what's on your to-do list for today?"

King stopped doodling on his notepad. His doodling was a habit that often annoyed his superiors. It indicated he was bored.

"Well, Hunky Joe and I have some burglary victims coming in at ten to try to ID some property we recovered from those Bethesda thieves last week. If we can get some victim claims, we can close a few more cases."

"That's good," smiled Taylor. "And how about you, Mike?"

Mike Tihila looked up from the sports page in front of him. "Just working my cases. Victim interviews, follow-ups, you know, keeping busy."

Taylor laughed. "Yeah Mike, we know how you keep busy. So what's good at the track today?" The five men smiled; Tihila's hobby was horses and horse racing.

Taylor next looked at George Neville. "So, what's up with you?"

"Cleaning up some cases," Neville replied, "writing supplements, doing paperwork."

"Good," Taylor replied, "but I'll need you to run over to Wheaton Station and pick up some reports. Other than that, nothing's up. Let's keep it that way."

It was almost eight o'clock when the meeting ended. Everybody got up carrying their coffee cups. King and Ed Slavin went to the coffee pot for a refill. Slavin was known as "Hunky Joe" to his friends. He was from Pennsylvania and had worked in the steel mills as a young man. His six-foot-four frame was all muscle, and he was fearless. He was the type of cop you wanted with you if you were going into trouble.

He went over and unlocked the property storage room and removed cardboard boxes with case numbers and names on the sides. These he placed on the now empty roll call table.

King called to Slavin, "Hey Ed, let's wipe down that table first. I saw Brown drop an Italian cold cut sub all over it yesterday. It still smells like onions."

Slavin pushed his glasses higher up the bridge of his nose. "Okay, where's the Windex?"

Windex, supplied by the department, was the universal cleaning agent of the unit. King shrugged his shoulders, and the two began to prowl through the office, searching for the elusive spray bottle. Finding a specific item in the Crimes Against Property office was no easy task. Two dozen desks were arranged in rows, like a classroom, and they were covered with folders, papers, cups, and ashtrays. Around and under each desk were chairs, trash cans, paper evidence bags, boxes of case files, and all the other detritus accumulated with heavy caseloads and minimal housekeeping.

Slavin and King poked about until Slavin found the Windex bottle in the lieutenant's office. King grabbed some brown paper towels, and the two of them cleaned the top of the gray roll call table. Then they emptied the boxes and began laying out the recovered stolen property in rows. The property was mostly costume jewelry, watches, a few pornographic videotapes, and other items that the young burglars had in their possession when arrested.

It was now almost nine o'clock. Slavin and King had gone through dozens of cases looking for reported stolen property that was similar to what they had recovered. If they could get identifications of the items lying on the table, they could close several more cases. Not only would that enable the state attorney's office to seek longer sentences for the thieves, but it would increase the closed case stats for the month. This was important. Detectives and their supervisors justified their positions by case closures, arrests, convictions, and recovered property statistics.

The office telephone rang and Slavin picked it up. "Crimes Against Property, Detective Slavin." He listened for a few seconds and placed the call on hold. He looked over to King's desk nearby. "Hey, King, it's for you. It's a DC detective."

King punched the flashing button on his desk phone. "Jim King," he announced.

"Hey King," the voice on the other end started, "this is Sergeant Bill Rollins down in 2-D in DC. I think you'll be very interested in this. Last night, at about eight-thirty, there was a burglary on Battery Place Northwest, just off MacArthur Boulevard, not too far from American University. A doctor and his wife came home and surprised a burglar inside. The doctor tussles with the bad guy and gets shot a couple of times in the chest. The bad guy runs away. Now get this; the doctor and his wife go to their car, a big Chevy, and head towards Sibley Hospital, which isn't too far away. The doctor drives. It's dark and the wife doesn't know how bad her husband is shot, okay?"

"I'm listening," replied King in a soft, tense voice. He thought he knew where this was going, hopefully another step closer to his Ghost Burglar.

Rollins continued. "Well, the doctor, I can't remember his name right off, is driving down the street with his wife, and they see the bad guy walking across the lawn of a house a few blocks away from their house. The doctor, who has two bullet holes in him, recognizes the bad guy. So he drives up on the lawn and whacks the bad guy a good one with his car. His wife is furious at him and hollering. Then he drives back onto the street and continues on his way to the hospital. I mean the doc doesn't even slow down. I guess he knew time was important. Anyway, about a block from the hospital the doc passes out and crashes into a tree. The wife jumps out and flags down a passing car for help. So he's finally taken to Sibley Hospital and dies on the operating table."

"Wait, wait," King interjects. "You're saying that the doctor ran over his assailant?"

"Yeah, but hold on, it gets better," Rollins replies. "Police are already at Sibley on some other matter, so they do a quick interview with the doc's wife. As soon as they get the basic details, they call it in to radio dispatch. I respond and so do a couple of scout cars. I'm close, so I go in and drive around the neighborhood looking for a dead body in a front yard. I mean, I don't have a lot of details to go on. By then neighbors have called about hearing gunshots and a car driving across lawns and maybe somebody hurt.

"So I see tire tracks in the grass in front of this house. I get out and walk along the tire marks looking for anything. Guess what I find? In the bushes beside a house, I spot a guy laying there all curled up, but he ain't dead. He's hurt bad, but alive. He sees me and my flashlight, and he tries to move. I get up close to him, and I know this guy had a gun; it could be on the ground nearby. He ain't moving too fast, but I was. I put my big old boot on his right hand real hard, and I stuck my .38 against his head. I told him, 'You're under arrest, asshole.' He just stopped wiggling and gave up. He was too beat up to resist. He'd been hit by a Chevy and knocked twenty feet or so into the bushes."

King started to say something but was cut off by Rollins. "So Jim, listen to this. By now there's a uniform officer there with a local resident who heard the shots and our boy moaning in the bushes. The uniform and I cuff and search this dude. He's got some gold coins and two little silver pigs in his pockets and a penlight. Nearby we find the gun and a big screwdriver. But no wallet or ID."

"Jesus H. Christ!" King blurted out.

"So, listen to this part," Rollins continued. "He's hurt, so we call an ambulance, and they transport him to, would you believe, Sibley ER. The ambulance has to go there, because it's the closest. Of course, that's where the shot doctor is. There, the doctor's wife sees him on the gurney in the ambulance and IDs him as the shooter. I mean, how often does that happen?"

King couldn't think of anything to say. He certainly wasn't expecting this phone call this morning.

Rollins continued. "So, he gets transferred to DC General, and I'm with the bad guy in the ER to recover his clothes for evidence—you know, blood, paint off the car, whatever. You know what else I find? A pair of wire snips and a key to a Mercedes! Could be his or could be stolen. Anyhow he's got no ID on him, so I ask him who he is and you know what he said to me?"

"No," King automatically responded.

"Nothing, he just looked away and wouldn't say a word." Rollins let this sink in before continuing. "We found three other burglaries in the same neighborhood, and in two of them the phone wires were cut. I'm pretty damn certain that this asshole is the Silver Burglar we've all been after. I think this is your guy, Welch, you kept talking about. What do you think?"

"Well it sounds really good so far. Where do we go from here?" King asked.

"Okay, here's the deal. The shooter is being released from the ER soon. He was only bruised up, no internal injuries. He should have been dead, the son of a bitch. Bottom line, he'll be brought down here where I am, at DC police headquarters, for processing and booking. That should be in an hour or so. If this is your guy Welch, you know more about him than anybody. I'm worried he'll get lawyered up and get released on personal recognizance or something. You know DC courts, anything is possible. I need you to get down here with his photos and the info that proves he's a fugitive. I don't know, maybe you can help keep him from making bond. Can you do that?"

King was almost breathless. His mind was jumbled with questions he wanted to ask, but speed was important now. "Man, I'll be there in an hour. DCPD headquarters, Major Burglary, right?"

"Yeah, right."

"I'll be there. And thanks, Bill, you just made my day."

King hung up the phone. He looked for Sergeant Taylor, but he wasn't in his office. While he was doing that, King thought about what he needed to take with him to identify Welch. Slavin stared at him as he started ripping through a brown cardboard box that was on the floor by his desk. Written on the side was the word "Ghost" in black marker. King quickly pulled out folders and leafed through them, selecting certain items. When he had finished, he had a one-inch stack on his desk. This he stuffed into a manila envelope. King then looked over to Slavin with a grin on his face.

"Hey, Ed, I've got to go to DC now. They caught the Silver Burglar, and it looks like it's Welch. Tell Sergeant Taylor he was breaking into a house in northwest DC and got surprised by the owner and his wife. He shot the owner, who's a doctor, in the chest and ran away. The doctor got to his car and ran him over. DCPD now has him in custody. The doctor died, and the DC police want me down there to help ID the guy as Welch so he doesn't make bond."

"So you were right," Slavin grinned. "Go on man, that's great. Outstanding."

King hurried out the back door of the building and got into his unmarked, maroon, 1978 Ford police car. He placed the red light on the dash and pulled out of the parking lot.

King was at DC police headquarters building within an hour. Because it was Saturday, there were open parking spaces in the front along the curb marked "Police Only." King parked and flipped down his visor with the "Official Police Business" white plasticized sign held on by several rubber bands. He got out and walked quickly down the sidewalk into the building, carrying his file of information.

The building at 300 Indiana Avenue was a large 1950s structure of sooty gray concrete. It, and the adjoining District courthouse, took up the entire city block. King entered the main lobby. The two Art Deco elevators were not in service. They required operators, and none were on duty on the weekend. King was familiar with the building and knew where the stairs were that led to the second floor office of Major Burglary. He went up the stairs, two at a time.

He found Rollins almost asleep in a swivel chair, his feet resting on an open desk drawer.

"Hey man," King called. "Is he here yet?"

"No, not yet," Rollins said, opening his eyes, "but soon. Let's go down to the processing area and wait. I'm falling asleep here."

The two detectives walked two floors down a back stairway to get to Criminal Processing. This was where arrested suspects were fingerprinted, photographed, and assigned a police ID number. Nearby was the lockup, consisting of holding cells where arrested suspects were held until they went before the District court next door for a preliminary hearing. There, the initial bail was set.

The hall outside of the processing area was cold, poorly lit, and dingy. The painted concrete floors were seldom cleaned. The concrete walls had several layers of peeling enamel paint. Underground passages led off like catacombs to unknown places. Prisoners would be walked through these passages to a courtroom to be "papered" after processing. To be "papered" was an old term used only in Washington, DC. It meant that an arrested person went before a judge. The arresting officer would tell the judge of the crime and the probable cause for arresting that particular person for that crime. These hearings were short. The judge almost always relied on the police testimony. He would then set the bail for the accused person. If bail could not be immediately met, the prisoner would be walked back to the holding area to be later transported to the District jail in southeast Washington.

The arresting officer had to testify in person at the preliminary hearing. This often meant waiting several hours for the next scheduled meeting of the court. If there was no one in court to present the probable cause for arrest, then the defendant was often set free. It was standard practice for the judge to grant personal recognizance in lieu of a cash bond if the defendant had no prior criminal record, was not a flight risk, and was not wanted for other crimes. It was this last part that Rollins wanted King to be there for. Even in a murder case, some bail had to be set. Rollins feared that Welch could actually make bail and flee the area. Rollins was trying his best to make sure that did not happen.

The two talked about the previous night's crime while they waited. Rollins filled King in on the many details. He paused for a second and then, "Oh yeah, I remember. The doctor's name was Halberstam, a heart surgeon. I heard at the hospital that one of the bullets nicked an artery, and he bled to death internally. Too bad. He was a brave man."

King nodded. "Yeah, too bad. But it was bound to happen someday. This

Ghost Burglar guy pistol-whipped some people and raped two, maybe three, women. He's a violent son of a bitch. The doctor did everyone a big favor by running over that asshole. I just hope it is Welch."

Soon, they heard the police paddy wagon arrive. It backed up to the steel intake door. Two uniformed DC officers got out and walked to the rear of the grimy, overused police van. One officer unlocked and opened the wagon's two rear doors. The other officer stood back a bit, in case the prisoner made an attempt to escape.

The interior of the wagon was smooth, painted steel. A bench ran along each side, front to rear, about six feet long. There was nothing for anyone inside to hold onto. A prisoner, with his hands cuffed behind him, would slide around the smooth metal interior like a peanut in an empty can. Unless the paddy wagon's compartment was packed with people, it was almost impossible to stay seated. Even if the police officer driving were considerate, a lone passenger would experience a hard passage.

King and Rollins stepped out to the low loading dock. King looked into the wagon's interior. There was a man in a hospital gown lying on the dirty floor. It was difficult to see his face, as his head was under the bench at the back of the compartment. He was moaning. His bare legs and feet were exposed to the cold December air. The cheap, blue cloth hospital slippers had come off and were in a corner. It seemed that the prisoner's bumpy ride had done some further damage to his already bruised body.

One of the uniformed officers addressed Rollins. "Hey, this guy can barely move. Go into processing and get one of them chairs with wheels. We're going to have to roll his ass inside."

Rollins went into the building and returned a minute later, pushing an old secretarial chair with castors on the legs. He rolled it across the concrete pavement to the rear of the van. The two police officers climbed inside and levered the prisoner up by his shoulders. They tugged him out backwards, his bare heels dragging across the van floor. Once out of the van, they unceremoniously deposited him onto the chair. He groaned loudly and shivered.

King got his first look at the culprit's face. Although he now sported a mustache and was heavier, King recognized Bernard Welch from his several mug shots. His hair was rumpled, and his unshaven face was lined with the pain of his handling. But there was no doubt in King's mind. This was Welch.

King was disappointed. He had imagined this first face-to-face moment many times. He had thought of Welch as he appeared in the old photographs—younger, thinner, well dressed. He was none of those things now. King had expected something more, something different. Over the past three years, King had thought of the Ghost Burglar as someone suave, like Cary Grant playing a jewel thief in an old movie. Someone smooth, professional, confident. The guy in front of him now was ordinary, plain, and nondescript. You could pass this guy in a grocery store and never remember a detail about him. Maybe that was what helped him get away for so long. He looked like a typical, unremarkable nobody.

King looked over to Rollins. All he could think to say was, "It's him."

King and Rollins followed the two patrol officers as they rolled Welch into the processing area. The officers turned Welch over to Sergeant Thomas Dolan, the officer in charge. Rollins and King stopped outside of the barred processing area. They both unloaded their .38-caliber service revolvers and placed them into individual lockboxes, keeping the keys.

As they entered the processing room, King could hear Dolan speaking to Welch in a New York, Lower East Side, Irish-like brogue. "Another John Doe, huh. Well my boy, you can lie, but your prints won't. Okay, you two," indicating King and Rollins, "roll that scruffy-arsed fellow over here to the print table."

The two detectives pushed the chair with Welch to the stand that contained the ink pad, roller, and hinged metal frame that would hold the fingerprint cards in place during the operation. The big, beefy sergeant squirted a few dabs of thick, pasty black ink onto the print pad and rolled it smooth. Then, Dolan looked down at Welch in his chair.

"John Doe, you can stand up or you can lie on the floor. Take your pick. I can take your prints either way." The veteran cop's tone indicated that it would be much better for Welch to cooperate.

Welch looked up at the serious eyes of the sergeant. He tried to stand but needed the help of the two detectives. King and Rollins got on each side and, grabbing Welch under the arms, heaved him to an upright position. He grunted and bent over but stood on his own. The sergeant pulled a key ring off his belt and unlocked Welch's handcuffs. Welch slowly moved his hands from his back to his front and rubbed his wrists.

"Don't even think about making a break or being funny or anything like that, my boy. There's me and my two assistants, as well as these two strapping plainclothes men to handle you."

With that, the sergeant examined Welch's hands and looked at his fingertips. "Dirty. Here's a paper towel. Wipe 'em clean."

Welch did as instructed. The sergeant grasped Welch's right hand and rolled each finger and thumb in the sticky, black ink. Then, he shifted the right hand until it was over the fingerprint card that was framed in the metal cardholder.

"Okay now, relax, go limp. Let me do all the work. Don't try to help." The sergeant first selected the thumb and rolled it in the appropriate box. He next did the same to the other four right-hand fingers.

Dolan repositioned the print card to the next row of spaces for the left hand. The thumb and four fingers of the left hand were also inked and rolled onto the card. The card was repositioned again to the next row. This row was for the thumb and four fingers together of each hand.

When this procedure was completed, the sergeant removed the card and inspected it. "Well now, that looks a bit sloppy. We'll have to do it again. Wouldn't want the FBI to think we don't do good work."

A fresh FBI card was fed into the hinged metal frame, and the process was repeated. The sergeant removed the card and examined it. "Oh, much better. That's number one. Only three more to go."

The process was repeated, and then full palm prints were taken. This left Welch's hands totally black from wrists to fingertips. Dolan gave him some foam hand cleaner and paper towels to clean up with. He was able to remove most of the tar-like ink.

Dolan looked from Welch to the stack of fingerprint cards. "I wonder just who, exactly, it is we have here."

"You'll be surprised," Welch replied.

The two police assistants who had been watching the processing came and helped Welch hobble over to the camera station. He was placed in front of a large, antique box camera on a wooden stand. One of the assistants had already inserted the white plastic numbers into the black, grooved material of the identification frame. The frame had a thin metal ball chain that was hung around the arrestee's neck. He was positioned at the white tape mark on the floor, while the other assistant positioned the camera. As he did this, the assistant looked up and said, somewhat ironically, "Don't smile." The camera clicked, and Welch blinked after the flash had gone off. "Turn your head to the left and give me a side view," the assistant instructed. The camera flashed again. "All done."

Welch was returned to his rolling chair and allowed to sit as the three officers finished filling out the paperwork. After a few minutes, the sergeant looked at Welch and said, "Buddy boy, it looks like you need some clothes. You go into the lock up with that split-back gown on and you'll be somebody's bitch before the day's over. Somebody get this here boy a jumpsuit. I'd say a medium would do."

An officer went to a large, green locker and found a folded bundle, which he threw at Welch. The bundle landed on the floor close to his feet. No one moved to help him. Welch sat there for a moment and finally realized that it was up to him to retrieve the clothing. With great effort, he slowly bent over, snagging the bundle's wrapping string with his right hand while holding on to the chair seat with his left. He unwrapped the string and began to laboriously put the jump suit on.

Rollins and King left the processing room and retrieved their weapons. They began to climb the stairs back to the second floor. As they got to the top, a thought occurred to King.

"Hey Bill, have you called the US Marshals? Welch is an escaped felon from New York."

Rollins looked at King. "You thought I was sleeping at those task force meetings, didn't you?"

King smiled. "You mean you weren't?"

"Man, I know his history," Rollins replied, feigning indignation. "I called them before you showed up. They said they couldn't do anything until his identity was confirmed by the FBI." Rollins pulled a completed fingerprint card from an envelope he'd been carrying. It had "Federal Bureau of Investigation" printed in red across the top. "I told Sergeant Dolan downstairs to roll an extra FBI card. That's why he did two."

"Hey, I'm sorry," King apologized. "You know, I never thought about this beyond the arrest."

"I know. Listen, I wouldn't know it was Welch if you hadn't talked about it so much. And just for you," Rollins clapped his hand on King's shoulder, "I will personally hand-deliver this card to the FBI Print Section on my way home to go to bed."

When they returned to the Major Burglary office, Rollins sat at his desk to make some phone calls. King sat down at another desk and called his office to update Sergeant Taylor.

Rollins hung up the phone and looked at King, "Well, I've got some news. First, Homicide will handle it from here. Since it's a murder case and Welch is technically a John Doe, he won't be papered until Monday. Second, Detective Drummond took that Mercedes key to the scene and found Welch's car, almost across the street from where he was hit by the doctor. Would you believe it's a new, 1980 silver Mercedes four-door sedan?"

"A Mercedes, so that key you got fit." King cocked his head a little to the side. "Hey, was it stolen?"

Rollins squinted as smoke curled up to his eyes from his cigarette. "Well, no. It's listed to a woman named Hamilton in Great Falls, Virginia. That's a pretty nice area near Fairfax, I think. Anyway, a wrecker's bringing the car here, now. This might be a good address for Welch, so I called Tom Bailey in Fairfax County and gave him the run down. He's all excited, just like you. He said he'll give the car's listed address a low flyby. I told him you were here and you'd keep him informed, because I'm going home."

"Okay," said King, "what now?"

"Well, I'll walk you down to Homicide, since they're handling it from here. They'll probably search Welch's car when it gets here. Mo Finkelberg is there now. You know him?"

King nodded. He knew Detective Finkelberg from a previous case. Rollins got up. The two left the burglary office and headed to the central Homicide office, about one hundred feet down the hall.

"Hey, I just want to say thanks for the good work and the call," King said to Rollins as they walked along. "Now go home. I'll call you later with the details. Oh, and don't forget that FBI print card."

"Don't worry," Rollins sighed. "I won't forget."

King followed Rollins into the Homicide office. This office closely resembled the Burglary office, except it had fewer desks.

"Hey Fink, I got Jim King from Montgomery County in tow," Rollins announced. "He's the guy who figured out who that Ghost Burglar was over a year ago. And this Ghost Burglar guy also just happens to be the shooter in that doctor's murder last night. I called King down to ID him, since he's a John Doe at the moment."

Finkelberg was a big man, six-foot-four and almost three hundred pounds. His hair was thinning, and his stomach hung over his belt. When he talked, his black-framed glasses moved up and down. Finkelberg looked up when Rollins and King entered. "Hey, King, come on in. One hell of a case, isn't it?"

King nodded. "Sure is. Sorry it happened this way. The bad guy was supposed to end up dead."

"Almost did," replied Finkelberg. "The doc should have hit him a little harder."

"Fink, I gotta go home and get some sleep," Rollins interjected. "The 2-D uniform unit has done the arrest report."

Finkelberg waved Rollins away. "Go man, see you later. And thanks."

Rollins waved to both men as he disappeared.

"The coffee's over there," Finkelberg said, nodding his head towards a ten-cup chrome percolator, steaming on the windowsill. King walked over and found a Styrofoam cup with only a little dirt in it. He blew the dirt out and poured a half-cup of the strong, black coffee. Finkelberg looked at the large electric clock over the door.

"We should be seeing the shooter's car soon. What's the guy's name?"

"Welch. Bernard C. Welch Junior, actually," King replied. "He's an escapee from New York state prison a few years ago. Been an active, big-time burglar in Richmond, northern Virginia, Maryland, and DC for the past four or five years. He's the suspect in at least three rapes, several armed house robberies, and I don't know what else. Probably did a few thousand major burglaries in the DC metro area."

"Hey, one hell of a catch." Finkelberg's eyes widened a little. "Better do this one by the book. When we take a car into custody, we have to inventory its contents and lock up anything valuable. We get a lot of theft from our impound lots, you know what I mean?"

"Yeah, I know," King nodded, "but will that kind of search stand up in court?"

"Yeah, always has. It's our standard procedure." King mulled this over as Finkelberg answered a phone call.

A few seconds later, Finkelberg hung up the phone. "Okay, that was the tow boys. They'll be here soon, and the evidence tech is on his way. He'll check out the car. Let's go down and meet them."

In the garage the two officers waited for a few minutes until a Metropolitan Police tow truck arrived. The driver, wearing greasy khaki overalls and a jacket with a DC police patch on the shoulder, got out and began to unhitch a 1980, silver Mercedes into an empty parking space. King noted the tag was a current Virginia plate, UGB 355. The tow truck driver opened the door and set the emergency brake.

"Any keys to this?" Finkelberg asked the driver.

"Yep, got it from a plainclothes guy. It's on the driver's side floor mat."

The tow truck pulled off, and Finkelberg opened the door. "This is a nice car. I wouldn't mind owning it, except it's German." He laughed and tried to slide in to the driver's side front seat. He stopped about halfway; he didn't fit. After adjusting the seat, Finkelberg looked around, felt under the seat, and found the key. He opened the glove compartment and found a wallet, which he opened. It had close to two hundred dollars in cash and some cards. Finkelberg went through the cards and found a Virginia driver's license.

"This license says his name is Norman Hamilton, with an address in Great Falls, Virginia." Finkelberg searched the papers in the box and located a Virginia registration. He held it out to King. "This says the car is owned by a Linda Hamilton at the same address in Great Falls.

King looked at Welch's photo and address on the license. He compared them to the registration card. Both had 411 Chesapeake Drive, Great Falls, Virginia. Damn, he had done it again. King remembered that Welch had done something similar with a woman in Richmond several years ago. He had used her address and her ex-husband's name as his own, assuming the cloak of legitimacy.

Finishing his search of the vehicle's interior, Finkelberg got out and walked to the car's rear. He stuck the key into the trunk, and it popped open. As the trunk lid rose up, both men peered in. Inside was a jumble of cloth bags and what appeared to be a white bed sheet. Finkelberg reached in and opened the sheet. It was wrapped around sterling silver pieces.

"Bingo!" exclaimed Finkelberg.

There were two cloth bags with drawstrings. These contained more silver and some jewelry. There was also a white bag that was full of silver knives, forks, and spoons. King smiled as he watched Finkelberg look through the bags.

When Finkelberg looked up, King smiled. "Rollins told me there were three other B and Es last night in that same neighborhood."

Finkelberg stopped for a second. "This must be the stuff he got. This is great!" Finkelberg closed the trunk and locked the car. "But I've got to wait for the evidence guy to come. This'll take all day to inventory."

Once upstairs, both detectives began making telephone calls. King first called Detective Tom Bailey in Fairfax County. He gave Bailey the details on what had been found in the car, which made Bailey very happy.

"Come on over, Jim," Bailey announced. "We're typing up an application for a search warrant. Then we have to find a judge on a golf course, and then we hit the house. You're welcome to come along if you want."

"Sure, I'd love to come. Be there in an hour or so," King replied. "And thanks for inviting me."

"No problem, and listen Jim, I'm glad you were right about that Welch fellow. It's got to have made your day."

"Tom, it's made everyone's day," King assured him, "except Welch's."

King next called his office and updated Sergeant Taylor. Taylor agreed that King should go to Virginia to lend whatever assistance he could with the house search.

King walked out of the Metropolitan police headquarters building. The sun was shining. The sky was a bright blue, and the air was almost warm. King took a deep breath and smiled. He didn't even realize he was humming.

It was noon when Detective James King entered the Third Street Tunnel. This route took him under the edge of Capitol Hill and onto the Southeast Freeway, which ran along the Potomac waterfront. From there, he turned left onto 14th Street, which, skirting the Jefferson Memorial, led to the Rochambeau Bridge over the Potomac River. Once across the Potomac and in Virginia, the roads improved and there were fewer potholes. The District was notorious for the poor condition of its streets.

King drove west along the George Washington Memorial Parkway. This road ran along the Potomac River with wonderful views of the Tidal Basin, the Washington Monument, the Pentagon, the Iwo Jima Memorial, and the Georgetown Palisades. Only tourists stopped to look anymore; it was just another commuter route in and out of Washington, DC. King rolled along at sixty.

He knew the Washington area well. Not only had he been born and raised here, but he had worked his way through college driving a taxi cab and a furniture delivery truck. He had chosen this route by considering the day of the week, the time of day, the weather, and road construction. The G. W. Parkway lead him to the Capitol Beltway in Virginia and then to Chain Bridge Road. There were no traffic lights until he reached the Fairfax County road system.

His stomach was making noises. His wife had made him a lunch for today, but he had forgotten it in his desk when he ran out of the office. He stopped at a nearby fast food chain. As he stuffed the last of the burger into his mouth, he pulled into the police station parking lot. He drank some water and walked into the front door of the one-story building.

At the McLean police station, six-foot-three, sandy-haired Tom Bailey shook Jim's hand. "Great day, Jim," Bailey exclaimed. "It was about time we got a break. Lord knows we didn't get any before this."

"Yeah, Tom, we were due." King motioned to Bailey's red and black flannel shirt. "Got you on your day off?"

"Yeah, I was getting ready to go to my kid's football game when that DC detective called here. He said it was important, so I called him back. After he filled me in, I came in and started the ball rolling."

Bailey lowered his voice and asked, "You're sure this guy, Hamilton, is really Welch?"

"Yeah, Tom, no question," King assured him. "I saw him up close when he was brought in for booking. A little older than his mug shots, and he has a moustache, but it's him. I was there when DC searched his car. Found the trunk loaded with silver and jewelry. And guess what? The DC burglaries had phone wires cut, and he had wire cutters on him. Have you checked the house the car is listed to?"

"I got a detective to go by and talk to the neighbors, just general questions. They said the place is owned by Norman and Linda Hamilton. They're married and got three kids. Supposedly, he's a wheeler-dealer in the stock market, they think, but they're not sure. The ones that have met him say he's a nice guy but not very sophisticated. Kind of a country boy made good. Then I drove by it. It's a big place in a really nice neighborhood in Great Falls. Houses there are in the half million dollar range. On a chance, I knocked on the door, and the wife answered. She let me in and allowed me to walk through the house. There were metal melting pots in the garage and a new Mercedes sports car."

King only nodded. "Interesting. How long have they lived there?"

"Two, maybe three years."

"So, can we assume that his wife is involved in the crimes too?"

Bailey wrinkled up one side of his face. "Well, I guess. There's nothing concrete yet, but we'll see."

A uniformed officer at a phone said, "Hold on, he's here. Detective Bailey, I have Captain Ailes on the line. He wants to talk to you."

"Excuse me, Jim," Bailey apologized. "Get some coffee and have a seat.

This'll take awhile." With that, Bailey walked to the desk and took the proffered telephone.

King took off his old tan raincoat and laid it over a chair. It was wrinkled and stained after four years of wear. It would have to last another year. King straightened his tie and sport coat and got some coffee.

Time passed slowly. King sat beside a table, his back against a wall. He watched the several police officers make phone calls, type, skim through police reports, and consult with one another. There was nothing he could do but stay out of the way.

Detective Dave Roberts from DC's Second District walked through the office door. He grinned as he turned to King and clapped him on the shoulder with a beefy hand. "Jimmy, a hell of a day! We all done good, and you're not as crazy as we thought."

"Thanks for the compliment," King laughed. Roberts and King were friends, and he knew Roberts had believed him when he proposed Bernard Welch as the prime suspect in all the related crimes in the area.

Bailey finished his call and approached the two men. "Anything back from the feds on the prints?"

Roberts shook his head. "Not yet. You know them. Maybe tomorrow, if we're lucky."

Bailey and King nodded knowingly. The FBI was not held in high esteem by the local police. The FBI might consider themselves elite, but the police on the street considered them amateurs. When it came to real crime, they had little experience. They were essentially bookkeepers with a lot of money to buy informants. Even at that, they usually picked informants who didn't know much or who were up to their necks into crime and getting FBI protection for dribbling out crap information. But the FBI did have excellent labs to process evidence, there was no denying that.

"In Richmond, didn't Welch hide all his stolen property in a rental storage place and when he had enough he'd pack it up and sell it out of state?" Bailey asked King.

"That was his MO then. As far as I know he seems to have followed that same pattern here," replied King.

"Well, that house in Great Falls has a three-car garage, a basement, and a new addition. It's bigger than any storage facility. Mrs. Hamilton told me her husband, Norm, keeps all of his stuff there." Then Bailey looked thoughtful for a few seconds, his eyebrows turned down, his mouth pursed. "I better arrange to have a truck available, just in case." As Tom began to turn away, he stopped. "Jim, show Dave where the coffee is. Oh, and we got pizza coming soon."

Roberts followed King to the coffee dispenser. It was one of the new Bunn, double pot models, made of stainless steel. Roberts looked around the Fairfax detective office in open admiration. "Boy, this sure is nice. Makes my place look like a dumpster behind the mini-mart."

"Yeah," King laughed, "I bet they even sweep the floors every week."

The two walked over to the table King had occupied earlier. "Rollins called me at home," Roberts explained as he sloughed off his heavy car coat and sat down by King. "Told me to come in early and get my ass over here to see what goes down." He took a sip of black coffee from the small Styrofoam cup. "It's a capital murder case, but we ain't fried anybody in DC for years. We're interested in everything that happens here, particularly if his wife was involved."

"I've been thinking about that. You guys found his car parked in the neighborhood right?" King speculated.

Roberts nodded then sipped his coffee as King continued.

"Well, that means he was alone. If she were the wheel man, she would have driven off. That indicates his wife was not with him. So, if she's part of his operation, she didn't have anything to do with the shooting. Even if charged criminally, she would probably never be convicted."

Roberts sipped his coffee, taking in King's comments. "Oh hey," he snapped his fingers and looked at King, "you were there with Finkelberg and looked in the trunk of Welch's car, right?"

"Yeah," King nodded, "quite a bit of stolen stuff in there. Probably from the burglaries before the shooting."

"Well, Welch's wife, she's the Mercedes owner," Roberts smiled slyly. "She gave us permission to search the car. So we're good on that, especially since we already searched it."

King laughed knowingly. DC had covered their ass on that one. They were lucky. But it was all falling into place now. This would be a successful prosecution. He was amazed how quickly the whole thing had come together. A few years ago, it would have taken days or weeks for the separate jurisdictions to start to cooperate. Now, it was almost instantaneous. All because of the cooperation of the cops in the trenches, who had taken matters in their own hands and worked together. After three years on the burglary task force, they knew and trusted each other.

The two men sat at the table observing the goings on around them. Eventually the pizza arrived. By the time the pizza was gone, it was after four o'clock.

A short time later, Bailey approached them. "Okay, we got the search warrant signed," Bailey informed them, all business. "I've got you guys cleared as observers only. It's allowed because of your extensive knowledge of the property stolen in your jurisdictions, and you were on the task force and cooperated with us one hundred percent. So it goes like this, we make entry first and secure the house, make sure it's safe. After that, you can enter and observe only. You have no authority here. I don't want challenges to the search warrant or chain of custody because unauthorized people helped serve it or handled the evidence. Understand?"

King and Roberts nodded, knowing that this was standard procedure in any jurisdiction. They also knew that the responsibility for a smooth operation was all on Bailey's shoulders.

Bailey turned and walked to the center of the room. "Okay, everybody, we're about ready to roll. Although the wife has been cooperative, and we don't expect trouble, we will still do this by the book, just in case. No one gets in trouble when you follow procedures. So be alert, but remember, there is a woman and three small children in the house, so we have to be careful." Roberts made sure everyone understood before continuing. "I will go with the entry team to the front door and demand entrance. Once the door opens, I will present the search warrant. If the door does not open, we will use the battering ram. The entry team will go in and check everything. You know the drill. Once the house is secure, then everyone else can come in, including the observers. Got that?" The dozen and a half officers present in the room nodded. "Then let's head out," Bailey instructed as he led the way out of the room.

Everyone cleared the room and headed to their cars. The temperature had cooled as the sun had begun to set. It was still a mild day for December. The sky was turning yellow-orange. Several police cars pulled out in a long convoy. Traffic was light. King made it a point to get behind a Fairfax police car. At least the Fairfax cop would know where he was going.

The caravan moved along at a reasonable pace, there were few traffic lights. Within twenty-five minutes, they were in a neighborhood of big houses. Well-kept homes on large lots were visible in the twilight. Like a funeral procession, the several police cars wound through the neighborhood, finally stopping along a quiet residential street. Streetlights placed at each intersection began to light up.

King stayed in his car as instructed. He could see Bailey, followed by several uniformed officers, approach the front door of a large, brick rambler. It had only a few interior lights on. King noticed that a pair of officers circled the house to the left and another pair circled to the right. In circumstances where anything could happen, especially attempts to escape, it was prudent to have all possible exit points covered.

King watched Bailey climb the few steps to the front door and knock. A few seconds later, Bailey knocked again, this time more forcefully. With his window cracked, King could hear Bailey knocking. He must be using a night-stick. He could not see who opened the door, but the porch light went on. Bailey stood there reading from the warrant to the unseen person inside the opened doorway. The seven police officers behind him entered. Then, Bailey entered also.

While waiting, King looked at the home he was parked in front of. It was a long, tan, brick rambler, large by any standard. It blended into the prosperous neighborhood of relatively new homes. He immediately noticed a closed-circuit television camera mounted at the peak of the garage roof. This was a rare form of home security, seen at the homes of the wealthy, government officials, and diplomats. The idea of an exterior camera seemed comical at first, but on second thought, not so funny considering the profession of the home's occupants and the items that might be stored there.

After several more minutes, two officers came around from the back and joined the first two. He exited his car and walked across the wide lawn toward the concrete sidewalk that led to the entrance. Roberts met him there.

"Hell of a house, huh, Jimmy?"

"Yeah, the only places like this I've been in have belonged to victims," replied King.

"Hey, did you see the big addition on the rear?" Roberts had been parked farther around the corner and, therefore, was able to see the other side of the residence.

"Not from where I was."

"One of the uniforms said it had an indoor pool inside."

"Jesus" exclaimed King. "Are you sure?"

"I don't know. That's what the guy said. But if it's true, that son of a bitch

Welch was doing better that I thought."

Bailey came to the front door and waved them inside. As they entered, he stopped King, Roberts, and the four uniformed officers. "Only the wife and three little children are here. I've told her to stay in the kitchen area with her kids. She asks that we not upset the little ones. She has not been handcuffed, because she has to tend the children and she has been very cooperative." Handcuffing all occupants and placing them under guard, de rigueur in search warrants, kept the occupants from interfering with the police search, stopped escape attempts, and protected the officers from attack. It was up to the officer in charge to determine if this procedure was necessary.

"This house is large and it's full of stuff," Bailey continued. "Everything is stored here, so it's going to take a long time. Remember, you guys are observers only. Walk around, take notes, and watch, but don't help. I know that'll be hard. If you see anything we might miss, let me know, okay?"

The two detectives nodded. They understood that they were present only as an act of professional courtesy. Bailey advised the other four officers to accompany him to the garage. Roberts and King followed also.

The garage was along the hall to the right. When they entered, they saw a late model Ford station wagon with wood trim and a new Mercedes sports coupe. Against the wall was a workbench. As the group proceeded into the garage area, Bailey pointed to some items on the floor near the workbench. "What do you think of that?"

The two detectives looked down. "Holy Christ!" exclaimed Roberts. "A melting pot thing."

King saw a propane tank, like those used on outside grills, hooked by hose to a metal stand with a burner. Nearby, were several thick ceramic crucibles. One was black and broken around its top. Two were new and two were dark brown and black on the outside. One of these had an interior silver coating. The other had gold flecks on the inside. On the workbench nearby were goggles, heavy asbestos gloves, and a set of long tongs made for handling the hot crucibles. There were also stainless steel cafeteria trays with indentations. These were for pouring the hot metal in to make ingots. King recognized much of this equipment, because his great grandfather had been a blacksmith and often melted lead and poured it into molds to make fishing sinkers. King scanned the room and was surprised by its neatness. There was little dust or debris, unlike a blacksmith shop. Apparently, Welch liked to keep his illegal operation tidy.

Bailey then led them back inside the house and to another door in the hall. This was the entrance to the lower level. The basement was large, extending the full length and width of the footprint of the home, maybe eighty by forty feet. It was a mostly finished living area. The majority of it was recreation room. There was also a full bath and a small bedroom. About a third of the basement was unfinished, containing a laundry room, a workshop, and a large storage room with a dead bolt lock on the door.

Bailey pointed to the opened storage room door. Inside, were many cardboard boxes stacked up. Some of the boxes were opened. King looked into the boxes nearest him. One was filled with porcelain figurines wrapped in newspaper. Another had pocket watches. A third contained a fur coat used for padding around an antique china doll. Leaning against one corner was what looked like a flintlock Pennsylvania long rifle.

"This," Bailey announced with a large grin on his face, "is his storage locker."

Roberts stared around the room with a blank look. "It's not very full."

"No," conceded Bailey, "but presumably he's only been working since late September. By spring, he would have filled it."

King stared around thoughtfully. "You're saying he stored everything here, in his house, until he stopped in the spring?"

Bailey gave an affirmative nod. "Yep, he'd stockpile it and make one trip out of state to sell it."

King cleared his throat nervously. "Ah, Tom, where did he take it?"

"To Duluth, Minnesota." Bailey paused a second, enjoying King's confusion.

King and Roberts looked at each other and, like a comedy routine, said simultaneously, "Duluth, Minnesota?"

"Yeah, Duluth. It's where his wife is from. Only, she's not his wife. They were never legally married."

Who would have guessed it? Welch was an East Coast guy. Everything he had ever done had been on the East Coast—New York to Virginia and, even once, Florida. Nowhere else. King had researched Welch's history. He had never, ever gone away from the Atlantic coast. King had mailed more than one hundred posters to antique auction houses up and down the East Coast. He had never figured on anything in the upper Midwest. In fact, he had been thinking about mailing posters to Illinois and Ohio next. That was to be the extent of his shot-in-the-dark efforts.

"Okay, look around. See what you can," Bailey looked at the detectives.

"I've got to get this stuff out of here."

Knowing that they were now in the way, the men wandered out of the room. "You know, Welch used to be a plumber," King mentioned to Roberts. "I'll bet he knew about melting metal because plumbers use molten lead to seal sewer pipes."

Roberts stared back at King for a moment. "Yeah, I guess. But if you melt it into bars, you have to sell it in bars. There's no place around here that I know of that buys homemade gold and silver bars. Before they pay you for it, they have to assay it. That means you have to ship it out of state to a commercial refinery. After the refinery is happy with the quality, then they mail you a check. That means a paper trail to follow. I'll bet that's how he got his operating cash while he was waiting to get the other stuff to Duluth in the spring."

"Sounds about right," King agreed. Roberts was silent for a moment. "By the way, how far is Duluth from here, anyway?"

"I don't know, a thousand miles maybe? It's in the top end of Minnesota, I think, near Canada."

The two looked around the recreation room. It was fairly conventional. The floor was tiled. The walls were paneled on the bottom with a cheap pine chair rail separating it from the top plasterboard that was painted a light green. Acoustical tile lined the ceiling. A couch, two upholstered armchairs, and a large, twenty-seven-inch color television furnished the room. The Seeburg jukebox in the corner caught King's attention. Refurbished, those things easily cost a grand. There were only a few bottles of alcohol behind the simple bar.

When they walked out of the rec room into the hall that lead to the stairs, they noticed a brown wooden box about the size of four telephone booths stuck together. It had a frosted glass door.

"What the hell is this?" Roberts asked as he opened the door. "Son of a bitch, it's a sauna!"

They looked inside. It had a slatted wood bench with lights and nozzles overhead. On the wall across from the bench was a control panel with buttons labeled "Jungle Mist" and "Hawaiian Rain."

"Well, I'll be damned," exclaimed Roberts. "This guy is no ordinary thief."

"Not in the least," agreed King.

These two detectives worked in one of the richest areas of the nation, encompassing northwest Washington, DC, Chevy Chase, Bethesda, and Potomac. They had visited many wealthy homes in their work. Such luxuries were rare.

But for a thief, even a good thief, to live like this was unheard of. Most criminals quickly converted their stolen goods into money for drugs, booze, sex, or gambling. They usually lived in squalor—mattress on the floor, clothes in a plastic trash bag, clogged toilets, drug and alcohol paraphernalia littering the area. A thief living like this was a first for King and Roberts.

"You know, this is something," King started. "This guy, Welch, is a murderer, rapist, thug, and thief, but he lives like a regular stockbroker or something!"

"Jimmy, this guy is one of a kind," replied Roberts. "He was good at what he did. That's why it took so long to get him."

"I wonder," mused King, "if Dr. Halberstam hadn't run him over, how much longer would it have taken for us to get him?"

The two investigators wandered through the residence feeling like they were on a house tour without a guide. The inside of the house wasn't fancy. The white painted walls looked like builder grade. Ready-made, off-white curtains on standard rods. The furniture was nice but average. The kind of furniture that people would buy at a department store. Everything was neat and clean. Occasionally, they noticed an original oil painting or watercolor hanging on the walls. These could not be purchased in a department store at the mall. In the dining room were a couple of nice big silver pieces with English hallmarks. King made a mental note to tell Bailey about these.

It was standard procedure, when serving a search warrant like this, to take everything that might possibly have been stolen while staying within the parameters of the warrant. The search warrant might be the only chance the police would ever have to recover stolen property from that place. In a similar Montgomery County case, but on a much smaller scale, the detectives had removed everything from an apartment but the couch. Almost everything had been stolen. Items later found not to be purloined are returned.

As King and Roberts entered the large kitchen area, they saw Tom Bailey sitting at a table speaking to a woman wearing an apron. She was bottle-feeding an infant. Two small children were over in a corner watching *Sesame Street* on a color TV. The children seemed oblivious to the intrusion of the police. There was food on the stove and a few dishes in the sink. Bailey was making notes as he talked to the woman. The two men turned away, not wanting to interfere with the interview.

King was as shocked by the appearance of this woman as he was earlier today by the appearance of Bernard Welch. Linda Hamilton was not what one would call a traffic stopper. She looked like the housewife of an average blue-collar worker. King, from his research, assumed that Welch would be hooked up with a good-looking woman with fine features, somewhat akin to the Mercedes he drove. Someone young and slim, with long hair, long legs, and wearing tight clothes. Linda Hamilton was short and pudgy, with thin, bushy reddish-blond hair. She wore an old dark skirt, a frumpy printed blouse, scuffed black slip-on shoes, and a striped green apron with stains on it. She and Welch, with the three little ones, would look like a normal family at any playground.

King furrowed his eyebrows in consternation. He was as amazed to see the real Bernard Welch and Linda Hamilton as he was by the house and the loot in the basement. Maybe more so. This was a day of illumination and disillusionment for him.

King and Roberts finished looking over the house. The master bedroom and children's rooms were just as ordinary as the rest of the house. The furnishings were unremarkable, the type that could be found in most any middle-class American home.

They found their way to the new addition. It contained an almost completed swimming pool that was not yet filled with water. King would have worried about having a pool inside a home with three little children. He had worked two child drowning cases. He knew how dangerous it was to have children in close proximity to any body of water, including a bathtub.

Even while most of the house proved lackluster, King and Roberts were still impressed with the effrontery of Welch setting himself up in a place like this. Walking back from the addition, King looked over at Roberts. "You know, I am so used to going into thieves' pads that are dirty and roach infested. I feel out of place here."

"Know what, Jimmy?" Roberts said. "I was thinking the same thing. Places like this belong to good citizens, not to lowlife criminals. It just doesn't seem right. What do you think that addition cost?"

King stopped and looked back at the addition. "Well, that pool had to cost about thirty-five grand. The addition had to cost close to a hundred thousand. So a hundred-forty, hundred-fifty thousand?"

"Who says crime doesn't pay?"

"Well, Dave, it does," King explained, "but only in the short term."

As they came to the basement steps, they heard Bailey, still talking to Linda Hamilton. They turned and went down to the basement again. More officers had arrived with paper bags, boxes, masking tape, and black felt-tipped markers. One plainclothes man stood at the storage room door. He was writing down box numbers and what each contained. Three other officers were sorting and carefully packaging each box. Each of Welch's original boxes was placed inside of a new box brought by the police, so the original boxes could later be checked for fingerprints. By preserving the boxes as they were found, it could be proved that it was Welch who was responsible for the collection and storage of the stolen goods and no one else.

King and Roberts followed a uniformed officer carrying a sealed and numbered box to the three-car garage. There, a truck with an eighteen-foot van body was backed up to an opened garage door. Another detective with a clipboard was noting the box numbers as they were placed on board. Roberts told the detective with the clipboard about the items they had seen inside the living room and dining room. The smelting equipment had already been loaded.

King stepped outside into the cool air. It was now dark and well after seven o'clock. The evening had begun to grow chilly. Dew was settling on the lawn. King lit a cigarette and looked over the neighborhood. There were few streetlights. The main source of outside illumination was the exterior lights of the houses on the street. It was quiet, except for the whine of a commercial jet following the nearby Potomac River on its way to the airport. It looked like a few residents had gathered in a front yard directly across the street. The media had probably broken the story of the Halberstam shooting and arrest of Bernard Welch, aka Norm Hamilton.

I'll bet they were shocked to learn that such a criminal was living in their midst, thought King. And that, ladies and gentlemen, was why this area never got hit.

"Well, Jimmy boy, what do you think?" Roberts asked as he walked over to King.

"Dave, I think we were damn lucky. If everything hadn't happened exactly right, we'd still be looking for this son of a bitch."

"Yeah, I guess, but like you said, he'd eventually make a mistake. I'm just glad it's over. Now we can get back and work the cases we can solve."

"Dave, Welch made us all look bad."

"Yeah, for five years. You're right about that."

King finished the cigarette and flicked it away onto the lawn where it sizzled in the wet grass. The two went back inside the garage. The truck packing was going slowly.

"Let's find Tom, see if he's through with Mrs. Welch or Hamilton, whatever her name is," King suggested. "I'd like to interview her. Want to sit in?"

"Yeah, that'll be good," Roberts agreed. "Make my bosses happy, just in case she goes down for the murder or burglaries."

They reentered the house and went back down to the basement. Bailey wasn't there. Walking through the rec room area, they met Bailey coming down from the upstairs.

"Tom," King smiled and raised his hand in greeting. "Is it okay for us to talk to Linda Hamilton now? We want to be able to tell our people that we really did something today, especially now that we're on overtime."

Bailey smiled. Every officer had to justify the use of overtime, particularly when the overtime hours were being accumulated outside of the home jurisdiction and without prior official sanction. "Sure, go ahead. But she's feeding the kids now I think, so give her a few minutes."

"Has she been given her Miranda warnings?" Roberts inquired.

"Yes, first thing I did," Bailey replied. "But you should do it again to be safe."

King had another thought. "Tom, what do you think? Is she part of Welch's criminal operation?"

Bailey pondered this for a moment, his finger to his lips. As always, he was cautious about snap judgments. "Well, I don't know for sure. She says she wasn't, had no idea that 'Norm,' as she calls him, was a burglar. Thought he was a legitimate businessman."

King and Roberts both looked at him skeptically.

"I know, I know, that's hard to believe, but that's her story," Bailey explained. "She's cooperated with me one hundred percent. Gave up a batch of business and bank records dealing with the auction gallery and metal refineries they did business with. So I don't know. As of this moment, she is not under arrest. But you go ahead, talk to her, and let me know what you think when you're through, okay?"

King could tell that Bailey was troubled by Linda Hamilton. Here was the common-law wife of a murderer, thief, rapist, and fugitive and the mother of his three children. She was the listed owner of the vehicle used in three burglaries and a homicide. She was the owner, or co-owner, of the home that was bought with the proceeds from stolen property and from which Welch had operated his criminal enterprise. Plus, he had stored the stolen property in that very same home. She had benefited from this unlawful activity. She admitted to shipping some of the stolen property to refineries. She apparently had helped transport some of the stolen property out of state to her own hometown. How could she deny involvement?

Normally, this would be an easy decision, but Bailey was hesitating. His police instincts were troubled about something he saw in Linda Hamilton. Bailey, in essence, was asking King and Roberts to give him their opinions of Linda. Bailey was an imminently fair man. His decision tonight would be questioned and reviewed by everyone in Fairfax County, Washington, DC, Montgomery County, and the rest of northern Virginia. What Bailey did now would affect not only Linda Hamilton, but also the future of her children. King just hoped that Bailey was not basing his decision on his reluctance to separate the children from their mother and place them in foster care for what might be months or even years. Most cops were suckers when it came to little kids.

The three detectives parted, Bailey toward the storage room, King and Roberts up the stairs. They looked into the kitchen. Linda Hamilton was at the kitchen table feeding the two boys. She looked up at the men standing in the doorway with a pained expression that said, "Please, not now."

King nodded slightly and said, "We'd like a word with you when you're finished."

Linda Hamilton bobbed her head in acknowledgment but said nothing.

King and Roberts again looked around the first floor, killing time. They noticed that the paintings they had observed earlier were now gone. The few silver pieces from the dining room were also gone. They wandered around reviewing the items that were to be left in the home. There was nothing that was of great value. King assumed that Linda Hamilton had been responsible for the home's furnishings. Strangely, all the furniture was traditional; there were no antiques. Maybe that's because antique furniture was too big to fit in a Mercedes trunk, King smiled to himself.

King and Roberts idled about for several more minutes not talking much. Linda could probably hear what they said. When they drifted back to the kitchen area, Linda was still there with the children, cleaning up the dinner debris. They stood in the kitchen doorway as Linda wiped down the red, white, and blue patterned plastic tablecloth.

"Have a seat while I finish up," she addressed the two detectives. "Be careful, the table is still wet."

King and Roberts pulled out chairs and sat down. Linda busied herself with the two toddlers, laying them on the rug in front of the color TV. She wrapped them in a soft, thick comforter and stacked some throw pillows around them. Then she checked on the baby who was dozing off in an infant seat.

As she dealt with her three boys, King looked around. The appliances were the popular harvest gold color. The countertop was a lemon-yellow Formica to match the appliances. The floor was patterned vinyl linoleum with yellow designs. All of it looked like builder-grade quality material that came with the house. There seemed to be no mark of personality in the place. It was almost like a rental property. Move the furniture in, move the furniture out when the lease is up. A quick clean and paint job and no evidence of the former occupants. The kitchen, which should be the warm soul of a home, was bleak. It had no personality, no spirit. Basically, it was a place to sit and eat, like a fast food stop on the interstate.

The woman finished placing dishes in the sink. She came to the table and sat down, facing the two detectives. She looked at them and somewhat firmly asked, "How much longer will this go on? I'd like to get my children to bed."

"I'm not sure," King answered truthfully. "Another hour or two maybe. It's up to the Fairfax County police. But let me introduce myself. I'm Detective Jim King from Montgomery County, Maryland. This is Detective Dave Roberts from Washington, DC." Dave nodded to Linda Hamilton, but remained silent. "We're here as interested observers because of the many crimes in Montgomery County and the many crimes and the homicide in Washington that Bernard Welch is suspected of."

Her face was round, and her complexion was very pale, which made her chubby cheeks' reddish color even more prominent. Her eyes were red-rimmed and watery. Linda just looked down at her folded hands, saying nothing, and moved her head up and down, as if to punctuate each of King's pronouncements. She looked like she was praying.

Roberts looked at her with some compassion. "Mrs. Hamilton, before we go any further, I'd like to remind you of your rights. I know that Detective Bailey did this earlier, but I need to do it again. You have the right to remain silent. Anything you say can be used against you. You have the right to the presence of an attorney when questioned by the police, and if you cannot afford an attorney, one will be appointed for you. Do you understand what I have said?

"Yes," came out faintly from the bowed head.

"Do you wish to answer our questions?"

"Yes," she answered again, even more faintly. A tear dropped from her bent face onto her clasped hands.

Roberts looked over the table to King. "You start."

King turned his head to the left and bent it forward slightly so that he could speak to the woman on a more personal level, a technique he used in interrogations to gain the confidence of the person he was with. "Can I call you Linda?" he asked.

Another silent nod from the downturned head.

"Linda, how long have you known Bernard Welch, that is, Norman Hamilton?"

Linda looked up with her sad, damp, puffy eyes. "Since 1975, I guess. We started dating and then lived together in my apartment. He said he was married."

Her slow, halting speech began to pick up speed and her voice grew firmer as she began to remember. "His wife was mean and wouldn't give him a divorce. She had a court order that took everything extra that he made. So, he needed me to put everything in my name. Norman said he and his ex owned a business together and bought antiques and jewelry from estates. She got half of everything that went through the company, even though he did all the work. So, he would skim stuff out of the business. That's why he'd go in the evenings and take things, small things that fit into the car. Stuff that wouldn't be missed from the warehouse. He'd bring it home before she could get her hands on it." Linda paused. Her voice had been a quiet monotone, with the occasional sniffle that required wiping her nose with a limp paper towel taken from her apron pocket.

Linda looked up. Tears were slowly running down her plump, flushed cheeks. She lifted her apron and wiped the tears away. Then, with more emotion she went on. "I believed him! I loved him and he loved me. He needed me. I knew he was cheating his wife, but he said it was justified because she had a crooked lawyer who threatened to destroy him and his business. When the money came in, I paid income tax on it. I didn't cheat anybody, not even the IRS."

The two detectives sat quietly and listened, allowing Linda to talk on without questions from either of them. It seemed that she was unburdening herself of the doubts that she had been harboring for five years. She had been in a position where she could not tell anyone, not even her family of her situation. Welch had sworn her to secrecy. She was never allowed to visit his supposed place of business in Washington, because his estranged wife often came in to review the books. That's why he would go out at night to retrieve items from the warehouse. Then, he could be sure she would not be there.

King wondered what Welch did when he was allegedly "working" during the day. Possibly he was driving around casing neighborhoods. King briefly wondered if he had ever passed Welch on the street on the many nights that he quietly patrolled the neighborhoods looking for suspicious subjects. He and all the other cops would not have looked twice at a well-dressed guy in a Mercedes.

"God, I was stupid!" Linda's voice rose higher. "I should have guessed. It was just too good. I was afraid to do anything to set him off. He had a terrible temper. I mean, he could just walk away from me and the kids. Then what would I do?" She looked up imploringly, first at King and then at Roberts. Her voice quavered and dropped to a huskier tone. "I know I'm in trouble now for being a stupid coward. But after we had the babies and moved in here, I was really afraid of losing him. What was I supposed to do?" She stopped and again wiped her eyes with the corner of her apron.

King could see that the conversation was moving away from the main focus of the investigation. He looked at Roberts. Roberts looked at King and closed his eyes briefly, barely moving his head left to right as if to say, "Poor, dumb broad."

King considered another tack. "You're from Duluth, right?"

Linda nodded yet again.

"Then the reason you went there to sell the stuff in the basement was?" He let the unfinished question hang in the air.

Linda looked at him and began to answer slowly. "Well, Norm didn't want to sell any of the antiques around here. He said he was too well known by the dealers. Word would get back to his wife. Then she'd catch on and sue him. He didn't want her to know anything about me, so she could never connect anything to him. That's why everything was in my name." She looked over to her children. The infant was fast asleep now. The two other boys were lying on the pillows, wrapped in the comforter. One was asleep. The other one was still watching TV, sucking his thumb.

Linda turned back to the investigators. "He'd store everything in the basement. Then, in the summer, we'd rent a big truck and haul everything to Minnesota. Nobody knew him there. We have a house there, in Duluth. We spend the summers there. Norm would go and take things to an auction place. I gave the name to Detective Bailey. The auction place would sell the stuff off over the year and mail us checks."

"How much were those checks for?" inquired King.

Linda thought for a few seconds. "They varied from a few thousand to ten thousand every week."

Roberts got interested. "Okay, and the smelting equipment in the garage. What about that?"

Linda's eyes had stopped watering for the moment. Talking about business did not seem to have as big an impact on her. It seemed that she did not have much emotion invested in it. Only when the conversation moved into her relationship with Welch did she become upset.

"Well, that was Norm's thing. I didn't like all that fire and melting metal. It scared me. Norm burned himself a few times. Nothing bad, just splatters, but it worried me. I made him wear goggles to protect his eyes. Every Sunday, he'd melt it, and then I would pack the gold or silver and mail it to a refinery in California. A couple weeks later, we'd get a check. I deposited it in our bank. I've got all the records."

King interjected. "What about the stones? You know, the diamonds and rubies? The gems that came out of the jewelry he melted?"

Linda seemed perplexed. "He sold some loose stones to jewelers in Duluth, but I never saw much of that. There may not have been a lot of that, I don't know."

King tried another approach. "Did Norm ever go to New York to visit his family?"

"I think he did, but he'd never take me. He said his wife was from that area and would find out if I showed up with him." Linda's fingers began to flutter, and she clasped her hands together to stop the nervous tremors. Her voice began to rise in pitch and became stronger. "Lord, was I dumb! I believed everything he told me! I was stupid, stupid, stupid." Again, she sobbed, her hands covering her face. King noticed a thin wedding ring on her left hand. That was probably stolen also, but he did not have the heart to mention it now. Linda removed the limp paper towel from her apron pocket again and blew her nose.

King thought for a moment during this lull in Linda's statement. He again steered the conversation back to the matter at hand. "Linda, I have to ask you this. Did you know anything about Norm's criminal activities, his gun, or his escape from prison?"

Linda looked at King, her face contorted, making her plain, red, blotched face even less attractive. "No. Lord, no. I'd have left him and taken my babies back to Duluth if I'd have known. Rapes, murder, stealing? No, No, No! I was never brought up that way. He said he needed a gun in his business because he worked in DC and carried money around. He said he was held up once before in DC. He needed a gun for protection. No. I was never a part of that. I swear, I swear!" Linda cried again, less quietly this time.

King looked across the table at Roberts. "Anything else?"

Roberts shook his head. "No, not now. Maybe later."

"Linda, go take care of your children," King said. "There will be more questions later, I'm sure. Thank you for your help."

King and Roberts walked out of the kitchen leaving Linda, small and alone, crying at the table. They went seeking Tom Bailey and found him outside of the garage, watching the last of the boxes going into the truck. The back of the truck was almost full. Bailey was speaking to a uniformed officer.

"Listen, Al, drive slow, especially around corners. I don't want this load shifting and ending up as a bunch of small pieces all over the floor. I want a cruiser in front and one behind you the whole way, okay?"

"Gotcha, Sarge," Al nodded. "I'll be careful."

As the truck pulled away from the house, Bailey walked over to King and Roberts. "Well now, what did you think of Linda Hamilton?"

King looked at Roberts first and back to Bailey. "Tom, I read Linda as a naive country girl. I don't see her as part of this, at least not actively. She gave us a story of being a used female kept in the dark by Welch. She's the ugly duckling from Hicksville who meets a rich prince charming. She's afraid to ask too many questions and pop the dream bubble. Maybe she suspected, maybe she didn't. I don't know. It's pretty much the same story that school-teacher in Richmond gave, and the detectives down there believed her. Bottom line here is, for her, criminally, there's not much to go on at the moment. Dave, what do you think?"

Roberts pulled a cigar out from inside his coat. He rolled it between his fingers for a few seconds before he spoke. "I've been on the job for a long time. I've seen just about everything. From what I've heard tonight, she doesn't fit the mold of an accomplice. We know that Welch worked alone. There's nothing I'm aware of, in any of the cases, that indicated there was a second person with him. If I had to make a bet, I'd bet she was being used and was too dumb, or too scared, or too much in love, to realize it. Maybe all three. The best you got is accessory. That's what I think," Roberts finished as he lit his cigar.

King had another thought. "Tom, you said she handed over her bank and business records, right?"

"Yes, she did."

"Okay, unless you have some compelling reason at this time, I'd say let her slide for now. Have somebody look over her records. You can always ask a grand jury to indict her. Since she's not Welch's legal wife, she can be made to testify against him in return for immunity from prosecution."

Bailey looked up at the garage ceiling and considered the advice of the two detectives. After a few seconds, he nodded his head, his mouth moving from a frown to a firm straight line. "I agree. Those were my thoughts, too. I'm glad you guys got the same feeling I did. Thanks. It's time to wrap this thing up. I've got to give Linda a list of the items we took away. I hope we got everything."

As Bailey started to go, King raised his voice a little. "Tom, I'm heading home now. Talk to you in a couple of days."

"See you, buddy," Roberts added. "I'm splitting, too."

Bailey waved to the detectives and went back into the house.

King and Roberts walked slowly down the driveway toward the street. It was much colder now. Their breath created small clouds as they exhaled. "Jim, this was one hell of a day," mumbled Roberts between puffs as he relit his cigar.

King stopped and reached into his shirt pocket. He removed his last Winston cigarette. "Yeah, it was. You know, I never thought about the finish. I mean, I figured that we'd get Welch someday, but I never thought about how it would happen. He was just too greedy, he'd have to make a mistake some time, but he thought he never would. Probably believed he was smarter than all the cops in the world. In the end, he actually caught himself. Now he's going to pay big time and lose all this." King waved his hand to encompass the large house.

Roberts looked back at the house through a cloud of cigar smoke. "Jimmy, we're the good guys, and the good guys always win. Don't you watch them cop shows?" Roberts had a broad smile on his face.

"Yeah, Dave, I know. Just sometimes it takes too long, and sometimes the price is too high."

When Bernard Welch was arrested on December 5, 1980, the circus began. The public's insatiable interest in this brazen criminal and the bizarre circumstances of his capture generated a media frenzy. Daily newspaper reports and radio and TV newscasts kept the public abreast of the unfolding events. A day seldom passed without some mention of Welch, his million-dollar Virginia home with a huge indoor swimming pool, his two new Mercedes, or the four million dollars' worth of recovered stolen property. Details emerged of police searches; thousands of victims viewed mountains of recovered items; a summer home in Duluth, Minnesota, which also held an indoor swimming pool, was searched, and even more stolen property was discovered; and testimony, court hearings, and other legal proceedings began. Welch gave interviews, his attorney gave interviews, victims gave interviews, and the police gave interviews.

Legal maneuvering began on December 8. At a preliminary hearing, Welch stood doubled over in pain from his injuries resulting from being struck by Dr. Halberstam's vehicle. He asked to be transferred from his cell at DC police department headquarters to a hospital for treatment. Judge Robert A. Shuker, aware of Welch's escape from a New York state prison, denied his request and ordered a no-bond preventative detention, a bail bond regulation that allows for no bail to be set for those who have a history of crime and violence.

The next day at a second hearing, Welch announced he was unemployed and had no money for a lawyer. The judge appointed Sol Z. Rosen to defend him. Rosen was a 43-year-old, tough-talking, Brooklyn-born, wily veteran of the District's legal system. He was known in the system as a "Fifth Street Lawyer." "Fifth Street Lawyers," a group of independent attorneys who made their living defending the poor, got their moniker in the 1930s and 1940s because they rented small offices on Fifth Street near the District courthouse. The "Fifth Street Lawyers" were not popular with the police, because they often defended the criminals that police had to deal with on a regular basis.

Rosen first challenged the lack of bail for his client. Welch, being a prison escapee with convictions for twelve felonies at the time of his escape, living under several assumed names while a fugitive for six years, and currently charged with murder and four burglaries, more than qualified for preventive detention. Prosecutors had only to list Welch's criminal history and utter the words "no condition of release would reasonably assure the safety of the community." The judge was also informed that burglary warrants had just been filed from Montgomery County, Maryland, and Fairfax County, Virginia, as well as one for prison escape from New York. Rosen's request for bail was swiftly denied.

At the same hearing, Rosen challenged Elliott Jones Halberstam's ambulance identification at Sibley Hospital. He contended she was "obviously in shock and frightened" at the time. Further, she never actually saw the face of the intruder inside the house. Therefore, Rosen argued the police put her in a "suggestive situation," and her identification of Welch amounted to a "one man lineup." Judge Shuker denied that motion also.

The house at 700 Valley Drive in Duluth, Minnesota, was entered on December 9 using a federal search warrant. Over two thousand items—jewelry, antiques, fur coats, and silver—were seized. Two DC police detectives accompanied FBI agents on the search looking for the "fruits and instrumentalities of the crime of burglary and books and records of financial transactions of Bernard Charles Welch." The recovered stolen property was returned to Washington for victim identification. The Internal Revenue Service was especially interested in the financial records.

Working furiously to review recent burglary reports, police from several jurisdictions matched stolen property descriptions from the loot found in Welch's two homes to 237 burglaries. Montgomery County Police announced that Welch was the prime suspect in hundreds of burglaries and three burglary-rapes. One rape victim was a 74-year-old homeowner.

On December 15, 1980, Rosen, tried another tactic, requesting a competency hearing for his client based on a pattern of compulsive behaviors for the past several years. Rosen offered that his client's persistent thieving might be "rooted in mental illness." He also noted he often had a hard time conversing with his client, which might make defense efforts difficult. Rosen realized that Welch's only possible defense was an insanity plea and hinted to the press that he was considering a plea of "not guilty by reason of insanity." Outside of the court, Rosen stated to the *Washington Post* that, "[Welch's] behavior seems so bizarre, to say that someone is involved in hundreds, if not thousands, of burglaries. How many pills do you have to take before you get high? How much do you have to eat before your hunger pains are satisfied? Maybe the devil made him do it. Maybe he's hearing celestial voices saying, 'Go burglarize.'"

Three days later, Judge James A. Belson ordered a court psychiatrist to conduct a mental competency examination of Welch. The judge directed that Welch be examined at DC jail, a maximum-security facility, instead of St. Elizabeth's Mental Hospital, where such procedures were normally conducted. St. Elizabeth's, in southeast Washington, was notorious for lax security.

On December 20, the court psychiatrist submitted a one-page report to the judge that stated Welch was "rational" and "mentally able" to "participate [with his attorney] in preparation of his defense." Welch had hoodwinked so many others, why didn't he fool the psychiatrist? Did the doctor see through his charade, or did Welch not even attempt to trick him?

On December 25, 1980, it was reported that Linda Sue Hamilton, who lived with, but never married, Bernard Welch, was granted limited immunity from prosecution. Limited immunity prevented prosecutors from using information supplied by Linda against her. If law enforcement agents independently developed information against her through other means, she may then be prosecuted. The US Attorney's Office did this in return for her testimony against Welch. She had already appeared before a DC Superior Court grand jury investigating the Halberstam slaying. The US Attorney's Office believed that Linda was the only person who could reveal the details of Welch's operation. Furthermore, she had given the police permission to search her car, which Welch had used in his crimes. She had also allowed police to look through her home before they obtained a search warrant. A tremendous amount of evidence was obtained in those two searches. If she were to be prosecuted, she could later claim that she had been coerced by police to allow the searches, which would jeopardize the case against Welch. The leverage against her used by the government was her prosecution. Without such an agreement, she could have faced many years in prison as a coconspirator of her common-law husband. She had three children now and could not afford that gamble.

Linda also couldn't afford the liens levied by the IRS. The IRS filed a federal tax lien for $24.2 million in back taxes, penalties, and interest against Bernard Welch and Linda Hamilton. Of the total, only $7.6 million was assessed against Hamilton, because even in the midst of Welch's criminal enterprise, she had filed and paid some taxes.

Low hanging clouds the color of asphalt covered most of the area. Although the predicted snow had not occurred, the January morning was still cold. It was almost eleven in the morning when Detective James King again pulled up to the home of Mrs. Barbara Smith in the village of Chevy Chase, Maryland.

King got out and walked up the ancient concrete sidewalk that led to the roofed front porch of the large, renovated, Victorian home. There was a "For Sale" sign in the front yard with a smaller sign that read "By Appointment Only" hanging underneath it. Homes like this were now selling for a million dollars or more in this area, but King knew the real reason Mrs. Smith was selling her house. He knew it was just one more result of her rape. She had believed she was safe in her big home in its exclusive area. This crime against her had rattled her highly structured and ordered existence, and this incident would stay with her for the rest of her life. It would always live in the back of her mind, shaping her decisions, especially if she stayed in this house.

He rang the bell and waited patiently for a response. Mrs. Smith knew he was coming.

She was scheduled to view a DC police lineup today. He was to take her to the place where she would identify her rapist. She was not looking forward to seeing her attacker again. She had been raised in a time and society where rape cast a social stigma on the woman. Some even believed that it was almost as much the woman's fault as the man's, so many females never reported a rape. But now, in this modern time of the feminist movement, many women felt it was necessary to stand up and fight back instead of curling up into a

ball. For women like Mrs. Smith, identifying their attackers was a form of ter-
rified therapy. They faced the demons that infested their thoughts and dreams.

The wind was picking up. Dead leaves were beginning to blow across the
front yard. King huddled deeper into his wrinkled trench coat. Soon he heard
a faint vibration of someone moving within. His hearing was extremely acute.
It was an inherited trait that had saved his life more than once in his police career.

Mrs. Smith opened the door, looking tired. King observed the dark circles
under her eyes. She had artfully applied makeup to mask the signs of sleep-
lessness, but it had not worked well.

Her demeanor was less tense than the last time he had interviewed her
over a year ago, just after her rape. He remembered it vividly. The information
he had gleaned from her had convinced him that Bernard Welch was not only
her rapist but was also the elusive Ghost Burglar who had been ravaging the
Washington area for four years.

She was the one who gave him the lead on the false teeth. The warden at
the Adirondack Correctional Facility in Dannemora, New York, confirmed
to King that Welch did, indeed, have a full set of dentures. That information
allowed everything to fall into place. It was the final piece of the puzzle that
made King certain, in early 1979, that Welch was the criminal more than a
dozen jurisdictions were after. How many white males in their late thirties
stole art and antiques, had a northern accent, did not smoke, were the right
height, weight, and hair color, had the same method of operation, and had
upper and lower false teeth? Only one had fit the bill—Bernard C. Welch.

King had staked his police credibility on that logic. The capture of Bernard
Welch had proven King correct, a sweet professional victory.

"Come in, Detective King," Mrs. Smith smiled wanly.

He nodded and stepped inside.

"Would you like a cup of coffee before we leave?"

"No, thank you, ma'am," King replied. "We've got to be down at DC Police Headquarters by noon, so there isn't time. But thank you kindly for the
offer."

She smiled briefly at his genteel manner. "Well, wait here then, and I'll
turn off the coffee and get my coat."

Mrs. Smith returned from the rear of the home, turning out lights as she
went. She walked to the hall closet and opened the door. As she reached inside,
he noticed that the closet interior was as neatly arranged as the rest of the home.

She shrugged on a black and gray plaid, mid-length wool coat then turned to the hall mirror and put on a floppy, black wool beret hat. She tucked in some loose strands of hair and picked up her black leather purse from the table.

Mrs. Smith turned to him. "I'm ready."

He nodded silently and opened the door. She walked to the home's burglar alarm pad and entered the code to arm the system. He stepped outside and waited as she closed and locked the front door's dead bolt lock with a key.

They arrived at police headquarters just before noon. King directed Mrs. Smith to the elevators at the left end of the lobby. They rode to the third floor in silence and stepped out into a square recessed area that comprised the elevator lobby.

King led her to the lineup witness waiting room. It was a long, narrow area with no windows. There was trash, soda cans, coffee cups, and balls of dust under the worn, prison-made wooden benches lined up along one wall. The room was half full of people. It was few minutes past noon.

Some of the people present were other victims of Bernard Welch. These were the ones who were unfortunate enough to have seen him while he burglarized, raped, or beat them. They were young and old, male and female, accompanied by friends or family and police officers from their home jurisdictions.

Most of the civilians were sitting on the wooden benches, so King directed Mrs. Smith to the end of an unoccupied bench near the door. The police stood in small groups talking. King recognized several of the detectives there, and after seating Mrs. Smith, he went to talk to them to find out what was going on. He was informed that nothing had occurred yet, but there was a sign-in sheet on a clipboard he should fill out. Mrs. Smith was witness number six, end of the line. That meant they should be finished by one o'clock, if all went well.

After talking to the other detectives for a while, King returned to Mrs. Smith. She was sitting, staring at the opposite wall, expressionless. She had entered some internal quiet zone. She slowly twisted a tissue in her hands, unconscious of her movement. He could understand her discomfort of being here. He did not disturb her. He was perceptive enough to see her need to be in mental isolation now. It was probably her way of distancing herself from this cruddy building, the cruddy event that had happened to her, and the cruddy ordeal she was about to go through.

Time went by slowly. It was twelve-twenty and nothing had happened yet. No police official had appeared to address the witnesses and that was unusual. Usually lineups were held fairly promptly, but more minutes just ticked by.

At 12:30 p.m., the dented, dark green steel door that led to the lineup viewing room opened and four DC detectives exited. They rushed past the bored police officers standing in the witness waiting room without a word of explanation.

King saw that one of the four was Detective Sally "Spider" Kirk, who worked in the Major Burglary unit. Kirk had earned the nickname of "Spider" in high school because of her tall, willowy appearance, and only those who knew her well were allowed to use the moniker. King knew her and liked her. She was funny, smart, and a good cop.

Curiosity forced him to follow the group out the door. The three male officers turned left, walking rapidly down the hall. Kirk went right and hurried towards a stairwell that led to her office below. He thought these were strange actions from people who were supposed to be organizing the lineup. He jogged to catch up to Kirk. When he was a few feet away, he raised his voice to get her attention.

"Hey, Spider, what's happening?" he asked, trying to keep pace with her. "I'm down here with a rape victim witness. Why the delay in the Welch lineup? What's the word?"

Kirk turned her head to see who was speaking. By the frown on her face, he could tell she was not happy. She slowed a little, but kept walking. He was beside her now, still heading towards the stairwell.

"Jim, it's a major fuckup," she answered in a low voice, eyeing the other people in the hall. "I can't go into details right now, I'm in a hurry. Let's just say we're trying to fix it. The lineup will be delayed for a bit, but hang in there, it'll happen." She looked at him imploringly before he could start with more questions. "Please, I've got to go." Kirk sped up as she reached the entrance of the stairwell and ran down the stairs.

King stopped at the top of the stairs and listened to Kirk's hard-heeled penny loafers click on the concrete steps as she descended. He reran her words through his brain. From them, he knew that Sally was now following orders— "we're trying to fix it." So, some authority had her, and three other detectives, on a mission to try to fix the Welch lineup snafu.

A lot of police time and effort goes into the planning and production of a good lineup. The lineup room has to be reserved. Police personnel have to be relieved from other duties and reassigned to the task. The jail has to be notified ahead of time to have the suspect ready, transportation arranged, and appropriate civilian clothes procured. If other jurisdictions will be involved, they have to be notified. Witnesses have to be summoned. Filler people have to be discovered, selected, and advised what to wear. All this has to be coordinated so it comes together at the same time and place. A big lineup can cost thousands of dollars and hundreds of work hours to stage. Therefore, once a procedure has been set in motion, police are loath to not follow through with it.

Important police lineups have a similar formula in all jurisdictions. The prime suspect is mixed in with a group of noncriminals. The lineup filler people have the same general appearance as the suspect. They do not have to be exactly like the suspect, but they do have to be the same race and close to the same height and weight, with similar hair and clothing.

Fillers are often police, court, or local government employees. Noncriminals are used as fillers so that if a witness picks the wrong person, the defense counsel cannot claim that the person identified must be the actual perpetrator and not the defendant. Photos of the lineup participants are taken, so that if the validity of the lineup is challenged, it can be proven by police that it was fairly constituted. A positive identification by a crime victim is legal court evidence, often leading to a conviction. A negative ID is useful to the defense for acquittal.

Since a lineup identification can be used as evidence in a criminal trial, it is a one-time function. After it is held, any witness who viewed the suspect in the lineup cannot view another lineup with the same suspect. Courts have ruled that a second lineup would be invalid, in that the witnesses might select the suspect not because he was recognized from the crime, but because they had seen him in the previous lineup.

King mulled over the little he had gleaned from Kirk as he slowly returned to Mrs. Smith. The problem couldn't be mechanical. Kirk would have said as much, no secret there. And a mechanical problem would be fixed by maintenance workers, not officers. The issue couldn't be with the noncriminal fillers. If one had failed to show, the cops would walk through the local buildings, grab some poor schmuck, and walk him over. They had a legal right to do that in emergencies. King was left with the only possibility of what could be going wrong with this lineup—Bernard Welch.

Although he detested Welch, King did not underestimate him. That crafty son of a bitch must have figured some way to screw up the system. But what could he do? He could not hide or refuse to come. He was in DC jail, and those guards didn't take crap from anybody. He knew that the jail guards would drag Welch's scruffy ass all the way to the lineup stage, if necessary.

In the long run, Welch's antics would not help him. The evidence of his crimes in six jurisdictions had been found in his home, plus the murder of Dr. Halberstam. Even DC courts would convict him on that one. So if he was the cause of this lineup delay, it was just Welch being Welch, trying to show he could still beat the system, because he was smarter than the jail, smarter than the cops, and smarter than the courts. His ego was driving him now. Sure, he could win a battle here and there, but he could not win the war. He was doomed to spend the rest of his life in prison.

King reentered the waiting area thinking about what he should tell Mrs. Smith. As he walked in the door an older DC plainclothes cop with a potbelly sticking out of his unbuttoned wrinkled suit coat was standing at the end of the room. He had just begun to speak.

"Ladies and gentlemen, we're sorry for the delay. We have had some technical difficulties, which we are trying to fix so that we can move ahead and hold this very important procedure. It shouldn't take too long, so please bear with us. Thank you."

Some objections and complaints were raised by the crowd, but the potbellied detective was already closing the old steel door behind him.

King sat down beside Mrs. Smith. She was still in her reverie, staring straight ahead. He decided to level with her. She deserved that. He touched her arm.

"Listen, Mrs. Smith, whatever is wrong here is not technical. I'm not sure what's going on, but whatever it is, I don't like it. I've been to a lot of lineups, and this type of delay has never happened. Trust me on this, something's not kosher here. I suggest that we leave now and wait for another day."

Mrs. Smith still had what was left of the Kleenex in her hand. She fingered it like an old lady in church working her rosary beads. Small balls of tissue landed on her lap. She continued to stare at the wall, not indicating she had even heard his statement.

He tried again. "Mrs. Smith, there is something really wrong here. I think we should go. If you don't identify him now, you'll never have another chance.

I think we should...."

"No, Detective King," she interrupted him, still staring at the wall, not making eye contact. "I want to stay. I'm here now. I want to get this over with. I've been dreading this day for weeks. I want to be finished with him. It's now or never. I could not do this again. I'm staying." Her voice was quiet, but forceful. She bit off her words, as if delivering a verdict.

He understood. She was taking a stand. This was her Alamo. She would face her enemy on the only battlefield she had.

He was a captive of her decision. And what if he were wrong anyway? If he dragged her away and the lineup worked, he'd be in hot water back at the office. His supervisor would say he had been impatient and rash. It would force Montgomery County into the expense and trouble of conducting its own lineup. He would be blamed.

He had tried to state his case, but he had done a poor job of it. He could not explain his gut feelings. He believed that this procedure would be a disaster, and all he could do now was sit here and wait. He hoped it would work out for Mrs. Smith, but knowing Welch and what he was capable of, he doubted it.

More time passed in the waiting room. One o'clock came and went. He found some bad coffee for Mrs. Smith and himself.

Two o'clock passed. The potbellied detective did not return.

At two-thirty, another plainclothes officer appeared. The sergeant came out of the lineup room and stood before the chipped green metal door. He cleared his throat to get everyone's attention.

"Sorry for the long delay, folks. We're almost ready. So, in a few minutes we'll call you in, in the order that you arrived. We will take witnesses only. No friends, family, or police officers will be allowed inside. Sorry, that's the rule for this lineup." Unconsciously or not, the sergeant had accentuated "this."

There were murmurs from the waiting police officers. The sergeant's last statement was very unusual, but there was little they could do. DC was calling the shots; it was their turf and their nickel.

"So, we'll call you in one at a time," the detective sergeant continued. "It should go pretty quickly. That's all. Thank you." He quickly turned and reentered the lineup viewing room door without addressing any questions.

King sat there beside Mrs. Smith. His suspicions were greater now than ever, and he didn't like how the process was unfolding. Normally, the police officer escorting the witness was allowed inside the lineup area to watch the procedure. Why not this time? Something was definitely wrong. He spoke to Mrs. Smith again in one last attempt to persuade her to leave. A lot rode on her identification—not only her case, but a series of other cases in Montgomery County, Maryland.

"Mrs. Smith, I don't like this. Something's wrong here." He leaned in close because of the noise created by the other people in the room, and he did not want her to miss the urgency of his tone. He was sincere in his concern, and he was right, he knew it now. "We can still walk out. I can arrange a lineup in Montgomery County. We plan to extradite Welch to face our charges, which includes your case. I think that would be best. Let's go."

Mrs. Smith sat there, unmoving. Her eyes were closed and her head bent as if in prayer. Her fingers kept working the last shreds of her tissue. A few seconds passed and then she lifted her head slightly and turned toward the detective. Her expression was sad, like that of the Madonna in Michelangelo's Pieta sculpture.

She slowly shook her head. "No, it's almost time now. I know I'll recognize him. I can never forget his face, what he did to me, and what he made me do. I see it every night." She had made her decision. "I'm staying. You can go. Please understand." She was gentle, almost pleading. King gave up. He sat there beside her, silent now, waiting for her to be called.

Finally, there was movement at the front of the line. The witnesses were taken into the lineup room individually, while their escorts remained in the anteroom. King knew that once the victims were inside the lineup area, they would be given the standard lineup instructions.

"The suspect in your particular case may or may not be in this lineup formation. He cannot see or hear you. There is a glass wall between you and the lineup participants. Those on the lineup stage cannot see through the glass, but you can see them. Each person on the stage will be standing under a number. They will be instructed to turn left and right. If you recognize the perpetrator in your crime, please say the number he is standing under. If necessary, we will have the lineup members say a few words for voice recognition. There is a speaker in this room, so you can hear the voices. When we are finished, you may exit the room and go on your way. Do not speak to the other witnesses after you exit. We will notify your jurisdiction of the results." The officer would then open the curtains covering the window, so that the witness could see the row of men standing on the brightly lit stage.

Each witness at the Welch lineup took about three minutes in the room. When they came out of the room one cried, one smiled, and the remainder seemed confused. They quietly murmured to their waiting escort and slowly left after gathering the coats, bags, and books they had brought with them. A DC detective came out and quietly spoke to each escorting officer as their witnesses finished.

After twenty minutes, it was Mrs. Smith's turn. She was the last witness left in the room. Detective King walked her to the doorway. The only thing he could think to say was, "Good luck." She smiled a little Mona Lisa smile of confidence, but said nothing. She walked into the viewing room looking straight ahead, her back stiff with resolve She was about to face the man who caused her a year of nightmares.

The door closed behind her, and King waited. He smoked. He sipped the remains of his cold coffee without tasting it. He checked his watch. One minute passed...then two...and then three.

King was at the door when it opened. He did not wait, but pushed his way inside the dim room. Mrs. Smith was crying. He looked through the glass at the stage. The men were still in their lineup positions. King had to look over the group twice before he saw Welch in position number four. Even then, he was only sure it was Welch because the other six men were not.

King stared at the strange vision. Welch looked nothing like himself, but was made up like a bad actor in a high school play. He had on a man's short, black wig and a fake black mustache. His eyebrows appeared to be actually drawn on. The other lineup members appeared normal, without garish costume.

At last, King finally understood what the "technical glitch" was. Welch had shaved his head, eyebrows, and mustache. DC police had decided to go on with the lineup anyway, trying to make him appear normal. Instead, he looked like a chemotherapy patient trying to unsuccessfully hide his hair loss. Welch appeared abnormal, almost unrecognizable. Even King, who had seen Welch a month ago, had difficulty picking him out. How was a scared witness, seeing someone while being beaten or raped a year or more ago, supposed to pick this freak out of a lineup?

King turned to look at the three plainclothes men in the room. "Did she pick him?" He knew the answer before he spoke. The three shook their heads as one and turned away, trying to distance themselves from him inside the small room.

King stood there, stunned, looking through the window as the formation began to dissolve. Welch was led off in handcuffs. King saw the reflection of Mrs. Smith in the window as she walked slowly out of the room, trembling, wiping tears from her cheeks. King was immobile, struck dumb as thoughts buzzed through his head. A cold anger began to churn inside of him.

Mrs. Smith and the other victims had been betrayed by the District of Columbia Metropolitan Police Department. Some asshole lieutenant or captain had made the decision to hold this travesty. Whoever that was would go home tonight, drink his scotch, and tell himself that it wasn't his fault no one had picked Welch. He had done everything possible to fix the screwup that DC jail officials had allowed to happen. King knew that it had to have happened at the jail. They did not have razors in the holding cells in the basement here. Hell, they didn't even have soap or toilet paper. Whoever the son of a bitch was who had made this decision should have had the balls to cancel this mockery.

It only took a few seconds for all this to run through King's mind. His anger welled up like vomit in his throat. He turned and looked at the three detectives still standing there holding clipboards. Their expressions were blank, but they knew what he was thinking; they could see it on his face. No wonder they did not let the police accompany the witnesses in; they would have had a fight on their hands.

"Hey, he arrived from the jail like that," one of the detectives tried to alibi their actions. "We tried to make it right, okay?"

"No, it's not okay," King answered in a harsh, nasty whisper. "Had I known this was the problem, I would have dragged my witness out of here. You've ruined our case. This lady," he pointed out the door in the direction Mrs. Smith had taken, "was raped by Welch. I hope whoever ordered this stupid circus to go on enjoys knowing that he helped screw her over again! I hope the asshole…" King ran out of words. He wanted to say more, but he saw through the door that Mrs. Smith had left the waiting room. She needed support now; he should be with her. At the moment he was all she had.

"Thanks for nothing, assholes." King turned and stomped out of the room.

He scooped up his trench coat and hurried down the hall after Mrs. Smith. He caught up to her as she arrived at the elevators and grabbed her arm to stop her. She turned to him, her face in anguish, crying openly now.

"Mrs. Smith, talk to me, tell me what happened." King used an old police maneuver to keep crime victims from becoming hysterical. Get them talking, get them to unload their grief. He understood victims. He had majored in criminology and psychology, but more importantly he had lots of experience. He had been a cop for thirteen years and worked with victims almost every day.

Still holding her left arm, he guided her to a tall window overlooking the plaza, which offered them a little recess for privacy.

"Tell me," he repeated, his voice low and calm, "what happened in there?"

Mrs. Smith cried a sobbing, broken sound. Her face was lined with distress. She stared through the grimy window and moved her mouth. She made another sobbing sound but then words came tumbling out. "I went in, and they…they opened the curtain. I saw the one who looked strange. I mean he looked weird. I said to myself, that can't be him. He's too weird looking. They just put this one in to fool us." She cried again, but softer this time.

King gave her a minute to compose herself then prompted, "Yes, go on. Tell me the rest."

"There was a guy beside the weird one." Her tears were slowing as she concentrated on telling her story. "That's him, I thought. He's changed some in a year, but that's him. I picked him, number five. I asked the police, 'Did I get him? Did I get him right?' and they said I didn't." She cried again, louder.

King put his arm around Mrs. Smith's shoulder, an instinctive action to comfort a person in crisis. "Ma'am, listen to me. You weren't the only one to be fooled. All the other witnesses picked the same guy." It was a lie. One rape victim had correctly identified Welch, but King wanted to comfort her because this debacle was not her fault. "Welch shaved off all his hair at the jail. That's why they delayed the lineup, to find a wig and fake mustache to put on him. And that's why he looked strange. It's not your fault. That sneaky son of a bitch tricked everybody again, especially the people who should have known better." There was little else he could say, so he waited for her to cry herself out.

After a few minutes, her crying subsided to a random sniffle. King reached into his right hip pocket and removed a clean, white cotton handkerchief, a habit held over from his old patrol days. In that era, police cruisers were not equipped with first aid kits. If he beat the ambulance to the crime scene—an auto accident, shooting, or stabbing—the only thing he could produce to help the injured was a clean handkerchief. He had lost a lot of hankies that way.

He handed the folded handkerchief to Mrs. Smith. "Your mascara is running," he said quietly.

"Oh, I must look awful!" Her eyes began to well up again. She took the handkerchief and started dabbing her eyes and cheeks, smearing the colors of her makeup on the white cloth.

"No ma'am, not really," King replied with a slight smile. "You look like my wife at a wedding."

Mrs. Smith laughed, though it came out as more of a hiccup.

"Why don't you go to the ladies' room and freshen up?" King suggested. He wanted to give her some private time to compose herself.

She turned to him and patted his arm. "Your wife is a lucky woman." She walked toward the restroom around the corner.

He leaned his back against the windowsill and waited. King considered how he would tell his supervisors about the lineup. He'd have to do a supplemental report when he got back to the office, detailing the fiasco. He'd be late getting home again.

King noticed a young female walk along the hall heading in the direction of the lineup room. As she passed the lobby, she looked left and spied him leaning against the far wall. She almost reached the end of the elevator lobby area before she stopped and turned around.

"Aren't you a policeman?" she asked.

He looked at her and realized that she was probably a news reporter. She was carrying a steno notebook with a cheap pen stuck in the wire coil at its top. Cops used clipboards. Reporters used steno pads.

"Yes, and you are a newspaper reporter, correct?" he said in his baritone voice, as pleasantly as possible, a pleasantness he did not feel.

"Yes, correct," she smiled, creating deep dimples in each cheek. "Jane Mayer, *Washington Star*. Weren't you at the Welch lineup earlier?"

He considered her question. It was simple on its face, but if he answered, he'd be sucked into an interview. That would be bad news for him back at his headquarters. The old-timers had been on his case about the amount of publicity he had gotten with the arrest of Welch, since he was the first detective to suspect Welch of being the Ghost Burglar, and his authoring of the Montgomery County precious metals law requiring buyers of precious metals to inform the police of the sellers and the items bought. King did not need to aggravate his superiors any further.

But he was still pissed off at the lineup debacle. He did something almost rash—he answered the question but pulled back from totally throwing himself into the fire.

"Yes, I was," he conceded, "but no name, and anything I tell you is not for attribution to me, okay?"

"Okay, deal," she agreed. The reporter easily picked up on the slight edge of anger in King's voice. The lack of attribution was a pain, but since he was angry, maybe she could get a good quote from a "police official" to spice up the story.

"So, where are you from, Fairfax or Montgomery?" He was obviously a detective, but dressed too well to be a DC cop.

"Montgomery," King grinned, "but I didn't think it showed."

"Oh yeah," the reporter smiled back, "you don't blend in well down here." She continued, "I know about the head shave that Welch pulled today. What did you think of that?"

Another dangerous question for King. He could blast the DC police hierarchy for allowing the lineup to proceed. He could rant about the incompetence of the DC jail for allowing Welch to have a razor in his cell before the lineup. King wanted to say these things, but it would be stupid to do so. A lowly detective corporal castigating a neighboring police department and penal system in the newspapers could kiss his police career goodbye. He'd be lucky to end up on the night shift at a landfill somewhere.

"Off the record," King tried to be circumspect, "I am not the person to comment about how the DC police department conducts its business."

The young reporter held her pen poised over her steno pad, writing nothing. He had said "off the record"; she knew the rules.

King knew reporters were like pigeons. Pigeons all flock together looking for crumbs when someone eats lunch on a park bench. The only way to get rid of them is to throw a piece of food far away. Reporters scour the scenes for any juicy story tidbit. If you give them a good enough quote, they'll leave you alone. So, he threw out a tidbit to the reporter.

"On the record, let me say that what happened was obviously the ploy of a guilty man." He paused, marshaling his thoughts before continuing. "If we could bring out before a jury that he wanted to change his hair, it might make them wonder. Who else would shave his head in the middle of winter?" He stopped. He had said enough. He had put the blame on Welch and not the

DC officials, a move that would make the Montgomery County good-old-boy system proud.

King then saw Mrs. Smith come around the corner, returning from the restroom. He had to keep her from meeting this reporter. The last thing she needed was to be interviewed about her failure to recognize her rapist. As the reporter was looking down, writing her last sentence, King shook his head in Mrs. Smith's direction, signaling her to stay back and move out of sight.

Mrs. Smith caught the gesture and moved back around the corner. The reporter looked up at King and smiled her dimpled smile. She stuck her ball-point pen back into the wire spiral of her steno pad. "Thanks," she said, stuffing her pen and paper into her bag. "Time to get back to the office. Maybe I can get home early tonight."

King waved goodbye and stayed by the window. He waited until the elevator doors closed on the reporter. Then, he walked around the corner and found Mrs. Smith several yards down the hall beside the water fountain. She had been pretending to drink from the fountain. She looked up at him as he approached, her expression quizzical. "Who was that?"

He grinned ruefully. "That was a reporter from the *Washington Star* newspaper. She cornered me. I figured you wouldn't want to be interviewed now."

"You figured right," she answered, a look of relief washing over her face. "If I had to talk to her, I'd cry all over again. And I just fixed my face, too." She looked up at King and actually smiled.

She appeared to be more herself now. Her makeup was almost perfect again. Only the slight redness in her eyes indicated the tears that had recently been shed. To any casual observer, she seemed calm and composed. But King knew better. It was only an act, a thin veneer of courage like an eggshell; crack it and the delicate insides would be exposed.

"Mrs. Smith, I'd like to say something about what happened today."

She turned her head and raised one eyebrow.

"The evidence against Bernard Welch in the murder of Dr. Halberstam is iron clad," King stated. "He'll get life with no parole. He will never see freedom again. He'll die an old man in prison. There is no doubt in my mind that he was your attacker, whether or not you could identify him in a wig. He not only fooled you today, he fooled everybody. So, ma'am, you're in good company, and the fault is not yours."

Mrs. Smith listened, without comment, as King continued. "And one more thing. If I was having a bad day when I was little, my mother would tell me, 'If you did your best, angels could not have done better.' It helped me then and it helps me now." King paused and took a deep breath. "Okay, that's it from Jim King's good advice column for today."

"Detective King, as tough as you try to be, you are a nice man."

He laughed. "Hey lady, don't spread that around. I've got a reputation to maintain."

Mrs. Smith laughed too.

Mrs. Smith's rape case was closed without trial. Since there was no lineup identification, there was insufficient evidence to prosecute. Welch eventually pleaded guilty to four burglaries in Montgomery County, Maryland. The twenty-year sentence he received was just a gesture. Thousands of burglaries with Welch's MO were closed by police departments in Maryland, Washington, and Virginia. The exact number was never accurately calculated. Even the amount of property he stole was never truly known, although it was estimated to be around $100 million.

A few weeks after the lineup in DC, King received a small package. It contained a new handkerchief with the initial "K" on the corner. A small note was inside that read, "Detective King, I am replacing the one that you gave me and I forgot to return. Thank you for all your concern." It was signed, "Barbara Smith."

Bernard Welch (#5), wearing a wig in a Jan. 5, 1981, D.C. police lineup for rape/burglary because he shaved his hair and mustache. Welch often wore masks during his crimes.

Once Welch was arrested and the story broke in the press, Sol Rosen received several inquiries from sources interested in Welch's life story. Rosen asked attorney Martin E. Firestone to represent Welch's literary interest to prevent any conflict of interest in his criminal defense. One of the first deals Firestone handled for Welch was an interview with *Life* magazine.

In mid-January, *Life* magazine interviewed Bernard Welch in prison for its February 1981 issue. After the interview was conducted, Jonathan Z. Larsen, *Life*'s news editor, teased that the article would reveal "[Welch] is quite proud of his accomplishments as a burglar.... He is a man who takes great pride in his profession. He talks about his career in crime quite eloquently, how he practiced it and escalated his endeavors." Larsen further revealed that Welch expressed a "virtual obsession" with theft but "sidesteps the issue of" his involvement in the death of Dr. Halberstam.

Life did not reveal publicly that Welch would be paid for the interview. This news leaked out anyway.

A group of well-known writers and journalists wrote an open letter to Henry A. Greewald, editor-in-chief of Time Inc., publisher of *Life*. In the letter, they deplored *Life* for paying Welch $9,000 for the interview. Some of those who signed the letter were Daniel Schorr of Cable News Network, Fred Graham of CBS News, Ron Nessen, the former press secretary to President Gerald Ford, and John Weisman, the Washington Bureau Chief of *T.V. Guide*. Pulitzer Prize-winning journalist, David Halberstam, brother of Dr. Michael Halberstam, also lashed out at *Life*, saying, "It is contemptible checkbook journalism.... It amounts to a tribute to Welch for his crimes."

Life, assailed from all sides for this alleged checkbook journalism, defended itself by stating it only paid for the nine photos of Welch, not the interview. The one thousand dollars per picture agreed to was double what *Life* usually paid for photographs. Elliott Jones Halberstam, also interviewed for the story, felt betrayed by the magazine. Had she known that Welch was also to be interviewed in the same article, and worse, paid for his photos, she would not have spoken to the reporter nor supplied photos of her husband for the same story.

On January 14, 1981, a DC Superior Court grand jury indicted Welch for first-degree murder, four burglaries, four grand larcenies, burglary while armed, and carrying a handgun without a license. Fairfax County, Virginia, indicts Bernard Welch for the rape of a 32-year-old woman in December 1977. The indictment also included the charges of burglary, maiming (a felony still used in many East Coast states that were originally British colonies), and use of a firearm during the sexual assault.

Rosen filed a motion to have the murder trial moved from the Washington, DC, area, because of the extensive publicity. Government prosecutors opposed the change of venue request due to adverse publicity, citing the *Life* interview. The prosecutors contended that Welch "sought notoriety by bragging about his criminal prowess." Moving the trial to a different location may have given Rosen a better chance of winning the case, but Welch's interview—his own need for recognition—voided that possibility.

In late January, advance issues of *Life* containing the Welch interview arrived on the newsstands. In an eight-page spread with nine photos, Welch proudly described his life of crime. He boasted that his crimes in the Washington area "would read like a *Who's Who* of Washington politics." In the article, Welch stated he believed he was not really stealing from people, "I wasn't ripping off people; I was ripping off insurance companies." Welch also intimated that he was a victim because his personal world has been "destroyed" by his arrest for murder. "I had everything going for me and [Halberstam] had everything going for him. But now he's dead and I'm in prison. They say I destroyed his life, but he destroyed mine."

Welch also boasted about his illegal accomplishments, describing his six years in Washington as the "best of his life." "I've been super, super active over the last several years." He also bragged that he once had a $1.8 million Paine Webber brokerage account and admitted to melting precious metals in his home on Sundays. "What you saw there was just peanuts. Something went out of that house every week. If it wasn't gold bars, it was silver bars; if it wasn't silver bars it was jewelry." Bernard Welch further stated to the interviewer that "[my] only bad habit, is that I steal."

Six independent drugstores in the Washington, DC, area refused to sell the *Life* issue containing the Welch interview. A few days later, other drugstores pulled the issue from their shelves, reflecting the local sentiment that Welch should not profit further from his crimes. In response to the magazine boycott, Elliott Jones Halberstam stated to the media, "That's wonderful. I love it. That's what should be done."

On January 27, 1981, Bernard Welch pleaded not guilty to the murder charge and other counts against him before Chief Judge Carl Moultrie, the first African-American judge in DC Superior Court. A trial date of April 1 was set.

Detectives Jim King and Steve Clarco watched the crowd through the glass doors of the DC Police Training Academy. As they arrived earlier that morning, they wrinkled their noses at the familiar sulfurous smell of Blue Plains. Blue Plains was a large tract of land owned by the District government, and it was home to the training academy as well as the DC impound lot where all the towed, stolen, and abandoned vehicles of Washington ended up. But the area was most noted for the Blue Plains Wastewater Treatment Plant.

The treatment facility was sited next to the Potomac River, at the southern most point of the District of Columbia. It was as far away from downtown DC as possible, and in the poorest part of the city; an excellent political solution to a necessary evil. All the effluent of the entire metropolitan area came to this facility to be separated, treated, and disposed of in an effective manner. Everything that is, except for the smell. Blue Plains was infamous for its odor. It overlaid the area like an invisible fog, inhaled, tasted, even felt on exposed skin. It was said that you could tell when a resident of the Blue Plains area entered a room without seeing them. Experiencing the police training academy near the sewage treatment plant was one of the joys on becoming a DC cop.

When King and Clarco entered the academy building early that morning, they went to the auditorium, which also served as a basketball court. The academy had been built in the 1950s. Its worn, brown wood floors creaked when walked on, and the room had a faint, musty men's locker room smell. Six-foot folding tables had been set up, and the recovered, stolen property from Welch's Great Falls, Virginia, home and Duluth, Minnesota, home was on display. All of the items had been labeled with little white tags, some attached by strings and some in plastic bags.

The FBI had volunteered to help Fairfax County and DC police with the viewing project. The local police believed the volunteer effort was the FBI's ploy to get some little credit for nabbing this interstate criminal since, as the cops put it, "they hadn't done shit" to track or capture Welch for five years. Still, King had to admit that the display was a tremendous logistical effort. Thousands of items had been listed, labeled, and displayed in an orderly manner.

Originally, there had been thirteen thousand individual items seized by Fairfax County at Welch's home, by DC in the trunk of his Mercedes, and by Duluth, Minnesota, authorities at the couple's Hidden Valley residence. Some of these items had been positively identified and were considered as evidence for upcoming court cases. How much that amounted to, King did not know, but there were still thousands and thousands of items to be viewed.

King had seen a bunch of college kids running around, making last-minute adjustments. He asked a gray-haired DC detective from Central Burglary who the kids were. The detective shook his head mournfully. "Would you believe they're rookie FBI agents? Just up from Quantico Training Academy and al-most ready to graduate. Looks like they recruited them straight out of high school. King laughed. "The feds volunteered them to help out. Poor SOBs. They probably think this is exciting."

King and Clarco walked the exhibit prior to admitting the public. When King had last seen this stuff it was packed in boxes in Welch's basement, but being tightly packed, it did not look like this much. Now, displayed on tables, it looked more like the estimated four million dollars of goods. There were two dozen mink coats; Tiffany lamps; dinner china; porcelain figures; oil paint-ings; engravings; pocket watches; jewelry; Oriental rugs; silver, pewter, gold, and ivory items; and more. An amazing diversity of items. One of the police officers cracked that if the Smithsonian Museum ever held a yard sale, it would look like this.

Much of the gold jewelry had been melted down by Bernard Welch prior to his arrest. There were two gold ingots on display for demonstration pur-poses to prove to the public that the police were not holding anything back.

The two crude bars were estimated to be worth $10,000 each, and that was just the going price per ounce. The majority of the items were not precious metal or things that could easily be melted in Welch's pot, such as pocket watches and large silver pieces.

King went looking for coffee before everything got started. "Hey, kid," he called to a fresh-faced young man walking by. "What time did you guys get here to set this all up?"

The young man, in his early twenties, wearing a white shirt and blue tie, looked serious, "Sir, we organized everything yesterday. We brought it up here this morning at 0600. We had it all done before 0800."

King nodded. "Where you from?"

"Nebraska," the man proudly replied.

King smiled. "Well, nice job."

The rookie agent grinned at the small compliment coming from a veteran detective. "Glad you like it." He walked off, obviously pleased.

King finally found coffee in a vending machine in the academy lunchroom. It was horrible, but he drank it anyway. He needed the caffeine.

The crowd arrived early in Blue Plains, waiting patiently in line. They quietly compared their Ghost Burglar stories. They were mostly older, mostly Caucasian, and mostly well dressed. A few were in wheelchairs, some used canes, and one carried an oxygen tank. They resembled the sick and infirm waiting to visit the Grotto at Lourdes, France, hoping to receive a miracle, a cure for their injuries.

At nine o'clock the academy doors opened. "Okay, folks, it's showtime," one of the officers near the front yelled back into the auditorium.

Police officers, male and female, some in uniform, some plainclothes, manned the tables set up near the front doors. As the burglary victims entered, they were directed to the table assigned to their particular jurisdiction. Their names would be checked off against a roster of suspected Ghost Burglar burglaries. Then a police officer from their home jurisdiction escorted each victim through the aisles of property-covered tables. Each of the involved departments had sent several police officers to perform this task. There were more than sixty metro area police personnel from ten different departments present in the auditorium.

King drew the second couple to arrive at the Montgomery County table, Mr. and Mrs. Diamond. He had actually worked their case last year. They were a pleasant older couple and remembered his name.

"Oh, Detective King, how nice to see you again," gushed the smiling Mrs. Diamond in a New York City accent. "I hope we find some of our things, especially Arthur's Chinese snuff bottle collection. He spent a lot of years and money getting them."

"Yes, I hope so, too," King murmured with a smile. But he knew it was improbable that they would discover any of their missing valuables here. Their burglary occurred in 1979. Their stuff had probably been sold at the auction gallery in Minneapolis last summer. All the items being shown at the academy had been taken between October and December 1980. Still, the Diamonds had paid their dues—being victimized by Bernard Welch—and had a right to tour the show.

King followed the Diamonds as they perused the assemblage of personal possessions. He carried a steno pad to note the tag numbers affixed to the articles they thought might be theirs. Later, the claimed items would be compared to the items reported stolen in the original burglary report. If a match could be confirmed by description, photo, engraved initials, manufacturer's name, marks, scars, or any other criteria of identification, then that item would be returned to the victim at some future time. Unless the victim's burglary had occurred in the autumn of 1980, King knew any claim would be denied almost out of hand.

The Diamonds were honest, but disappointed. They claimed nothing. Some items were similar to their stolen property, but not exact. King let them examine the pieces more closely. Each time, they looked longingly at the items but said, "No, it's not ours. It looks like ours, but it's not ours." After almost half an hour, they finished the last table.

"I'm sorry you didn't find anything," King apologized. He was sincere. The Diamonds were good people, victimized by Welch.

Mr. Diamond shook his hand. "Well, it was a good try anyway. Thank you for showing us around." King walked them to the door and said goodbye and then returned to his table to get the next customer.

The auditorium was getting crowded now. The spaces between the tables were full of citizens and police. It was becoming like an auto accident on the beltway, passing traffic bogged down by the gawkers. Even when it was explained to the victims that, since their theft had occurred one, two, or three years ago, there was absolutely no chance of any of their property being present, they insisted on looking anyway. Like the Diamonds, they had paid Welch's steep admission price, so the police allowed them to gawk. As the wait became longer to traverse the aisles, some people became impatient and left without going through.

The morning continued on, with hopeful people streaming through the doors. There were a few successes but not many. Those people who identified items walked away happy, but most were not so lucky.

Then the media arrived like locusts descending on a field of wheat. They were everywhere, cameras, lights, microphones, and tape recorders pressed into the face of anyone willing to speak. Everyone was cornered, both citizens and police, but especially Jim King. The local media had been alerted that Detective King was one of the primary investigators of the Ghost Burglar cases and had actually named Welch as a suspect over a year before he was captured.

King knew a few of the local reporters from past cases, but there were others present he had never seen before. He tried to avoid them all, but a local guy, a radio reporter he liked, found him alone and got him talking on tape. Other media types soon gathered around, and they recorded, filmed, and took notes. King was encircled, like a piece of candy on the sidewalk discovered by ants. King made an unguarded comment to the effect that, had it not been for Dr. Halberstam's initial resistance and final act of dying rage against the person who had shot him, the police would still be chasing Bernard Welch.

It was an impolitic, but true, statement. Other nearby cops heard the remark and winced. King really did not care. It was time for area law enforcement to admit that Dr. Halberstam had solved these cases for them. If some people couldn't admit that, screw them. Internal politics was not King's strong suit.

The line of victims and the media diminished as the day wore on. By four o'clock, there were few victims left. Someone estimated that close to 4,000 people had filed through. Where that number came from, no one knew. It was probably a news reporter's guess; they always liked dramatic numbers for their stories. No one had actually counted. There were an estimated 3,300 burglaries that Welch had committed since 1975, which included the Richmond and Washington areas together. King was doubtful that even a third of the victims had shown up.

It had been a long day. King and Clarco were glad to leave. They packed up their boxes of reports and headed to the car. The other Montgomery County officers were also leaving. One day of this was enough. There were too many disappointed citizens to deal with. King was tired. Thank God he had the next few days off.

Clarco drove back to the office. King sat in the passenger seat and was quiet. He dozed off. Regular sleep at home was difficult. He only managed an hour or two a night. His nine-year-old daughter had died of brain cancer four months ago. It had been a long, grueling three-year illness. Since her death, he had begun to lose interest in not only the Welch case, but in everything. It was time to…what? He didn't have an answer to that. Hell, he didn't even know what the question was anymore. He could feel himself spiraling down mentally, like those gun-camera films of planes in World War II. Shot up, broken, parts falling off, spinning down, smoke pouring out until they crashed in a big ball of fire. That's how he felt—smoking, spiraling out of control, preparing to crash.

In his almost asleep, almost awake landscape he almost dreamed. It wasn't really a dream, but it was not rational thought. His mind was disconnected from his body. He drifted from idea to idea. His firstborn daughter slowly dying. The people who were hurt by Welch. How useless all his efforts were to solve either problem. Time to leave police work? Go where? Do what? He thought of these and other things. None of it made sense. None of it mattered.

Maybe if he drank more booze at night, he could sleep. He would buy a bottle of vodka on the way home and drink it tonight. Then, his mind would be quiet. He'd fall asleep on the couch in front of the TV. He'd sleep. His wife wouldn't like that, but he didn't care anymore.

Martin Firestone, Welch's literary attorney, announced that Paul Sann, a New York–based crime reporter, editor, and author, has been awarded the rights to Bernard Welch's life story. A trust agreement was drawn up stating that Sann would share the proceeds with Welch's three male children by Linda Hamilton and a female child he fathered[1] with Susan Swanson, Linda's niece. The aim of the trust was to benefit the four children, so it was hoped the IRS would not put a lien on it, even though they could.

After researching Welch, Sann called him perhaps the "greatest one-man crime wave of this century. [Welch] may well be the master burglar of all time." The various police agencies involved with Welch's cases agree. They now estimated that Welch was responsible for over 3,300 burglaries in the Maryland, Virginia, and Washington, DC, areas.[2]

In March 1981, Welch gives a two-hour interview to the *Washington Post.* Welch denied he was involved in the shooting of Dr. Halberstam or any of the burglaries that evening. He said he will plead not guilty, explaining, "This is not my crime." He lamented that he could not receive a fair trial because of pretrial publicity. "[The press] have already found me guilty.... I just don't believe I'll ever get a fair trial in the Washington area."

When asked by the reporter why he shaved his head, mustache, and eyebrows before the police lineup, Welch claimed it was because he had dandruff, not to fool the witnesses.

Welch used the *Post* interview to complain about what he claimed was his abusive treatment at the District jail. He makes a not-so-veiled threat regarding what would happen if he was convicted and sent back to prison, warning, "Prison made me.... When I was in there I furthered my [criminal] education. If they send me back to prison you can believe that I'll school everybody I can so they will do better when they get out."

Welch also alleged his attorney, Sol Rosen, had agreed to be paid his legal fees out of the proceeds from the book deal. Such an arrangement would be a clear conflict of interest. If the charge were sustained, it could lead to Rosen's disbarment, and even more pertinent to Welch, on appeal, a higher court might overturn Welch's conviction because of this conflict of interest.

Rosen, having previously lectured Welch on the perils of speaking to the press, stated, "I'm surprised that Welch talked to the [*Post*]. It was without my consent or knowledge." But he can also use the talkative nature of his client to their advantage.

Still seeking a change of venue, Rosen subpoenaed reporters from the *Washington Post* and the *Washington Star* newspapers, demanding that they bring to court all newspaper clippings relating to the case. Rosen used the number of clippings to try to prove how excessive the media reporting had been.

On March 30, 1981, Judge Moultrie called a special hearing on the allegations made by Welch in his *Post* interview that Rosen had an agreement to receive payment from the profits of a book about Welch's life. Present at the meeting are Welch, Rosen, Assistant US Attorney Alexia Morrison, and a court transcriber. Welch denied at the hearing that he had said anything about a fee arrangement for a book. Rosen informed the judge he had no such agreement with Welch. Rosen requested that his attorney fees be paid by public funds, since Welch had filed an affidavit that he was indigent. Judge Moultrie agreed.

Welch's story was overshadowed in the press the very next day. On March 31, President Ronald Reagan and three others were shot by John Hinckley, a crazed gunman, in Washington, DC.

Judge Moultrie denied the defense motions to move the trial location due to massive publicity on April 1, 1981. He rejected the defense's argument that an unbiased jury could not be found because of the media coverage and the recent attempted assassination of the president.

Rosen's final motions requested that the trial be closed to the press and the trial date be postponed for thirty days because of the attempted assassination on President Reagan. Judge Moultrie denied both motions, and jury selection began. Judge Moultrie individually interviews each of the prospective jurors in his chambers to ensure that each is unbiased.

Before the trial began in April 1981, Welch granted another interview, this time to the Associated Press. He bemoaned what he saw as his inevitable fate. "I will be convicted," he declared. "Everybody has convicted me already.... How can I get a fair trial when everybody is writing I have done this and done that?"

In this interview, Welch also discussed Linda Hamilton, his common-law wife, and what her life had turned into since his arrest. "I feel sorry for her, the way the IRS, the media, and the police have all found her guilty by association. Linda's only crime or mistake was in loving or trusting me."

Welch seemed to reiterate her innocence. "We met and I treated her with respect and I turned on the charm...I have used several women in my life of crime, but only a fool could or would think I would tell a woman I was an escaped convict or an active criminal. I wasn't going back to prison for being stupid."

In a pretrial hearing, Linda Hamilton was called as a prosecution witness. The defense contended that she had been coerced by police into permitting a search of her Great Falls, Virginia, home and her car in DC. Linda disputed this allegation, stating that she allowed the initial searches because she had nothing to hide. She reiterated she was ignorant of the secret life of her common-law husband. She then made eye contact with Welch and flushed. Outside of the courtroom, after her testimony, she collapsed, sobbing.

On April 6, 1981, five months after the murder of Dr. Michael Halberstam, Bernard Welch's trial began. Defense attorney Sol Rosen submitted a motion in court that witness identifications be struck and the evidence from Welch's Virginia home disallowed. This would prevent the prosecution from introducing as evidence items from Welch's basement that linked him to the murder weapon. Judge Moultrie overruled the defense's motion and the trial began.

Assistant US Attorney Jay B. Stephens began with a powerful opening statement. "[Welch] was prepared for every eventuality, except one. He did not consider the eventuality of Dr. Halberstam. Two shots through his chest and three in his coat did not stop him." Pointing to the defendant, Stephens stated, "In his last heroic act, [Halberstam] himself marked for you his killer."

The next day Elliott Jones Halberstam, the widow of the slain doctor, took the witness stand. Rosen, in an attempt to keep the jury from hearing her statement, objected that anything Mrs. Halberstam said regarding Bernard Welch was hearsay. Although she never saw Bernard Welch in her house with her own eyes, she was the only one to hear Dr. Michael Halberstam identify the suspect. Judge Moultrie ruled the doctor's statement was a "dying declaration," one of the few instances where the law allows hearsay evidence, deeming her testimony of these events admissible.

Her testimony is poignant and moving. Mrs. Halberstam, teary-eyed, stoically told the jury of the shooting and the mad drive toward the hospital. She stated that her husband exclaimed, "That's the guy!" and drove up a curb and over a lawn, pursuing a man in a dark blue parka jacket.

"I was holding on because I was afraid the car was going to flip over.... I saw Michael hit him. I heard a thump. I saw a form falling."

The courtroom was silent as Mrs. Halberstam continued quietly in her deep Mississippi drawl, telling of the crash, the rush to get help, and her husband being brought into the emergency room. "The next time I saw him," she cried, "he was dead."

Mrs. Halberstam then testified that the man she saw forty-five minutes later in the ambulance was the same person her husband identified as the one who had shot him and was later struck with their car. When she recalled telling the police, "That's him. That's the son of a bitch that did it!" Rosen objected, claiming the comment was "unduly suggestive" and a violation of Welch's constitutional rights. Judge Moultrie overruled Rosen and allowed Stephens to continue. The district attorney finished by asking Mrs. Halberstam to point out the man she saw her husband hit. Mrs. Halberstam stated, "That's the guy," as she pointed toward Welch at the defense table.

The jury was clearly affected by Mrs. Halberstam's testimony. She was emotional, but her sincerity was real. There was no doubt that she was speaking the truth.[3] Some members of the jury wiped tears from their eyes.

Then it was Rosen's turn to cross-examine Mrs. Halberstam. He asked Mrs. Halberstam if she had seen Welch in the house.

"No," she answered.

Rosen asked if she saw anyone run from the house.

"No," she answered again.

With those answers, Rosen declared that he had no further questions. He could not be harsh in his questioning of Elliott Jones Halberstam, otherwise the jury could view him as cruel and callous. Welch had already admitted to the press that he was struck by Halberstam's car. That meant Rosen could not challenge her identification of Welch in the ambulance. He could only try to establish that Dr. Halberstam, in his critically injured state, misidentified Welch as the burglar.

The next day, the prosecution called Linda Sue Hamilton to the stand. Having been granted limited immunity, the slightly plump, strawberry blond woman testified that she knew Bernard Welch as Norm Heiman and had no knowledge of his criminal career, past or present. She admitted that on the evening of the murder he was out all night and never came home. She reasserted that she gave police permission to search her house and her car because she had nothing to hide. Rosen declined to cross-examine.

The prosecution then called a bevy of Battery Place neighborhood witnesses.

One heard gun shots. Another saw a man wearing a blue parka run past her bedroom window with his fists clenched. Another saw headlights, heard a car engine rev up, followed by a thump, and then called the police. Other neighbors testified to hearing a car drive up on their lawn and hit something, after which they checked out front and heard moans from the bushes.

Called next was a DC police detective. He testified that he drove from the Great Falls home of Welch to the Battery Place home of Dr. Halberstam. The trip officially took twenty-three minutes. Although a seemingly minor detail, this unchallenged bit of fact punctured a future defense contention.

From the witness stand, another police detective identified the items found in Welch's pockets at the time of his arrest—four gold French coins, two small silver pig figurines, and a penlight—and a .38-caliber Smith and Wesson stainless steel revolver. All were government exhibits. Another neighborhood resident who was also a victim of a burglary that same evening identified the four gold coins and silver pig figurines as being hers.

In addition to the neighbors, the prosecution also called Mamie Stallworth, a housekeeper on Battery Place, who had seen Welch in the neighborhood on December 5, 1980, and identified him in an earlier lineup. Ms. Stallworth testified that she had first seen a white man with brown hair, thick sideburns, and a mustache driving a silver Mercedes at 1:40 p.m. She was out front sweeping the porch as he slowly drove by, stopping briefly to look at the Halberstam house. A while later, at 5:45 p.m., she left the home where she was employed and attempted to drive out of the cul-de-sac, but her car was blocked in by a silver Mercedes. The same man was driving the same car. She blew her horn twice, but he chose to ignore her. She then rolled down her window and yelled at the driver, "You stupid ass dummy, can't you move your car so I can come out, please?" He backed up and she drove slowly by him, passing within eight feet. She identified Bernard Welch as the man she saw in the silver Mercedes Benz. As she drove away, she looked in her rearview mirror and saw the silver Mercedes reenter Battery Place near the Halberstam home.

A DC police detective took the stand next to show two videotapes. The first video featured Mamie Stallworth at the December 9 lineup, three days after his arrest. She quickly picked Welch out of the group. The next video showed the voice lineup. Nine different men said, "Lie down or I'll blow your fucking head off." On the tape, the jury saw Mrs. Halberstam pick three voices as being similar to the intruder, one of which was Welch's voice.

Rosen cross-examined the detective and elicited from him the fact that Ms. Stallworth had seen a photograph of Welch on television the evening before the lineup. After court recessed for the day, Rosen stated somewhat cryptically that discrediting Ms. Stallworth's ID was the "same as shooting ducks in a barrel.... We got a lot of stuff that will knock her [testimony] out. We will prove [Welch] was in Virginia until about 5:00 p.m., then downtown."

The prosecution also brought to the stand four witnesses who lived within a few blocks of the Halberstam home. Their homes had also been burglarized the evening of the murder. These victims identified more than two hundred pieces of property found in the trunk of Welch's Mercedes parked on the street near where Halberstam ran him down. The items, displayed as evidence, covered two tables in the courtroom. The evidence included silver goblets, bowls, trays, gold jewelry, pearls, US and foreign currency, and even a mold for a gold dental bridge.

At this point in the trial, Rosen had to come to grips with the fact that he had lost the burglary part of the case. He now needed to concentrate on Welch's murder charge.

FBI agent Phillip Chaney took the stand and testified that the .38-caliber Smith and Wesson five-shot revolver found near Welch when he was arrested was the same one taken when his home was burglarized a month earlier. A Colt .357 magnum revolver, handcuffs, an FBI badge, jewelry, and a photo of Chaney's children, also stolen from his home, were found in Welch's basement when it was searched.

Two District of Columbia police evidence technicians testified next. One reported that a ballistics test proved the revolver found near Welch was the same weapon that shot Dr. Halberstam and that a match was made with a slug recovered from the doctor's body, three from the Halberstams' garage door, and one from a neighbor's garage. An FBI analysis indicated that the left rear pocket of the jeans Welch had been wearing when arrested revealed gunshot powder residue. This residue was deposited on the gun barrel and cylinder when it was fired and then rubbed off when the weapon was shoved into the pocket.

The other DC police evidence technician identified the bloody shirt, coat, and tie worn by Dr. Halberstam when he was shot. He explained the meaning of the bullet holes in the clothing, stating that the powder residue found on the clothing indicated that the two fatal shots were fired at close range, "three inches or less."

The last witness for the prosecution was the District of Columbia deputy medical examiner. He discussed Dr. Halberstam's autopsy and confirmed he died from two gunshot wounds to the chest. One bullet entered the left chest, hit a rib, pierced the left lung, and buried itself in the muscles of the back. The other bullet entered the left side below the armpit, piercing the same lung and exiting out the back.

Welch repeatedly rubbed his face as he listened to the testimony of the evidence technicians and the medical examiner. He twisted a ballpoint pen in his mouth and bit his nails. For the first time in the trial, Welch seemed nervous.

The government rested its case.

Rosen immediately asked for an acquittal. It was a long shot, but most of his case was, so he doesn't have much to lose. He contended that the government had not proven its murder case against his client, providing neither eyewitnesses to the crime nor direct proof that Welch did the shooting. Judge Moultrie swiftly denied the motion.

Rosen began the defense by calling two building contractors and a housekeeper who stated they saw Welch at his home on the afternoon of the murder, but not that evening. Upon cross-examination, the witnesses admitted that Welch did leave his home in the afternoon to replace empty propane gas tanks. One of the contractors recalled, under cross-examination, that Welch was wearing a blue, down-filled parka and jeans in the afternoon, the same clothes he was wearing when arrested on the evening of the murder.

In a bold move, Rosen recalled Mamie Stallworth, the housekeeper who said she saw Welch in front of the Halberstam home, trying to break her earlier identification of Welch. She was the only person who could place Welch in the area before the murder. If she could be confused or made unsure in her story, it could cast doubt as to whether it was Welch who pulled the trigger. Rosen needed to create reasonable doubt in the minds of the jurors, make them believe his client was misidentified.

But Ms. Stallworth was a tough old cookie. To one of Rosen's questions she replied, "Mamie may forget names, but she never forgets a face." Looking at Welch she stated, "That's the man… I'm very positive it was." Rosen did nothing to neutralize her earlier, damaging testimony.

Rosen then called Linda Hamilton as a defense witness. She confirmed that she and Welch operated a gold and silver buying operation from their home, but she never really knew where Welch got the goods that they later sold. She believed the business, and her relationship with Welch, to be legitimate. This was Rosen's real reason for recalling Linda. He needed to balance out the tearful testimony of Elliott Jones Halberstam.

"How long have you known Bernard Welch?" Rosen questioned Linda.

"Five years," she answered nervously.

"He is the father of your three boys?"

"Yes."

"Do you love Bernard Welch?"

"Yes." Linda's eyes teared up.

"Do you want to see Bernard Welch go to prison?"

"No," she said, tears trickling down her face.

"You don't believe he's a murderer?"

"No," she sobbed.

After only five witnesses and two hours of testimony, Rosen rests. He could not let Welch testify. If Welch took the stand, he would have opened himself up to a devastating cross-examination by the prosecution. His criminal history would be revealed, and then there would have been no hope in winning this already seemingly hopeless case.

On April 10, 1981, both sides presented their closing arguments. Assistant US Attorney Alexia Morrison summed up the evidence and testimony of the government's case and knitted it together into a tight net around Welch. She closed by reminding the jury that "all the evidence ends in an arrow that points at the defendant.... Label this man a burglar, a thief, and a pistol-carrying murderer.... There has been in court an identification of sorts, for Michael Halberstam has come into this courtroom by his actions, swerving his car to hit his assailant, Bernard Welch."

"That's the guy"—Dr. Halberstam's dying declaration—are the words that are hung around Welch's neck like a scarlet letter. Morrison pointed her finger at Welch and said, "That's the guy. That's the guy who left his home in Great Falls, Virginia, on December 5 and robbed four homes in the District. And that's the guy who didn't have enough and then went to the home of Dr. Michael Halberstam. That's the guy who shot Michael Halberstam, and that's the guy who was recognized by Michael Halberstam."

Morrison finished by telling the jury that all the circumstantial evidence led to the logical conclusion that Bernard Welch is the person who shot the doctor. "The government has borne its responsibility to prove its case beyond a reasonable doubt."

By contrast, Rosen's closing argument to the panel of nine women and three men was weak. He had no case to tie together. All he had was theory and assumption. He had presented no credible witnesses, no real alibi, and no evidence. He couldn't—none of those things existed for Welch. He could only attempt to put doubt in the minds of the jury. He argued that the wire snips and screwdriver found on Welch were tools "he obviously needed around his house," which was under construction. He posited that the gun found near Welch might have been thrown there by "the real killer in this case." Rosen contended that the prosecution had not provided "one scintilla of evidence to prove the defendant had committed the murder." It was a case, he stated, "based on speculation and conjecture.... There has been...no eyewitness... no fingerprints or any tangible evidence to link Mr. Welch to the crime." He said his client was "an innocent bystander" misidentified by the agitated and injured doctor who may not have been thinking clearly. He stressed that "the government witnesses have picked the wrong man." Rosen did the best he could with what he had to work with. He couldn't do anything about the burglary charges, but he tried to save his client from life in prison.

That afternoon, the jury began its deliberations.

Rosen met with reporters outside the courthouse. "We've got a 50-50 chance," he mused. "All I have to do is leave a reasonable doubt in some of the juror's minds." He needs only one juror. One doubtful juror would cause a hung jury, requiring a new trial. He commented that Welch was in a "pretty jovial mood and wants to finish the trial."

After just two hours of deliberation, the jury returned. Welch and Rosen stood and faced the court. As the jury entered, one of the female jurors was crying. Welch turned to Rosen and whispered, "Is that a good sign?"

The jury foreman announced the verdict: guilty of premeditated murder in the first degree, and guilty of nine counts of burglary, grand larceny, and carrying a pistol.

When he heard the outcome, Welch showed no emotion, only let out a small sigh.

Judge Moultrie set sentencing for May 22, and the court bailiffs moved in quickly to handcuff the prisoner and escort him out of the courtroom.

Sol Rosen announced to the media after the trial that he would appeal based on the judge allowing the jury to see the stolen items found in Welch's auto. He admits that "the case was overwhelming.... It was like facing an army. My God [it] was just the two of us against the world.... I think Welch expected the verdict. There was just so much cumulative evidence.... He thanked me for a good job."

Dr. Halberstam's two teenage sons, who attended every day of the trial, were there to hear the final verdict, to see that "the system works."

"He's a nothing. He's a murderer. He's trash!" Elliott Jones Halberstam commented to the media. She was glad for the outcome, but also bitter and angry. "I've known people like him all my life. Where I came from...the back woods of Mississippi...you know they had rotten teeth, they killed deer out of season. If he'd been from Mississippi, he'd belong to the Klan."[4]

After the trial, the press interviewed several jury panelists. They revealed that there was no question of Welch's guilt. Within the first thirty minutes of deliberation, they had all agreed on a guilty verdict. They reviewed the evidence for another hour and a half to make sure they hadn't rushed to judgment. They voted three times on each of the eleven charges. Each time, the vote was unanimous.

"It was not a tough case. All the [prosecution] evidence presented was overwhelming," said one juror, adding that Rosen had "mighty little to present."

"Our hearts went out to her," another jury member added in reference to Elliott Jones Halberstam's testimony. "She was very convincing, which is the only thing that counts." Linda Hamilton hadn't been as convincing. All of the jurors thought she knew more than she was saying and didn't buy that she knew nothing about Welch's criminal activities.

A few days after the jury delivered the guilty verdict, Elliott Jones Halberstam, acting as executor of the Michael Halberstam estate, filed suit against Bernard C. Welch and Linda Sue Hamilton for $81 million. The suit sought $77 million in punitive damages and $4 million in compensatory damages, contending that Hamilton was in a "joint criminal venture and conspiracy" with Welch and shared responsibility for the crime. Mrs. Halberstam realized that the estate will never collect any money from this suit, but she conceded, "That's not the point." She called the suit her revenge.

"I don't mean to be facetious," Linda Hamilton responded wearily, "but she will just have to get to the end of the line," referring to the previous IRS lien of $24 million against herself and Welch and various mechanics' liens and unpaid merchant suits tying up both houses and all three cars.

Soon after the trial, Welch fired Rosen as his attorney and formally complained to the District of Columbia Bar Association that Rosen was an "ineffective counsel." Having been "fired," Rosen requested of the court that he be allowed to withdraw from the case. He denied Welch's contention and commented philosophically to the press, "Every defendant has two trials, one in court, and then he tries his lawyer. This is phase two."

When Rosen later learned the details of Welch's complaint to the bar association, he discovered Welch complained that he had failed to prepare his defense adequately and spent most of his time promoting the book idea. Welch also complained about the statements Rosen made to reporters before and after the trial. Rosen fired back at Welch in a statement to the *Washington Post*, saying Welch's allegations were "the last gasps of a dying man.... He hopes to embarrass me. He's a mean, vicious guy. He'll stop at nothing to achieve his ends and just doesn't care who he hurts. The charges are spurious. Everything was okay during the trial, and all this is after the fact." Rosen further responded, "When you sleep with dogs, you wake up with fleas.... I did everything I could to defend the case."

Bernard Welch turned forty-one on April 28, 1981. Having alienated Linda Hamilton and fired his attorney, Welch spent his birthday alone in his jail cell.

On April 30, Judge Moultrie granted Rosen's request to be removed as Bernard Welch's counsel. He appointed Alan B. Soschin as Welch's new attorney.

In a confidential court memo dated May 21, 1981, Welch requested that Judge Moultrie perform a wedding ceremony for him at the time of his sentencing. Amazingly, Welch did not name Linda Hamilton, the mother of his three sons, as his future bride, but rather her niece, Susan Swanson. The same young niece who had moved from Duluth to Welch's home in Virginia after giving birth to a child out of wedlock. Neighbors said the child had an uncanny resemblance to Welch, and it was rumored that he was, indeed, the father. Welch's new attorney, Soschin, strongly advised that such a ceremony wait until after sentencing. Welch eventually agreed, and it was rumored that Judge Moultrie took a dim view of Welch's request.

Linda Hamilton could no longer tolerate Bernard Welch's now confirmed infidelity with Susan Swanson. Carrying on an affair for more than a year, renting a nearby apartment to accommodate it, and now asking the judge to marry them. Naming Heather Swanson as his child in the Hamilton children's trust he tried to set up in February. Whispered rumors back in Duluth about the landscaper's wife, the seamstress, and who knows who else? What a sap she'd been.

Surprisingly, Linda was still allowing Susan Swanson to live with her in the Great Falls house. Linda's frustration and exasperation finally boiled over, and she got into a major shouting contest with her niece. This kitchen debate degenerated into a knockdown, drag-out, hair-pulling match, and then Linda went for a butcher knife. Diane Jenkins, the housekeeper, was still in the home at the time, doing her work. She successfully pulled Linda off Susan and disarmed her before she could do any serious damage with the knife.

On May 22, 1981, Bernard C. Welch Jr. was brought before Judge Moultrie for sentencing. Welch, appearing tired, was escorted into the courtroom by the US Marshals. Again, as on his birthday just a month earlier, Welch was alone. Susan Swanson, his prospective bride, was not present in the courtroom. Linda Hamilton also did not attend. Even Elliott Jones Halberstam missed the sentencing because of her mother's recent death.

Assistant US Attorney Alexia Morrison addressed the court. "The defendant's total disregard for the rights of others is perhaps best exemplified in his conscious decision first to carry a gun and second to use it to mask his misdeeds by murdering any witnesses he encountered." She appealed to the court that Welch was "not a candidate for rehabilitation" and that his sentence should be for as long as the law allows since he was a "parasite and a greedy marauder."

Soschin asked the court for a sentence that would allow for rehabilitation and eventual return to society. He reminded the court that "our corrections system is not set up to intentionally exile [people] from their family and friends."

Judge Moultrie agreed that "an extended incarceration would serve the needs of the public," sentencing Welch to a minimum of 143 years before being eligible for parole. This sentence was to begin after he served his ten years for the New York escape. If he were to live that long, Welch would be eligible for parole when he was 184 years old.

The sentence is basically one of life in prison without parole. The judge just told him he will be locked up until he dies. It appeared to have as much effect on him as a pronouncement that he had a hole in his sock. Welch made no statement or sign at the pronouncement of the judge. It did not seem to matter. There were no tears, no twitches, no tremors. If there was a time that proved Welch had no emotions, this was it.

Soschin immediately advised the court he would appeal, simply stating, "The sentence is too long."

That same day, the US Marshals transported Welch to Lewisburg Penitentiary in Pennsylvania. Welch was housed in Lewisburg until appropriate long-term placement was determined.

Shortly after Welch is taken away, Sol Rosen spoke with the press, stating somewhat gleefully, "Justice triumphed!" Rosen finally revealed that Welch admitted to him that he had shot Dr. Halberstam. Welch also offered Rosen fifty thousand dollars if he could get Welch transferred to St. Elizabeth's Mental Hospital so he could escape. Rosen also released his reply letter to the bar association regarding Welch's complaints. Welch asked Rosen after he was convicted to prevent his transfer to federal prison and request that Welch be incarcerated in the District's Lorton Reformatory. Welch knew escape from Lorton would be easier. Rosen stated, "[Welch] is of the opinion that he can break out of any prison and does not intend to serve his sentence."[5] Perhaps this explained Welch's lack of reaction to his sentence.

In early June, Bernard Welch moved to the US Penitentiary in Marion, Illinois. Considered the new Alcatraz and escape-proof, Marion was the federal government's toughest prison, reserved for the most rebellious and the most hardened criminals in America. About 25 percent of its population were lifers with nothing to lose. The 370 inmates had small, individual cells and were let out for only one hour a day. The perimeter guards were equipped with shoulder-fired rocket launchers to shoot down helicopter escape attempts.

Shortly after he arrived at Marion, Welch received a bill along with a dunning letter from a collection agency. They were attempting to collect the thirty-five-dollar fee for his ambulance ride to Sibley Hospital after Dr. Halberstam ran him over. The letter threatened that if action wasn't taken soon, his credit rating would be affected.

But Welch also received good news at Marion. Susan Swanson missed him so much she decided to move to southern Illinois with her daughter Heather to be near him. Welch pulled some strings back East and had his mother send ten thousand dollars to Susan to finance her move. Against the advice of friends and relatives, Susan relocated to Marion and got a job at a nearby nursing home to support herself and her daughter. The arrangement worked well at first, but visiting time with Welch was limited to a few hours a week because he was in protective custody and Susan wasn't his immediate family. Even with the cash for the move her resources were very limited and she had absolutely no family nearby to fall back on. And at this point, Welch wasn't even at Marion that often. He was still being transported back East for different trials. Ever faithful, Susan enrolled Heather in the public school and kept working at her low-paying job.

Things weren't going well for Linda Hamilton back in Virginia, either. She had been living off loans from family and friends and had not paid the mortgage or utility bills for the Great Falls house in months. One of her sons needed an operation, but she had no health insurance or money. She couldn't go back to work, because day care was too expensive, and the IRS would take any money she earned. She considered her relationship with Welch over, reiterating, "He said he's planning to marry my niece."

On July 10, 1981, the real estate ad for the Welch-Hamilton house in Great Falls, Virginia, appeared in local DC papers: "For Sale: 7 BR, 6 1/2 ba., 4 f.pl, 50 ft. indoor pool, sauna, 14 skylights, contemp. style. New, but with a fabled history. Reduced to sell at $975,000—was $1.3 million." The ad failed to mention the $7.6 million IRS lien, $89,000 in mechanic liens to unpaid contractors, an estimated $85,000 to complete the unfinished pool and addition, construction debris in the yard, and an oven that didn't work. That summer, Linda moved from 411 Chesapeake Drive to 10417 Cavalcade Street in Great Falls.

The summer of 1981 also ended Welch's dream of having his book written. Paul Sann, the New York writer and editor, was barred from visiting Welch at Marion. Prison officials declared "no meaningful relationship was established prior to incarceration," so Sann was removed from Welch's approved visitor's list. With no access to Welch, Sann all but ran out of options for completing a book on Welch's life story, as Welch's mother, Genevieve, refused to talk to him.

In September 1981, Welch was transferred to Montgomery County, Maryland, to face twenty-one charges ranging from burglary to rape. At great expense, Welch had been shuttled all over the East Coast to be brought up on charges such as burglary, rape, armed robbery, and assault by numerous different municipalities and government agencies. The rationale for the multiple trials was that if Welch's District convictions were overturned and he was released, convictions in other municipalities would keep him in prison. No jurisdiction already hit by Welch wanted to see him ever set foot outside a jail again, and no jurisdiction trusted any other to keep him adequately locked up. Montgomery County State's Attorney Andrew Sonner knew he could get a conviction and prison time for Welch. Special arrangements, such as twenty-four-hour watch to keep Welch secure, were made at Montgomery County jail.

After the Montgomery County trials were over, Welch was to stand trial in Fairfax, Arlington, and Alexandria counties in Virginia for rape, burglary, and firearms violations. Welch also had to face the pending New York escape charge.

In December 1981, one year after the murder of Dr. Michael Halberstam, Virginia police reported the number of burglaries had fallen 45 percent since the same time the previous year. The decrease was attributed to the declining price of gold and silver, the enactment of laws regulating the buying and selling of precious metals, the establishment of neighborhood watch programs, the increasing installation of alarm systems, and the arrest of Bernard C. Welch.

A plea bargain agreement was reached in January 1982 in Montgomery County, Maryland. Welch received thirty years for one armed robbery and three burglaries. The rape cases were not prosecuted because of minimal evidence and the lack of witness identification at the infamous "no hair" lineup one year ago.

With the prison sentence delivered by Montgomery County, it was insured that Welch would stay in prison even if his DC murder sentence was overturned. Now, northern Virginia area jurisdictions awaited the verdict of Welch's appeal of his DC convictions. If his appeal was granted, Virginia would go forward with their cases and Welch would still end up doing life in prison. If the appeal was denied, Virginia jurisdictions would not proceed with their trials, thus saving the counties millions in court costs.

Welch and another prisoner at Marion, Garvin White of Fresno, California, put together an escape plan in July 1982. It involved sharpshooters, high-powered rifles, an airplane, and lots of money. On September 7, 1982, a pilot, Dennis Murray, flew Dale White, Garvin White's son, and Starr K. Thompson in from California. White and Thompson proceeded to the prison while Murray waited at the airport with the plane. The two men then opened fire on the guard towers with deer rifles from nearby woods. Six inmates tried to scale two barbed wire fences while the guards were distracted. Four of them reached the no-man's-land between the fences, and two were left still climbing the first fence when the tower guards returned fire and the escaping prisoners were rounded up. Welch was not among the escapees. He helped with the planning and financed the escape but did not participate.

The resulting grand jury named Bernard Welch as an unindicted co-conspirator. Local officials were also quite sure that Susan Swanson, as a confidant of Welch's on the outside, had something to do with this. She was subpoenaed by a federal grand jury and interrogated repeatedly about this case but was never charged with anything. "All my life I've been uncomfortable around cops," she told Welch, "and you send the biggies to my door." Susan decided to leave Illinois the next spring. She gave up her vigil for Welch and took her daughter back to Duluth.

On March 20, 1983, the Great Falls house was sold at a bank foreclosure auction for $375,000. The mortgage holder and contractors received the majority of that amount. The IRS got $80,000. Ironically the vacant home had been burglarized, and its burglar alarm system and a bidet were stolen.

The IRS sold the house on Valley Drive in Duluth on July 28, 1983. The residence, with its indoor pool, was valued at $149,000. It sold at auction for $102,600. The mortgage lender received $35,000 still owed on the loan. The IRS got the remaining $67,600.

In September 1983, the DC Court of Appeals turned down Welch's appeal to overturn his convictions for first-degree murder, burglary, and grand larceny. Because the court upheld the original DC conviction and sentence, Welch was never tried by the Virginia courts for the rapes or the thousands of burglaries he committed there.

The effects of Bernard Welch's depredations extended well into the future. For some victims, the effects lasted for only months, for others years, and still others a lifetime. The actions of this one felon touched countless people in uncountable ways. When he went to prison, many felt safer, but his life of crime was not yet finished.

Shock waves reverberated off the towers of steel and glass in Chicago's financial district before the first raindrops fell on the western edge of the city. A churning squall muscled its way northeast toward the great lake as the residents of a unique prism-shaped building settled in for the night.

This particular high-rise was a twenty-six-story triangular box set on end. The rough-poured concrete walls were textured by the imprint of the wooden forms used to cast them. Random, narrow slit windows made each side of the building resemble an IBM punch card. The building, designed by Harry Weese and built in 1975, was a prime example of Brutalist architecture with its bleak, Soviet Bloc look.

The stark structure at the intersection of Van Buren and Clark Streets stood in the heart of the Loop, right on the 'L' tracks. The setting would have been ideal for exploring the sprawling city, except the residents of this all-male enclave didn't get around much anymore. They were prisoners housed in the Chicago Metropolitan Correctional Center (MCC), a detention center for federal offenders. Various floors of the building held prisoners with different security requirements, ranging from work-release inmates needing minimal security requirements to dangerous felons and escape-risks needing maximum security.

The innovative triangular layout of the building allowed each floor to be overseen and secured by only one guard. Fourteen one-man cells were located on the outside walls of the structure with an open commons area in the center, where prisoners could watch television, lift weights, read magazines, or play cards at a large table anchored to the floor. Individual rooms had a solid door with a small window. The door could be closed but not locked. The décor was battleship gray with a gray linoleum floor. Movies were shown on the unit from time to time, and the building had a law library for inmates who needed to conduct legal research.

Taking ten million dollars to build and operating for ten years, this fortress had yet to be broken out of.

The men on the sixth floor of this barless prison were in a federal witness protection program known as WITSEC, the Witness Security Program. The WITSEC unit housed informers and snitches. Segregation from the general prison population was a necessity. These prisoners were important witnesses in upcoming high-profile criminal trials, or they had information about future escape attempts or planned violence against guards or other prisoners. Sometimes prisoners got there by manipulating the system, insisting they had information to get special treatment and a change of scenery.

Of the dozen or so men in the MCC WITSEC unit, almost all had killed someone. Over half had at least one murder conviction. Many had escape attempts in their record, and several were members of the Aryan Brotherhood. For these reasons, the WITSEC unit was designated maximum security.

This wasn't Bernard Welch's first time in the WITSEC unit at the MCC. He had spent six months there in 1983 and really enjoyed the low-key treatment. Welch knew by now there was no chance of escape at the supermax federal prison in Marion, Illinois. It had been deemed the new Alcatraz, and he just couldn't find any weaknesses to exploit. Nobody ever broke out of there. The MCC in Chicago was another matter.

As during his past incarcerations, Welch had spent his first stint at the MCC studying. He closely studied the walls and windows of the building. He figured the weakest point in the structure was the area where the narrow, tempered glass windows were mortared into the poured concrete walls. The embrasure-style windows, mere five-inch-wide slits, were flush with the inside wall, but the outside wall tapered in at an angle to match the window thickness; much less than seven inches. This tapered wall was thinnest where it met the window. Welch knew this was something he could work with.

He talked his way back into the WITSEC program with his self-proclaimed knowledge of imminent prison breaks and violence to be visited upon the warden and staff of the federal penitentiary at Marion, Illinois, and the federal penitentiary in Atlanta, Georgia. Shortly after arriving in Chicago, Welch linked up with former Marion inmate Hugh Colomb.

Colomb earned his way into the MCC by also claiming to have important information to spill about past and future uprisings at Marion. While doing time in Illinois for a West Coast bank robbery conviction, Colomb stabbed a fellow prisoner to death in the cellblock area. He was convicted of voluntary manslaughter, making him one of the few WITSEC inmates who was not a convicted murderer.[6]

Welch and Colomb put together their escape plan, and the inmates in the WITSEC unit had a hand in helping Welch and Colomb escape, either by actively participating in the preparations or by playing dumb when the escape took place. George Newby, convicted of two homicides and drug dealing, procured hacksaw blades and drill bits from his girlfriend, DeAnna Yslava. In early May, she mailed a pair of gym shoes to Newby that had two hacksaw blades hidden in them. Larry Vaughn, a convicted murderer and former member of the Aryan Brotherhood, arranged for the getaway car and driver. Another inmate with Chicago contacts arranged three-way phone calls placed by Welch with Colomb on the second line and individuals outside the prison walls on the third line.

The individuals outside the MCC were just as crucial to the escape as the complicit inmates. To that end, the outdoor recreation area on the roof of the MCC proved to be a very important place. The WITSEC inmates would spend their allotted hour on the open roof some 275 feet above the busy Chicago streets. On the eleventh floor of a building across the street was a dance academy. The female students there would hoot and holler at the federal prisoners to get their attention. These women seemed more than willing to converse at a distance with the WITSEC inmates, who had the added perk of being able to wear civilian clothes all the time instead of prison-issue blue denim uniforms with stenciling on the shirt backs. The more enterprising WITSEC prisoners smuggled folded homemade signs up to the recreation roof with a phone number or address so they could be contacted by incoming calls or mail. And they were. Over a period of time, a couple of the women were recruited to smuggle contraband into the prison. Soon these women, along with prisoners' relatives, girlfriends, and other acquaintances became part of the escape plot.

Everything was in place as the violent thunderstorm pushed into the Loop area on May 14. The rain pounded heavily outside the concrete walls. Rumbles of thunder shook the floor occasionally, and the men amused themselves by counting the seconds from lightning flash to thunderclap. Welch walked through the commons area and climbed up the ten steps to the railed balcony that led to Colomb's room. He walked past the orange support column and directly under a canister light, which accented the thinning hair of the 45-year-old, as he neared the door with the white block numbers 602. As he entered the room a gigantic, nearby lightning strike blasted light through the tall narrow window of the outside wall. It was like an intense strobe or flash bulb had gone off in the small sleeping area, overwhelming the weak ceiling lights that stayed on until lights out. The noise and light show outside provided great cover for what they had planned.

Colomb had skipped the evening meal to spend time filing a point on the blunt end of a five-foot-long steel barbell. This barbell normally held the disc weights in the unit's workout room, but as a combination battering ram and pry bar, it was just the tool they needed. The momentum from the one-inch-thick rod would allow them to break and chisel their way through that vulnerable area in the MCC's walls, where the window met the concrete.

Welch and Colomb both donned the cheap brown cotton work gloves stolen from custodial supplies. These gloves would be especially handy for phase two of the operation, slipping down a rope made of bed sheets tied together. They had one sheet from each of the other inmates' beds, which had mysteriously disappeared, officials were told later, while their attention was elsewhere. An old vacuum cleaner motor that had been successfully altered to hold the smuggled masonry drill bits rounded out their arsenal of tools for the escape. This makeshift drill was what they used to make the starter holes in the concrete wall.

Welch started slowly, taking short, measured strokes to enlarge the pilot hole. Once the starter hole was satisfactory, Welch handed the bar to his more aggressive and impatient partner. Colomb went to work with a vengeance. After five minutes, he was sweating heavily. He removed his shirt, revealing the elaborate blue tattoo covering the breadth of his back. It was an intricate scene of a nude woman, a unicorn, and a warrior holding a battle-axe. This fantastic tattoo was his "colors," a badge of honor for services rendered on behalf of the Aryan Brotherhood.

Colomb continued ramming the twenty-pound solid steel bar into the joint beside the narrow window. He used leverage to break off pieces of the heat-treated glass window. His pace was rapid, but irregular; swing, thump…

swing, thump…swing, thump. Chunks of concrete and glass flew in every direction with each impact. The hole was getting bigger. Colomb staggered his rhythm, trying to mimic the thunder. Sweat ran down his muscled arms, over the jailhouse tattoos of swastikas, and spattering on the floor with each stroke of the bar into the wall.

Welch kept cracking the door opened between bangs to look toward the far end of the commons area. Inside the closed room, the bar hitting the wall was loud and strong enough to send vibrations through the solid walls of the facility. Welch knew the sound wouldn't carry upward easily, as two floors above them was the mechanical floor. The noise from heating and cooling fan motors, venting, and other building operations would drown out their pounding. Back in the WITSEC commons area, George Newby and another inmate, a motorcycle gang member with several homicide convictions, were doing their part. They got into a staged argument as one continuously and repeatedly vacuumed the carpet while the other kept turning up the television to presumably hear over the vacuuming. Plus the thunderstorm raging outside cooperated fully, masking more of the noise.

It would appear that luck was with Welch and Colomb, but they had more than luck on their side. Welch had paid out $50,000 for information, cooperation, and tools. Perhaps more importantly than anything else, Welch's money had paid for security. They knew the guard for their floor was being tasked elsewhere and would run into major distractions and interference from the WITSEC inmates. The guard's progress around the structure and up and down the elevator shaft was being monitored. If that lone guard had suddenly appeared on the sixth floor, Welch and Colomb would have been warned.

If other inmates of the MCC could hear the steel barbell bang against the wall of their escape-proof prison, they weren't telling anyone. There were rumors, and later statements, from federal investigators that staff members of the MCC had taken bribes of upwards of $25,000.

Yet, Welch was nervous. This escape was for him. This plan either worked, or he would spend the next 143 years to life in maximum security. And they were working on a floor full of snitches, protected snitches. And it was only a short time until next head count. They'd be missed. Then there would be a lockdown, a recount, and a search. They had to be outside and gone by then.

The hole was big enough for Colomb now but not for Welch, so Colomb continued to bang at the wall. He was admirably suited for this task because he had been lifting weights for years in prison. Small, wiry, with incredible staying power, he never seemed to tire. He continued his nonstop destruction of the wall until his larger partner could squeeze through. Finally, he laid down the steel bar and grabbed a piece of the half-inch reinforcing rod poking through the new opening. He used the dull hacksaw blade to cut through most of it and then bent it back and forth until the metal fatigued and broke. The last obstacle to their exit was cleared.

Welch and Colomb had earlier tied a dozen bed sheets end to end to make a continuous cloth rope. They threw it out the opening, and it unraveled as it fell toward the ground outside. Welch bent down to look out the hole. It was still raining, which was one of the reasons they had chosen this moment. Darkness and rain were good cover. He could see the trees and concrete plaza six floors below. A slip from this height and death would be a blessing. Bernard Welch took a long hard look at the rig that was supposed to support his 180-pound frame while he moved hand-over-hand down the knotted sheets in the pouring rain. He looked back at the jumble of jagged concrete and twisted steel reinforcing rod they had sawed and bent out of the way. The sheets were already pulling and stretching because of the weight of the rainwater.

They decided to use Plan B. Colomb went to the maintenance closet and dragged the floor buffer all the way into his room. They would use the 75-foot power cord as their rope to freedom. The electric cord was awkward but stout and as thick as a thumb. They wrapped the cord around the barbell close to the handle of the buffer then fed the plug end out of the hole and let it all spill down the outside wall. They lost two feet of cord when they had to tie it around the barbell. They took turns peering out the hole to see that the end of the cord was still fifteen to twenty feet above the courtyard. Knocking off seven feet of drop for dangling by their outstretched arms, they'd still fall at least ten feet onto concrete. At this point they couldn't worry about a broken ankle and having to limp or be dragged to the waiting car. They just had to do it.

Welch took a deep breath and went out the hole, feet first. The cotton work gloves would help him hold the slick electric cord. Once Welch had wormed his feet and legs through the opening, he grabbed the cord with both hands. He continued to wiggle past the sharp, jagged edges of the opening, cutting his bare arms and ripping his clothes as he struggled to squeeze through. Colomb made sure the steel barbell was wedged firmly across the hole while he waited for Welch's head to disappear. Then he followed his partner into the darkness.

The two men wrapped their legs around the power cord, attempting to lower themselves slowly, but the cord's smooth plastic coating, already gummy with years of floor wax, was now slick with rain. Even with the gloves, their trip down was more of a semi-controlled slide than the composed, hand-over-hand descent they had envisioned.

Welch tried to look down. The yellowish, sodium vapor, wall pack lights set into the building's ground level barely pierced the foggy rain. He couldn't see the end of the power cord. He concentrated on keeping his hands wrapped around the yellow cord in front of his nose. He briefly wondered if it would hold the 350 pounds of the two of them at once. He was sliding faster now. His legs and hands were getting tired and the cord slicker. The gray concrete walls were passing by quickly. He was brushing against the rough walls, and the skin on his face and arms grew raw from the contact. The knees of his pants were torn through. He was seeping blood from a thousand abrasions, but he felt no pain.

Welch squeezed his legs together and clamped down both hands to slow down. Suddenly, Welch's feet slid over the plug end of the electrical cord and met nothing but air. He closed his eyes and, in a last act of desperation, squeezed his hands together with all the strength he could summon so that he could stop when he reached the plug.

His hands quickly met the electric plug, which tore through his weakened grip, ripping a glove off. Then he was airborne in free fall. His legs were slightly bent, like springs. A blink later, his feet met the poured concrete of the plaza. Welch hit the ground hard and fell backward. Immediately he rolled away from the cord, because Colomb would land on him if he didn't move fast. He rolled over once, onto his stomach, and tried to stand but couldn't. His legs were tired and cramped from being clamped in a death grip around the electric cord. His hands were like claws and one was bleeding. Only now did he began to feel pain and let out a low groan.

Colomb landed just after Welch had rolled away. He managed to stay upright, but just barely. He bent over and grabbed his knees with both hands to stabilize himself. Still bent over, he shook his head in disbelief. He slowly straightened and looked up at the dangling wire swaying rhythmically above his head. They had only dropped about eight feet.

Lightning and thunder cracked above them, and the big city lights illuminated the clouds rolling overhead. The two wet men in torn and bloody clothes were alone outside the MCC. The storm was letting up. Colomb reached down and grabbed Welch by his shirt collar, lifting him into a standing position. Welch quickly looked around. To their left was Van Buren Street. That way led to the correctional facility's main entrance with a guard at the front door. Colomb looked over South Federal Street.

The getaway driver had been parked so he could easily observe what was going on in the MCC plaza. As soon as Welch and Colomb dropped to the ground, he started up the car and headed over to pick them up. As soon as Welch and Colomb spotted their ride, they slowly, almost drunkenly, jogged over to the waiting car.

Back on the sixth floor of the MCC, a WITSEC inmate entered the now empty cell and slowly pulled the floor buffer's wet electric cord up from the MCC plaza. He methodically coiled it on the handle of the floor buffer and pushed it back to the closet where it was stored. He didn't need to say a word as he passed by the other WITSEC inmates. The smile on his face said it all.

The news media had a field day reporting the daring jailbreak of Hugh Colomb, stick-up man, killer, and bank robber, and notorious millionaire burglar and murderer, Bernard C. Welch, from the escape-proof facility. In the media frenzy that followed, Chicago Metropolitan Correctional Center Warden O. C. Jenkins summed up his frustration best when he blurted out, "Why didn't somebody tell me who these bastards were?"

Officer James King sat at the sergeant's desk reviewing reports. He was back in uniform now, an acting shift supervisor at Germantown District Station, covering for his sergeant who was on extended sick leave at an out-of-state alcohol rehab facility. He should be on the road, tending to his flock of eighteen young officers, but he had to review the reports they wrote. The small cubicle where he sat was cramped, overflowing with papers, badly lit, and smelling of the last shift sergeant's dinner. The odor emanating from the trash can indicated that the meal had been Chinese.

"Jesus," King shook his head as he reviewed the reports. "Some of these guys had to have failed English in high school." He made corrections where he could and flagged some reports to go back to the officers for a rewrite. It was important for the reports to be factually correct as well as clear. These reports would be reviewed by lawyers, judges, and insurance companies.

The overhead speaker came to life just as he was wrapping up. "Corporal King, call on 2383."

King picked up the phone, punched the flashing button, and said, "Corporal King."

"Is this Detective James King of the Crimes Against Property Unit?"

"Used to be. The Crimes Against Property Unit was disbanded, and I'm no longer a detective, but I'm still James King," he explained.

"Good," the male voice sounded relieved. "Sir, I've called six numbers trying to find you. I'm Deputy US Marshal Patrick Dawkins in Chicago. My supervisor, Edward Kolster, told me to contact you."

Ed Kolster and King had been on the same shift at Bethesda District Station twelve years ago. Kolster had left to join the US Marshal Service. They still kept in touch.

"Oh yeah? Fast Eddie Kolster is your boss? How's he doing? Still got a quick temper?"

"Sir, he's fine, and yes, well, never mind. He is my supervisor."

King grinned. Kolster apparently had not changed.

"Listen, we have a problem," Dawkins continued. "Marshal Kolster said if anybody could help, it would be you."

King was puzzled. What problem could the US Marshal's office in Chicago have that he could help with?

"Okay, I'll try," he responded. "What's the problem?"

"Bernard Welch has escaped."

The blunt statement stunned King. Escaped? Bernard Welch? Not possible. Welch was supposed to be locked up tight in a federal pen somewhere in the Midwest.

Bernard Welch has escaped. That statement was so bizarre, so unexpected, King laughed. Not a little laugh, but big guffaws. He didn't mean to, but he could not control the involuntary outburst, and it took a while for him to stop. His eyes had begun to water, and he wiped the corners with his finger.

The earnest young law enforcement officer was silent on the other end of the line. King knew he should not have behaved so unprofessionally.

"Hey man, I'm sorry," he apologized. "It just caught me off guard. I know he's a crafty son of a bitch, but I never expected this. I thought we were done with him." King, regaining his composure and now fully aware of the scale and immediacy of the marshal's problem, slipped back into police mode. "Can you tell me what happened?"

Dawkins politely ignored King's outburst. "Well, as you may know, Welch was in the federal maximum security prison in Marion, Illinois. He wrote to a federal crime commission in Chicago and told them he had inside information about some prison escape that was in the planning stage. He said he could not talk about it in Marion, because he'd get shivved there. So, the crime commission brought him to the Metropolitan Correctional Center in Chicago's downtown Loop area to interview him. We know now that they were being snookered. It was all a hoax to get himself out of Marion, because no one escapes from Marion."

Dawkins continued matter-of-factly. "The rumor we've recently heard is that the whole thing was a setup for him to escape. We are told that he paid fifty grand to the Aryan Brotherhood to do the deal. You familiar with them?"

"Yeah, I've heard of them," King nodded. He had worked for the Washington, DC, prison system. He knew escapes were seldom a one-man operation and required careful planning.

Dawkins resumed. "This whole thing may have been planned by them. It certainly was well organized. What lends credence to the rumor is that when Welch escaped he was accompanied by a member of the Aryan Brotherhood. A tough customer, one of their enforcers, who was doing time for bank robbery, escape, voluntary manslaughter of a Marion inmate, and aggravated assault of a prison guard."

"The two of them were in the WITSEC unit and were able to get to an exercise room at night. They bashed a hole through the wall using a weightlifting bar. Then, during a thunderstorm, they shinnied down an electrical cord, six floors to the street level. No one saw them because of the storm, and it was late. They were in civilian clothes but had no money that we know of. They must have had a ride waiting because they disappeared."

King broke in. "When did this happen?"

"Day before yesterday."

"Okay, so what do you want from me?"

"Marshal Kolster said you knew more about Welch than anybody. Some of us think he'll head north, into the woods of the Upper Peninsula of Michigan, or maybe into Canada. What do you think? Where is he most likely to go?"

King thought for a second. "Well, I knew a lot about him as of three, no, five years ago. When he was a teenager in New York state, he was a hunter and a trapper, but that was a long time ago. He's older now and loves the good life. I can tell you this, he's smart. Wherever you expect him to go, he'll go the other way."

"Let's see," King paused again, thinking. "He doesn't drink, smoke, or do drugs. He's always worked alone, so I think he'll shake his Aryan Brotherhood pal early on. Welch is an East Coast boy. He's never really gone too far from his territory. If I had to guess, I think he'll head back east, somewhere between Virginia and New York, but he won't go back to where he's been arrested. At least he never has. So that rules out Virginia, Washington, DC, Maryland, New York, and West Virginia. It also excludes Minnesota, but that was just for sales, not theft. So that leaves what? Pennsylvania, Delaware, New Jersey?"

"That's a lot of territory, Detective King." King could hear Dawkins scribbling on a pad of paper, and he knew that meant Dawkins was on speakerphone and others were probably listening in.

"Not really. Now, this is all a guess," King continued, warming to the topic. "He likes large metropolitan areas where he can fade into the crowd. So that's what? Philadelphia, Wilmington, Delaware, and northern New Jersey, up near New York City,

The more King talked, the more he remembered. "I'll add this. He's got a pattern, and he always follows it because it's been successful, and here it is. I think he will be living in an apartment in some out-of-the way area, probably with a woman. He'll be using an assumed name until he can beg, borrow, or steal a legitimate name. He'll be driving a stolen car. He likes Fords and Mercedes. He'll be doing house burglaries, because that's all he knows. He'll drive fifty to one hundred miles from where he's living to do a burglary. Tell your people to look for early evening house burglaries with cut phone wires in really good neighborhoods around big cities. He'll steal good silver, good jewelry, and good antiques. When you find a rich neighborhood where antiques are being stolen, you'll find him."

King stopped but quickly started again. "The most important thing is he'll have a gun. A pistol, whatever he can get. And he'll use it. You know that?"

"Yes sir, we know that. So to recap, you think East Coast states, probably Delaware, Pennsylvania, or New Jersey, near New York City. Rich areas, cut telephone wires, and antiques."

"That's my best guess. One more thing. If he owes money to the Aryan Brotherhood, the only place he might have stashed any money is his family home in upstate New York, near Rochester." King could hear Dawkins writing again. At least he was taking notes.

"Okay, thanks Detective King. You've been a tremendous help." The young man hung up.

King sat at the desk, thinking. "Jesus, was it five years ago? It seems longer." Actually it was closer to ten years. It had all started in 1976, at that old police station in Richmond, Virginia.

Detective Sergeant William Rollins was waiting to testify in federal district court in Washington, DC, when a US Marshal found him and instructed, "You must come with me." The marshal informed Rollins that Bernard Welch and Hugh Colomb had escaped from a federal prison in Chicago and were headed for parts unknown, and they wanted Rollins involved with the case. Reports surfaced identifying Welch and Colomb buying camping supplies and empty gasoline cans in downstate Illinois. Rollins followed the marshal, and the DC case he was about to testify for was postponed.

Rollins worked for the Washington, DC, Metropolitan Police Department and, as such, could be considered not only a municipal civil servant but a federal one as well. Welch's murder of Halberstam was committed in Washington, DC, proper, so it was handled as a federal capital offense. Rollins was the first police officer at the scene of Welch's arrest in 1980 and was thought of as the best candidate to help chase down Welch now.

Rollins was put on leave from his DC Metro Police duties and immediately sworn in as a deputy US Marshal. He was assigned to work directly for the US attorney's office and the Marshal's Service paid his Metro Police salary. His first act as a deputy marshal was to call the Metropolitan Correctional Center (MCC) in Chicago and request that Warden O. C. Jenkins lock down the entire floor that Welch and Colomb escaped from and that nothing be touched or moved.

Rollins was on a plane that night to Chicago. He went immediately to the

MCC at 71 Van Buren Street. When he arrived at the facility and walked around the perimeter of the building and the plaza, the escapees' makeshift bedsheet rope was still hanging from the hole in the wall of the sixth floor. Rollins checked in with the desk guards and stated his business, but they barred him from entering the facility.

Rollins figured the staff here thought that this jailbreak was going to be handled as an internal matter, and they didn't realize it had gotten much bigger than that. Rollins said, "That's okay. I'll go to the US attorney's office here in Chicago and get a search warrant." In short order, Warden O. C. Jenkins was notified, and Rollins was let in.

Rollins started by interviewing all the inmates in WITSEC at the MCC. In the first go-round, all of them claimed to have no direct knowledge of or involvement with the escape. Then, with some persuasive interrogation techniques, such as using a polygraph and the threat of being sent back into the general prison population, the truth started to materialize little by little. A story developed that involved inmates, relatives, girlfriends, hidden hacksaw blades, drill bits, illegal drugs, homemade drills, and worst of all, bribery and the involvement of guards.

It became obvious to Rollins that some money had changed hands and guards were looking the other way when drugs and tools for escape were smuggled into the prison. Rollins informed the chief correctional supervisor in no uncertain terms that some of the guards under his command were going to jail. The questioning of these correctional officers concluded with a dozen arrests and a half dozen prosecutions.

After Rollins completed his interviews and submitted his findings, he returned to Washington to check in with the US attorney's office. Deputy Assistant US Attorney General Jay Stephens, who was the prosecutor in Welch's murder trial in 1981, stated, "We viewed Welch as a very clever, bright, conniving individual who has escaped from secure facilities before and who has every intention of attempting to escape again. We are doing everything we can to get him back." Indeed, Rollins was sent off again to resume the search for Welch and Colomb, a search that would take him through twenty-nine states and Canada in less than four months.

Bernard Welch and Hugh Colomb worked their way north from the Chicago Loop. The getaway car driver hauled the two escapees up into southern Wisconsin, staying close to the shore of Lake Michigan. He stopped in

Rochester, a small town of 1,200 west of Racine, Wisconsin, handed over some cash, and dropped them off. Arrangements had already been made for their stay in a rental apartment with a detached garage. It was a nice setup they could make use of until they got on their feet and establish new identities. They had very little cash, no car, and no identification.

Welch decided to get back to what he did best, burglary. Starting at a local hardware store, he bought two pairs of cheap brown cotton work gloves, a pair of small side-cutter pliers, a medium-sized flat-blade screwdriver, and a penlight with batteries. Welch started with a few burglaries in Shorewood, an affluent suburb north of Milwaukee, only thirty miles away. He was lucky enough to pick up some hidden cash taped to the bottom of dresser drawers. Even more importantly, he was able to steal a couple of handguns. There would be one for him and one for Hugh. He'd make another trip to the hardware store for ammunition.

On May 23, Colomb pulled an armed robbery of Kohl's grocery store in Shorewood. Here was an escaped convict from a federal prison, tattoos all over his body and forearms, brandishing a handgun in a daytime stick-up only one hundred miles north of the prison he broke out of nine days ago. There were at least two eyewitnesses—the robbed checkout clerk and a customer he threatened. If authorities had been paying attention, this crime clearly indicated the location of Hugh Colomb, but it went totally unnoticed by federal law enforcement authorities as they focused their attention on areas such as Washington, DC, Duluth, Chicago, southern California, and upstate New York.

Welch, the non-drinker, was having a hard time putting up with Colomb, who seemed to get drunk every night. Such behavior could cause major problems in the small town where they were trying to blend in. Colomb couldn't see that they couldn't talk at all with anyone about their past life, much less shout about it at night when he was plastered. He was just not sophisticated enough to live under a false identity very long. Welch knew he had to leave, and soon. The prospect of them splitting up had become the main topic of Colomb's rants. Welch had to get a car and a sizeable amount of cash so he could head back East and start making the big money again.

On the night of May 25, Welch was prospecting again. He spotted three unoccupied houses in Shorewood right next to each other. He robbed the first house of $5,300 worth of jewelry. The second house wasn't a very good producer, but when he was cruising through the kitchen of the third house, he spotted a set of car keys hanging from a corkboard. Jackpot! He needed a car; it may as well be a BMW. Welch also took $3,000 worth of silver and gold from that house before driving off in his new car.

Now Welch had a car and a good reason—Colomb's robbery and other high-profile hijinx—to leave the area. He knew it was only a matter of time before the cops followed Colomb right to their doorstep. He wished Hugh Colomb well but dare not let him know where he was headed.

He piled his belongings and burglary loot into the stolen 1977 BMW and headed south toward Chicago to get around the tip of Lake Michigan. He then headed east toward Pennsylvania. Welch went to Greensburg, a small town southeast of Pittsburgh. He knew there was no reason for anyone to look for him there. He had no connection to that area whatsoever. It was just an outer suburb of the metropolitan Pittsburgh area where he could prey on homeowners. Like before, he would hit the richest suburbs and drive away with the goods to sell at a later date.

On June 1, Bernard Welch Jr. and Hugh Colomb were placed on the US Marshals Service "15 Most Wanted Fugitives" list. California Supreme Court Justice Malcolm Lucas was informed that Colomb, who had promised to kill him if he ever got out, was no longer in custody. In 1977, Lucas was a US District Court Judge and had sentenced Hugh Colomb to twenty-five years in prison for an armed bank robbery. It was the maximum sentence he could hand down. The federal investigators believed Welch and Colomb might be headed to California at this point, and Judge Lucas was assigned extra security to protect him against the threatened retaliation.

Robert C. Leschorn, the search coordinator for the US Marshals Service, announced that Welch was reportedly seen in Duluth, Minnesota, and the Marshals concentrated their effort in that area. They also believed he changed his hairstyle by getting a perm. They thought he could even be wearing tortoise shell glasses to alter his appearance along with the curly hair.

A vehicle matching the description of the getaway car used in the MCC prison escape was reportedly seen in Duluth. John Hamilton, Linda Hamilton's brother, received an unexpected visit from a S.W.A.T. team, which was under the mistaken impression that he and his family were being held hostage by

Welch. They broke his door in and handcuffed everyone in the house until they sorted out who was who. They found no sign of Welch or Colomb.

By this time, Welch had made it to Greensburg, Pennsylvania, with a quick stop in Carlisle to steal the license plates from a parked car. He found an unsuspecting elderly couple, Dick and Janet Pershing, and rented their upstairs apartment. They were very pleased to get two months rent in advance, plus their deposit. Welch also created a cover story that was virtually impossible to check out. He used Robert Wilson as his alias, and he claimed to have worked at or on airfields for a number of years in Saudi Arabia, saving up tons of money since there was nowhere to spend it there. Now he was back in the United States to take a year off. A very plausible tale, and it was a glamorous cover story for the ladies, too.

On June 22, the US Marshals Service announced it believed Colomb was still with Welch. Since both men have extensive outdoor and camping background, it was thought they may have entered the one-million-acre Boundary Waters Canoe Area Wilderness in northern Minnesota to escape to Canada. Welch had made numerous visits to this area when he summered in Duluth. Chester Lonczak, the chief law enforcement officer for the Forest Service in Minnesota warned B.W.C.A.W. employees to be on the lookout for suspicious canoe campers. Wanted posters of both Welch and Colomb were nailed up at entrance points and in towns near the Boundary Waters. Lonczak said, "Indications are that he might go up there again. If they had a canoe, they could go anywhere."

The US Marshals Services director, Stanley E. Morris, publicized the offer of a $25,000 reward for information leading to the arrest of Bernard C. Welch and a $10,000 reward for the arrest of Hugh Colomb. Morris added, "It is not known at this time whether Colomb and Welch are still traveling together. It is possible that these two individuals have separated." Anyone having information regarding the whereabouts of Welch or Colomb was advised to contact the nearest US Marshals Service office.

US Marshals Service spokesman John Dempsey stated on June 23 that a special task force was still trying to find Welch. "The case is moving along, and we just hope the reward will shake something loose. Hundreds of leads have been followed up, and there's nothing conclusive yet."

As Welch settled into his new life in Greensburg, Pennsylvania, he started dating Janice Roos, a recently divorced sales clerk who worked at a local store. She was slim and very pretty. Janice started seeing a lot of Welch, whom she knew as Bob Wilson. Janice soon moved into the third-floor apartment that he rented from the Pershings. Janice was easily convinced that Bob Wilson was living off his savings from that Saudi airport job, and right now he didn't really need to work. The hobby he had of buying and selling coins, jewelry, and antiques seemed lucrative, but his hours were very strange.

On June 30, 1985, Welch burglarized a doctor's home on the other side of Pittsburgh in Hampton Township and, along with many other items, stole a handgun. The Pennsylvania Turnpike was very handy for Welch's thefts, as he was only seven minutes from the on ramp.

Near Hampton Township was another township by the name of McCandless. It was actually a city of 20,000 and just ten miles north of Pittsburgh. McCandless Police Chief Patrick McCabe mulled over a group of eight high-value, sophisticated burglaries that had taken place in his jurisdiction recently. The houses were empty, the phone lines were cut, and the items stolen consisted of watches, jewelry, antiques, gold, firearms, and sterling silver. Silver-plated items were left behind, set back in their places upside-down. He wondered what type of calculating crook was responsible for these crimes and where could he have come from?

Greensburg, Pennsylvania
August 6 and 7, 1985

Bernard Welch was having a good day. In the morning, he sorted through the rings, watches, and jewelry he had stolen from the trendy homes in the Pittsburgh suburbs. He had yet to find a suitable place where he could melt down the silver and gold he was accumulating from his latest evening forays. He was in a rental apartment at the moment. The apartment gave him a home base to work out of although not a lot of storage or workspace. But no more cheap motels and moving every few days. Greensburg, this little hick town just a few miles off the Pennsylvania Turnpike, was only a thirty-mile run to Pittsburgh. While Pittsburgh itself was an industrial rust bucket, it still had wealthy suburban areas with old money. Those places had loads of silver, jewelry, coin collections, and antiques. He had done alright there so far. Not as good as the DC area, but not bad for starters.

For now, his only source of income came from selling any precious stones he could pop out of stolen jewelry, but he was running out of customers. There weren't that many jewelers around who would buy loose stones, and if he kept going back to the same ones, they'd start getting suspicious. He decided to start selling off the valuable coins. Even though they took longer to sell than the gems and would only bring in enough to keep him going for a few weeks, coins were a lot easier to get rid of. Tomorrow he'd have to start hustling coins and looking for an isolated garage to rent, so he could start melting stuff down. He was getting such a big stockpile of silver and gold that his new girlfriend and roommate, Janice Roos, would get suspicious if she discovered it.

By the time he organized the coins to sell the next day and then repacked the remaining loot into several boxes and tucked them away into their hiding place in the ceiling, it was almost time to go. He had a dinner date with Janice. She got off work at six o'clock, and he was to meet her at a local steak house. He showered, dressed, and pulled up to the restaurant at exactly six-thirty. Janice was already in the parking lot, waiting in her car. Being that it was a Tuesday night, the place was not crowded. They had a nice dinner and were finished in an hour.

After dinner, he followed her back to their apartment. She parked in the one space allotted to the apartment. He pulled his BMW in close behind her Toyota. The apartment was really the third floor of an old house. The only way up to it was by the rear steps. The owners, Dick and Janet Pershing, lived on the first floor and were sitting on their back porch. Welch and Janice could not pass them without speaking.

"Oh, hi, Robert. Hi, Janice," called out Mr. Pershing. Welch had rented the apartment using an alias, so the Pershings only knew him as Robert Wilson.

"Hello," Janice, who led the way up the stairs, answered for them. "Enjoying the evening?"

Janice quickly found herself in a conversation about Mr. Pershing's garden. She was from the area, so the conversation soon evolved into local issues. Welch listened to the three of them chatter with a small smile on his lips. The others thought he was enjoying the banter, but the smile was just a mask.

While he listened without paying attention, Welch's mind was working on a different level. As an escaped convict, Welch always had to be on alert. He had watched to be sure he was not being followed on the way back from the restaurant. When he parked his car in the alley behind the Pershings' house he had taken in everything in the area. All was normal. There was nothing out of place, and there were no strangers around.

He had chosen his hideout well. As the Pershings and Janice chattered, he had to laugh at them and their simple, boring lives. They were so innocent. They had believed without question that he was Robert Wilson, taking a year off from government work. He said he worked at an airport in Saudi Arabia for two years and was tired. He told them he had saved enough money to hold him over if he was careful. This was a vacation for him, and when his money ran out he'd go back to work at the airport. He even hinted he worked for the CIA. Everybody understood that when you had a job like that, you couldn't discuss details. It would be unpatriotic of them to ask questions. They bought the con, hook, line, and sinker.

He immediately won the old couple over that first day back in June. He had walked up to inquire about their furnished room for rent. After showing him the third floor apartment, they stated the rent was $250 a month, two months in advance, plus a one-month security deposit. They were reserved and a little suspicious of him, until he peeled off $750 in cash (he had sold some diamonds to a jeweler earlier in the day) and handed it to them without saying a thing. Their eyes had widened in shock when they saw his wad of cash. They were so shocked that they didn't even ask to see any ID.

Janice had also been easy to fool. He knew she would be from the moment he met her at the mall. When she met him, she probably thought she had finally found her true love in this dinky burg. Janice was just as easy to con as all the other small town women he had used. These women believed anything you told them, especially if they thought they were in love. That's why Welch had never trusted women. They were ruled by emotion and that made them stupid.

The sun was almost down now. As usual, Welch pretended to be interested and smiled when necessary, but he was quiet while the others talked. He finished the lemonade and made an excuse for Janice and himself to leave. They said their goodbyes to the Pershings and climbed the two flights of stairs to the third floor. He followed Janice up the stairs, focusing on her long legs and short skirt. She was nice looking and had a nice body. After being in prison for five years, this relationship was not bad, for starters.

At the top landing, Welch and Janice entered the sparsely furnished garret apartment. It wasn't much, just a large room with a bathroom, kitchenette, and a tiny bedroom. A musty smell permeated the place, as if it had been closed up for years. All the furniture was old, as were the yellowish white curtains that hung on the room's four windows. One of the windows in the big room had an air conditioner stuck in it. Being on the top floor, the room was always hot in the summer. The air conditioner ran on low full-time. Welch walked over to the small, color TV and turned it on to try to catch some local news. He looked around the room; nothing had been moved since he left. He didn't trust landlords. They liked to snoop. So did curious girlfriends. That's why he carefully hid his loot.

The apartment wasn't the best setup for him, but it would do until he could get back into full swing. He had to reestablish his trade routes and start unloading the antiques he'd accumulated. The silver was a problem. It was too bulky to hide easily, and he had no place to melt it down. He knew better when he took it that he had neither the room to store it nor the means to get rid of it. But old habits die hard, and it was just too good to leave behind. He'd think of something to do with the silver soon. Until then, he would start selling the coins tomorrow.

Damn! he thought as he settled in for the night. He had left the BMW parked behind Janice's car. A double-parked car might draw attention. Not good, especially since it was stolen. He had been driving the BMW too long, but he loved the sleek sports car and the way it handled. In it he could outrun and outmaneuver any cop car on the road. But he knew he should get rid of it and buy one with real tags. That was hard to do without legit ID. When he got some more cash, he would get Janice to buy a used car and tags for him. She'd do that for him now. Tomorrow, he'd get enough from the coin collections and tell Janice some story to convince her to buy the car. For now, he better move the car.

He just turned to go back outside when Janice emerged from the bathroom. She smiled seductively at him, and he smiled back, instantly forgetting about the double-parked car. Janice turned out the room's light and said sweetly, "Coming to bed?"

Lust overcame Welch's thoughts in that moment. He turned and began taking off his shirt. "Right behind you, honey." As he followed her into the bedroom, undoing his belt, he decided to get up early tomorrow to move the car. The car could wait; he was safe here.

Tuesday night slid gently into Wednesday morning. The town of Greensburg, Pennsylvania, was always quiet at night, especially on a summer weeknight. It was not really a big place, with a population of about 17,000. The development of shopping centers and malls outside the city limits had killed the old downtown retail area. Many of the stores were boarded up now. The closure of the coal mine and local factories had contributed to the economic decline. The place was now basically a suburb of Pittsburgh; a bedroom community of law-abiding citizens. There was not much for the local police to do after midnight, except to check the commercial area and respond to the occasional barking dog complaint. It was even slower in the winter. The barking dogs were kept inside.

Only five officers of the twenty-nine-man department worked the midnight trick in Greensburg. The two officers working this evening, Patrolman Paul Burkey and Officer Joe Niedzalkoski, rode together forty hours a week. They knew each other's habits and preferences to the point that they almost thought as one entity. Neither one liked the midnight shift, but it was a job in an area where jobs were scarce.

At roll call, Burkey told his partner about some information he received from Detective Tom Tridico, a retired Pennsylvania state trooper who was now the chief investigator for the Westmoreland County District Attorney's Office. Tridico informed Burkey that he had received a tip about a car in town with a stolen license plate. Nancy Peterson, a county employee, had told him about her friend, Janice Roos, who was dating and living with a man named Robert Wilson. According to Nancy, Wilson was a mystery man. He drove an expensive car and had money, but did not work. He had come to town a couple of months ago and spoke very little about himself or his past.

Peterson had been in Robert Wilson's apartment before Janice had moved in with him, and she noticed he had an awful lot of guns lying around, especially handguns. Recently, Janice told her that she and Wilson were taking a trip to Virginia in the next couple of days. Wilson had bragged to the women that he had taken someone on a trip once before and they never came back. Nancy, worried about her friend's safety, had asked Tridico to quietly check out Robert Wilson.

Nancy supplied Tridico with the man's name, address, and car information. He had checked the Pennsylvania license plate number, and it had come back as stolen. Tridico thought maybe Nancy had copied down the plate number incorrectly. After confirming that Burkey was working the night shift, Tridico gave Burkey the information and asked if he could check the license plate to make sure.

Niedzalkoski agreed it was something to do on what was expected to be another slow night. Officers Paul Cycak and Terry Immel, who were in the other two-man unit that evening, agreed to assist Burkey and Niedzalkoski if the license plate was indeed stolen.

Burkey and Niedzalkoski began their patrol at eleven o'clock. The two officers first checked the commercial area and the several bars that were still open. They knew from experience that the first hour of the night shift would be the busiest. That's when they might get a traffic violation, DUI, or domestic dispute. After midnight, they would have the quiet streets to themselves.

Twelve o'clock came and all was silent on the police radio. Burkey and Niedzalkoski decided to follow up on Tridico's information about the stolen license plate. According to Tridico the stolen Pennsylvania plate was on a blue BMW parked behind 545 West Newton Street.

The officers drove into an alley at the rear of the three-story boarding-house. It was a large, red brick residence built in the early 1900s, when Greens-burg was a happening place. Money was easy then; farms, factories, coal mines, and steel mills were booming. This old pile of bricks had once been some-body's dream home. Now, it was a tired building chopped up into apartments to pay the costs of upkeep for the people who owned it.

It took the officers less than a minute to spot the blue BMW 630CSi. It was parked in a graveled area with two other cars. The license plate on the German car matched the information Tridico had given them. Burkey picked up the scarred Motorola microphone from the dash and asked the Greensburg radio dispatcher for a wanted check on the plate. The officers waited silently in the darkness. In a few minutes the dispatcher responded back that the li-cense plate was listed to a Ford sedan, and the plate had been reported stolen from Thrifty Rent-a-Car in Carlisle, Pennsylvania, several weeks ago.

With the tag theft confirmed, the officers decided to check to see if the BMW was also stolen. They walked to the car and, using their flashlights, searched for the vehicle identification number plate located at the lower left corner of the windshield. The VIN plate wasn't there. German automakers did not place VINs in the same place as American automakers. Burkey and Niedzalkoski didn't know where to look. It would be necessary to head back to headquarters to do a little research before they could investigate further.

At the station, Burkey asked the dispatcher to run the tag listings of the other two cars parked beside the BMW, while Niedzalkoski searched the book that contained the information about VIN locations for any car ever made. As he waited for Niedzalkoski to finish, the dispatcher handed him the informa-tion for the other two cars. The brown Toyota was listed to Janice Roos, and the Chevy was owned by Richard and Janet Pershing. From his discussion with Tridico earlier, Burkey knew that Janice Roos was the mystery man's girlfriend and Mr. and Mrs. Pershing were the homeowners.

Niedzalkoski discovered BMWs had their VINs inscribed on the steering columns between the steering wheel and the dashboard. Fortified with that information, they hurried back to Newton Street. This time, they found the BMW's VIN and called it in. In minutes, the Greensburg dispatcher informed them that the VIN number was listed to a 1977 BMW 630 CSi coupe reported stolen from Shorewood, Wisconsin, near Milwaukee, in May. Burkey grabbed the radio and requested Cycak and Immel for backup.

Once Cycak and Immel arrived on the scene, the officers knocked on the rear door of the home. An older man in pajamas opened the door and identified himself as Dick Pershing, the owner of the property. Burkey informed Mr. Pershing that the police had received a parking complaint about the blue BMW behind the house. The old man explained the car belonged to his tenant, Robert Wilson, who lived upstairs in the third-floor apartment with his girlfriend, Janice Roos. Mr. Pershing showed them to the wooden exterior stairway that led to the second floor. At the top was a door that allowed entry to the second and third floor apartments. Inside that door was an entry hallway that led to internal stairs that led up to the third floor. Mr. Pershing told them the second floor was vacant, so they would have to knock loud if the exterior door was locked.

The four police officers climbed the wooden stairs to the second floor and found the door locked. Niedzalkoski rapped loudly on the exterior door. After several minutes, a woman in her late 20s, with tousled hair and wearing a T-shirt and brief shorts, opened the door.

Burkey stated that they were there in response to a parking complaint about the BMW, and they were looking for the owner. The woman said, as she pointed up the stairs behind her, that the car owner was her boyfriend, who was asleep in bed.

Niedzalkoski nodded to Burkey and they grabbed the female by her arms and pulled her outside onto the exterior stair landing. Cycak and Immel secured her, and she was warned to keep quiet. Burkey and Niedzalkoski reentered the short hall. The internal stairs were unlit, as was the apartment above. The two officers knew if the mystery man above had a gun he could ambush them and there was no place to hide. They climbed the stairway as silently as possible.

The apartment door at the top of the stairs was open. The officers entered the room and probed the dark place with their flashlight beams. Through an open bedroom door, they saw a white male lying in bed. The officers moved quickly to the bedroom and shined their lights on the man's face. Burkey announced, "Police, don't move!"

The male, with curly, reddish hair and wearing boxer shorts, lay on his back with his hands on his stomach. He did not move as he squinted his eyes in the flashlight glare. Burkey, in front of Niedzalkoski, turned on the room's ceiling light and saw a 9mm automatic pistol on the nightstand beside the man. He picked up the weapon and said, "Robert Wilson, you're under arrest for possession of a stolen vehicle." The man remained still.

"Get up slowly and turn around," Burkey commanded.

Niedzalkoski threw the shirt and pants draped over a nearby chair on the bed in front of the suspect. The officers instructed him to get dressed and put on his shoes before they handcuffed him. The officers then asked the man if he had any identification. He silently shook his head no.

At the bottom of the apartment stairs Cycak and Immel were waiting with Roos. She stood as if her bare feet were glued to the floor as she watched her handcuffed boyfriend being led down by the officers. There was a worried, mystified look on her face as the trio reached the bottom. The curly-haired suspect stopped in front of the woman and said, "Well, this is it, I guess. It's over now."

He turned to Officer Burkey. "Can I kiss her goodbye?"

Burkey nodded, and the man leaned forward awkwardly, his hands shackled behind him, and kissed her on the lips. She barely responded. There was no expression on her face as the man kissed her.

After the short kiss, Burkey and Niedzalkoski led their prisoner out the door into the night followed by Cycak and Immel. Janice Roos stood at the door watching her now former lover being escorted down the wooden stairway.

The suspect was placed in Cycak's cruiser and transported to the station. Burkey and Niedzalkoski stayed behind and called for a tow truck.

Back at the station, Burkey continued his report detailing the incident. He knew that Police Chief Dominick Felice would want the completed report when he arrived in the morning. As Burkey worked on his report, Cycak came to him to say that the suspect asked to call the US Marshal's office to "straighten this all out." Immel related the same request from the prisoner and added that the man had also said he "worked undercover for the US Marshals." Then Immel laughed. "You know what? I asked him his real name, and he said it was Fred Rogers. That's the guy on television that does that kids show,

Mr. Rogers' Neighborhood."

Burkey and Niedzalkoski agreed that a phone call to the US Marshals was worth a try. It was about four in the morning when Niedzalkoski called the US Marshals Office in Washington, DC. He described the situation. The person on the other end said he wasn't interested and hung up. Niedzalkoski immediately called back, but no one in the marshal's office answered.

If the marshals didn't care about this suspect maybe the FBI would. Cycak had recently met Hillary Jenkins, a new FBI agent living in Greensburg and a former Chicago police officer. Jenkins had given Cycak his home phone number. It was a federal offense to transport a stolen vehicle across state lines, and since the BMW had been stolen in Wisconsin and recovered in Pennsylvania, it was proper procedure to alert the feds. Cycak called Agent Jenkins at home.

Realizing that Robert Wilson and Fred Rogers were aliases, the officers also called Westmoreland County Detective Tony Marcocci at home. Marcocci was the city's fingerprint examiner. He had worked as an FBI fingerprint examiner for two years in Washington, DC, before coming to Greensburg.

Marcocci arrived at the station just before five in the morning. The suspect was removed from his holding cell and brought to the processing room. Marcocci spoke to the man in his smooth, gentle voice, asking the questions necessary to fill out the several fingerprint cards. When asked his name this time, the suspect stated, "Robert Leroy Wilson, but that's not my real name." He told Marcocci to call the "Head US Marshal in McLean, Virginia," to get his true name.

Marcocci was surprised at the statement, but let it pass as he continued to ask questions. Wilson said he was born in Minneapolis, Minnesota, on April 3, 1949. He had been living in Wisconsin until moving to Greensburg two months ago. In a momentary lapse of restraint, the suspect confided to Marcocci that he normally would have never kept a stolen car so long. It just looked like a million bucks and handled so responsively that he absolutely could not cut it loose. That hot blue 1977 BMW with the stolen plates turned out to be his downfall.

Marcocci rolled the prisoner's prints and took an ID photo. He returned Wilson to the holding cell then got to work classifying the suspect's prints. Once done, he called the twenty-four-hour office of the FBI's Expedite Service Unit and gave them the suspect's Henry print classification numbers. He also faxed the print card to the unit. Although the print classification numbers would not be able to put a specific name to the prints, they would narrow the list down to a much smaller group by looking at certain characteristics of the fingerprints. When the suspect's physical description was included, more individuals would be winnowed out. Of those remaining, the dead and incarcerated would be eliminated and hopefully only one suspect would be left.

FBI Agent Hillary Jenkins arrived by six o'clock and began questioning the suspect. Wilson again told the agent to call the US Marshals.

Detective Mike Dell emptied the contents of the stolen BMW and inventoried the items. A 32-caliber Colt revolver was found under the driver's seat. A fake mustache and a Rochester, New York, police lapel pin were in the glove box. In the trunk were two rifles, a box of handgun cartridges, bolt cutters, pliers, gloves, jewelry, loose gemstones in a half-gallon milk container, and a pair of stolen license plates from New York.[7]

The milk carton half full of loose gemstones had an interesting story behind it. Mr. Pershing and others had observed Robert Wilson taking strolls to the local county park with numerous milk cartons and a shovel. Apparently he was having trouble locating willing buyers for his unmounted gems and planned to dig them up later when he had a better setup.

The FBI Expedite Service Unit called back and informed Marcocci that the suspect in custody appeared to be Bernard C. Welch Jr., a recent escapee from the Metropolitan Correctional Center in Chicago. FBI Agent Jenkins confronted the suspect with this information, and he readily admitted that he was in fact Bernard Welch.

Marcocci again questioned Welch. Welch kept telling him to contact the US Marshals. From the little information he had, Marcocci guessed that Welch was in the federal Witness Protection Program. He was correct—Welch *had* been in the Witness Security Program. Now the US Marshals only wanted Welch back in custody. They no longer had any use for information Welch might give them. The US Marshals and the Justice Department would never again believe anything Welch said.

During his interrogation, Marcocci did get Welch to sign a consent form allowing his third-floor apartment at 545 West Newton Street to be searched. During the search on August 7, ten lawmen— six local police officers, one FBI agent, and three US Marshals—generated an inventory of 811 stolen items. The items included watches, antiques, artwork, sporting goods, handguns, long guns, ammunition, coin and stamp collections, $375 in rolled coins,

$450 in cash, 93 silver dollars, 230 silver half-dollars, 329 silver quarters, and 645 silver dimes. There were hundreds of pieces of jewelry and more than 50 men's gold class rings. Most of the jewelry had the precious stones removed, and some individual items on the list were valued in excess of $1,000. The value of the stolen property totaled up at $175,000. This figure did not include the loose gemstones in the car or the unaccounted for precious stones that Welch buried.

Burkey and Niedzalkoski received multiple phone calls that day informing them they had captured one of the US Marshals most wanted fugitives. Burkey could only respond with a simple, "Incredible!"

They finished their report and turned it in to the chief. Police Chief Dominick Felice congratulated the two for a good investigation and praised them in the press, "They were lucky they weren't blown away by this guy. They didn't know who he really was, but they are good, well-trained police officers."

On the morning of the August 7, Welch was taken to the Westmoreland County Detention Center to await arraignment. Magistrate Michael Moschetti set his bail at one million dollars.

US Associate Deputy Attorney Jay Stephens, who had prosecuted Welch in the 1981 murder trial, was informed of the events that lead to Welch's arrest that day. Stephens probably summed it up best when he dryly remarked, "I don't think it was Bernard Welch's finest hour."

Later that day, US Marshals escorted a sullen, shackled Bernard Welch to a chartered plane that would fly him back to the federal penitentiary at Marion, Illinois. He would stay in that prison until his death in 1997.

Epilogue

Bernard Welch was unceremoniously dragged back to the Marion penitentiary in Illinois. He got a "Cool Hand Luke" reception from the inmates but found out in short order that his services were no longer required in the Witness Security Program. Escapes and escape attempts are grounds for immediate expulsion from witness protection. Welch found himself back on the high-security/high-profile K block at Marion with the federal spies, serial murderers, and celebrity felons. By now, even the less sophisticated inmates realized that his title of "witness" or "snitch" was just a charade to get preferential treatment and set up opportunities for his own escape.

Sergeant Michael V. Dell of the Grantsburg Police Department met with Lieutenant William Mullen and Sergeant Rak Micknowski of the Pittsburgh Police Department on August 16, 1985. Bernard Welch was also a suspect in a recent burglary/rape in the city of Pittsburgh. Several items taken in the search of Welch's Greensburg apartment were signed over to the Pittsburgh police officers for evidence in their rape case. The stolen goods would be taken to the Allegheny County Crime Lab to be analyzed and compared to crime scene evidence.

On August 27, 1985, the Greensburg Police Department exhibited the stolen items found in Welch's rented apartment and stolen car. The display of the property in the Greensburg City Hall was on a much smaller scale than the immense 1981 exhibit in Washington, DC. There were only about 825 inventoried items instead of 16,000. There were no long lines of victims waiting for hours to see if their stolen property was on display. "We don't want everybody and their brother viewing this," Police Chief Dominick Felice stated. The stolen items were only viewed by law enforcement officials and victims who brought along burglary reports with specific descriptions of missing articles.

Peace officers and burglary victims from all over showed up to view the property. People came from Rochester, New York; Pittsburgh, McCandless, Ross, Shaler, and Hempfield Townships in Pennsylvania. Victims and police also came from the towns of Avalon, Edgewood, Sewickley, and Greensburg, Pennsylvania. The police department in the Milwaukee suburb of Shorewood, Wisconsin, sent a detailed list of stolen items from their jurisdiction to be compared with the recovered merchandise. Over 70 percent of the displayed goods were reclaimed by the owners, and more than 40 burglaries were solved. This was largely due to the fact that Welch wasn't yet smelting silver and gold and was having trouble moving the stolen goods.

In October 1985, Hugh T. Colomb Jr. was arrested after a failed bank robbery in Canton, Mississippi. He was tried for the May 23, 1985, Kohl's store robbery in Shorewood, Wisconsin, on November 2, 1987. Welch was called to testify on Colomb's behalf. Having Welch and another former MCC prisoner flown to Milwaukee for the trial, along with the beefed up security needed in the courtroom to accommodate their appearance, cost the taxpayers of Milwaukee $45,000.

A week after the end of Colomb's trial, Welch sent a letter to the *Milwaukee Journal Sentinel* thanking the taxpayers of the city for sending him on an all-expenses-paid vacation from Marion Federal Penitentiary. He stated, "At this time, I would like to say I really enjoyed my trip to Milwaukee, and I considered it a vacation. I like the way no expense was spared and the prosecutor went first class all the way. I thank the people of Milwaukee for the money to make this all possible. Feel free in the future to call me back any time to testify." Noting that a Learjet transported him to Milwaukee, Welch added, "Learjets are the way to travel, but in the future could you please have a helicopter fly me from the airport to the county jail instead of a caravan of cars? Also, since I'm from the Northeast, could you please arrange my menu to have some seafood from New England?"

On June 15, 1992, the National Rifle Association was embarrassed to announce that Bernard C. Welch Jr. had signed up for and received a temporary membership in the NRA through the mail. Welch was still incarcerated at the maximum-security federal penitentiary at Marion, Illinois. The National Rifle Association rescinded Welch's membership as soon as they were informed that he was a murderer serving a life sentence in a federal prison. The NRA's by-laws ban felons from becoming members.

At the end of the civil trial brought against Bernard Welch and Linda Hamilton by Elliott Jones Halberstam, US District Court Judge Aubrey E. Robinson Jr. ruled that the estate of Michael Halberstam should be awarded $5.7 million. Between the IRS, this civil judgment, other judgments and liens, Linda owed various people and agencies almost $13.5 million. The verdict meant the Internal Revenue Service would be watching Linda and seizing any money she earned. It was a form of imprisonment from which Linda Hamilton could never hope to escape and would dog her until the end of her life in 2005.

But, there was one unintended consequence of the civil trial that Elliott Jones Halberstam could not foretell, but in which her deceased husband, Dr. Michael Halberstam, would probably have rejoiced.

In the 1970s, '80s, and '90s, terrorists were killing Americans in the Middle East. People were suing and winning large judgments against governments, such as Iran and Libya, whose sponsorship of terrorism and terrorist organizations, such as the Palestinian Liberation Organization and Hamas, had previously been ignored. The leaders in foreign lands seemed to have an immunity from the world's courts, that is, until a father and daughter legal team, Lewin and Lewin of Washington, DC, read the case of Halberstam vs. Hamilton.

The Halberstam vs. Hamilton decision declared Linda Hamilton a coconspirator in a joint venture with her criminal lover. Though she was not at the scene of the murder, Linda, as determined by the ruling, had knowledge of her partner's illegal activities, helped make those activities possible, and shared in the rewards.

Lewin and Lewin applied this principle to one of their civil cases. Seventeen-year-old, Brooklyn-born David Boim was murdered by Hamas in Israel, and his parents were suing. In this case, Lewin and Lewin named not only Hamas, but also its American-based support group. There were large donors, banks that held and transferred money around the world, and the financers who managed the funds. The people and organizations that gathered, controlled, and moved the donations claimed it was going only to Middle East charities. The court found that they knew what type of outfits the PLO and Hamas were and what the funds would really be used for.

The terrorism supporters in America lost. In 2004, the $156 million verdict was the largest US civil suit awarded that year. Funds and support for Hamas and other such nefarious groups dried up in America, dealing terrorists a crippling financial blow. This court decision is still being cited to combat the funding of terrorism.

On May 7, 1997, Bernard Welch was sent to the prison hospital complaining of severe chest pains, shortness of breath, and other symptoms. He died of heart failure on June 21, 1997, after six weeks in the US Medical Center for Federal Prisoners at Springfield, Missouri. He was 57. His body was cremated, and the ashes were given to his sister, Marilyn.

* * * * *

"I wonder what I'd be doing if that doctor hadn't hit me with his car. One thing for sure, the big house [in Great Falls, Virginia] would have been finished by now. All that money and I never had a chance to use the sauna or the swimming pool or that beautiful bathroom with the whirlpool tub. If I ever get out, I swear I'm going to break into that house one night just to see what it looks like finished…I'll take their silver and jewelry, too."

— Bernard C. Welch Jr. in a December 16, 1981,
letter to Linda Hamilton

This book is an account of a five-year crime spree that roiled the Washington, DC, area's four million citizens and ended like a Greek tragedy. In this story, there was only one hero, Dr. Michael Halberstam, who fought to protect his wife and home. There was one villain, Bernard C. Welch, a sociopath, murderer, rapist, thug, and thief. The rest were a Greek chorus of victims—Dr. Halberstam's wife and family; the three-thousand-plus victims of burglary, rape, and assault; and the many police officers who worked valiantly to solve the crimes. All were the innocent victims of a clever, soulless predator. The culpability of Bernard Welch's common-law wife, Linda Hamilton, is up for debate. Certainly, a civil court deemed her as being part of Welch's criminal enterprise, as did the Internal Revenue Service. Her connection to Welch doomed her and her three children to a life of poverty and struggle.

Bernard Welch considered himself invincible in the criminal world. If the amount of property he stole and the amount of grief he caused is any measure, then he does rank at the top of his class, a class of dishonor. In my estimation, he was nothing more than a clever and compulsive thief who enjoyed what he did.

Welch did not have the excuse of being hungry, lacking job skills, or a drug habit as an explanation for his actions. If we could see into his black heart, we would find that he derived pleasure in outsmarting the system, besting the laws, victimizing the innocent, and escaping the prisons he was placed in.

Some have commented that he was smart enough to have made it by going straight. Probably true, but even had he done so he would have become entangled in his own ego. Had he been a lawyer, he would have eventually been disbarred. Had he worked on Wall Street, he would have someday been charged with stock manipulation. Had he been in the military, there is no doubt he would have been court martialed. Whatever was in his twisted psyche that made him believe he was invincible also doomed him to eventual failure.

As a young man, Welch was a loner who spent much time in the rural areas of upstate New York, where he learned to hunt and trap animals. Not only did he make money from his prey, he also sharpened his skills as a hunter, craftier than his quarry. He must have relished the ego boost, gratification more important than the money he received for the pelts.

It was said at the time that Welch ignored the game laws in his hunting endeavors, failing to obtain required permits, taking animals out of season, stealing from other hunter's traps. and going over the legal limits. It is not far-fetched to believe he enjoyed this aspect of avoiding authority and being a law unto himself.

Looking back on his life, it is my opinion that he transferred all of these early traits from the animal world to human society. He certainly considered his human victims as prey to profit from as he had done in the woodlands. He used others to aid in his schemes just as he would employ hunting dogs. He used Anne Marie Hulbert (his wife), two fellow escapees, Mary Boone (the educator in Richmond), Linda Hamilton and her family, and Janice Roos to further his activities. He then abandoned them without a second thought when their usefulness was over. Up until the time of his final capture, Welch was still the loner, hunting for a living, being outside of the law. Only his location and prey had changed.

Some people speculated that the police might have admired Welch for his skills as a thief. To think that would, essentially, grant him the criminal world's equivalent of "rock star" status. We, the police, certainly did not admire him, but we did recognize that he was good at what he did. To suggest that we admired him would be akin to saying an oncologist admired cancer because of its devious and silent methods of causing pain and death. Welch was like a cancer in society, someone to be despised, not lauded.

One of the major difficulties in not capturing Welch sooner lay in the nature of police department organization in those days. The metropolitan area of "greater DC" was fractured jurisdictionally into a dozen or so separate police entities that seldom communicated with each other. Welch's method of operation took advantage of this inherent weakness as no other criminal had ever done.

Traditionally, the vast majority of crime is local. Criminals tend not to do their nefarious work outside of the areas they are familiar with. Therefore, local police departments are structured to combat local crime. In the past, there was little communication between the various police departments in the Washington, Maryland, and Virginia areas. These departments were like families living in a high-rise apartment building. They all lived together but seldom spoke to one another.

That is to say, there was little formal communication. There was always informal, officer-to-officer interaction, just as in an apartment building, where neighbors meet on the elevator. This mostly occurred when criminals overlapped the political boundaries. Officers working the street have always been aware that the bad guys are not concerned with invisible borders. The street cops talk to their compatriots across those invisible lines in an effort to stop crime.

Old-time officers, who rose through the ranks and were in charge during the 1970s, looked askance at this officer-to-officer, cross-border contact. Although they did not forbid it, they were suspicious of the motives behind it. Police departments and police, in general, tend to be a closed-mouth lot. They keep their crime problems to themselves. Not only does it look bad if the news media discovers a crime trend, but the media habitually plays it up to sell papers or lead the six o'clock news. While publicizing criminal events is the media's job, they sensationalize the story, often making the problem worse than it really is. This makes the local police seem mismanaged and ineffective. It also gives other, would-be transgressors ideas that they would never have otherwise conceived. Thus, a spate of copycat crimes can occur, adding to the public hysteria and further muddying the investigative waters.

One of the realities that police old-timers knew was that police departments are political constructs. They work within political boundaries and are paid by the local government with local tax dollars. The chief of police is usually a political appointee. Cooperation with another jurisdiction may help to solve crimes, but what if the arrest occurs in that other jurisdiction? The question then arises, "Why are our tax dollars paying you to solve crimes over there? That's their problem." This type of attitude creates competition between police departments and reduces needed cooperation between jurisdictions. This was the general model of the Washington area police information- and resource-sharing well into the 1970s.

Welch's tactics hit the capital area at just the right time. Whether this was planned or coincidental will never be known. Whatever the case, it was fortuitous for him and disastrous for us, the police and citizens. Collectively, we, the police, certainly had all the resources necessary to combat Welch early on, if we had only been able to marshal them effectively. Given the history and nature of the Washington areas separate and distinct jurisdictions, that was almost impossible at the time.

At the beginning, Washington area police departments ignored the Ghost Burglar situation. Not that they ignored the individual cases or victims, but they failed to treat them as an interconnected phenomenon. This attitude of benign neglect was encouraged by the on-again, off-again tempo of Welch's operation. When the crimes stopped in the spring, during the prolonged daylight hours, police departments essentially stopped working those cases. There were other cases that required urgent attention. This is the standard triage procedure of public safety—take care of the immediate problem and ignore the problem that nothing can be done about. Leave the fire that's gone out and rush to the one that's burning. A necessary tactic for the short term, but dangerous if the old fire has been left with embers to reignite.

During the daylight savings time months, there was no task force, no one to continuing to investigate, to plan, to plot, to try to connect the dots. The pile of last year's Ghost Burglar crimes went into a file to be ignored, while more immediate crimes were addressed.

Could we, the police, have done better? Yes, we could have and probably should have. But that's hindsight. To have asked lowly detectives and their immediate supervisors to assign one or two people from their very limited force to work old cases, while newer, solvable cases were screaming for attention was just asking too much. Street detectives and their supervisors knew that if they did this and their case closure stats went down, they'd be back in uniform working a beat. Someone else more willing to work within the system would soon be sitting at their desk.

In effect, police departments are highly structured, goal-oriented organizations. They know what worked in the past, and they typically continue in that manner into the future, that is, until orders come down from the top to change. Isn't this what history accuses military leaders of? Generals are often said to be fighting the next war with the tactics of the last war. So it seems the police "generals" at the time were guilty of the same fault.

Now, after a generation has passed, the Washington area police departments are more flexible, more willing to work together on common problems. Let us hope the new police "generals" continue to be more adaptive than their predecessors.

In the late 1970s. there was one final element that increased interjurisdictional cooperation, and it returns us to the activities of Bernard Welch.

Welch came to the Washington area at the cusp of the transition from a jumble of independent, isolated localities to a slowly evolving regional entity in the mid-1970s. The increasing boldness of Welch's burglaries and victim confrontations put pressure on the affected police jurisdictions to meet and share data. What had been informal communication between detectives became increasingly more inclusive. While there had always been regional police meetings of general topics, these had been few and sporadic. Once the Ghost Burglar crimes in multiple jurisdictions were identified by the media in 1977–78, police meetings on this topic became more regular. This is how the "Standard Time Burglar Task Force," as it was then known, evolved.

At first, it was just a few of us that met, usually around a detective's desk in his office. As word got around to other police officers in other areas who had experienced similar crimes, the meetings became bigger and more regular. There was never an official task force. As far as I know, there was never one single detective in any jurisdiction that was exclusively assigned to work these cases. While handling the Ghost Burglar cases, we received other cases as well. In my office, that amounted to thirty to fifty cases a month. We, the street cops, were still trading information as we had always done, albeit in a more organized manner. We were just trying to do our jobs as best as we could with the resources at hand. We were like a blind boxer in the ring. We were getting punched fast and hard. We couldn't see our opponent, but he could see us. We were trying to get the rhythm of the fight, anticipate the next punch, and find a weak spot. Trouble was, we couldn't find the adversary, and his hits were unpredictable.

In Montgomery County, the officers I worked with were also assigned Ghost Burglar cases. We worked together and did what we could. I was the point man, staying in contact with everyone. When it was Montgomery's turn to host a meeting, I arranged it, made the coffee, and paid for the donuts. I believe the same can be said for the other key investigators in other jurisdictions.

My department neither encouraged nor hindered my efforts. They ignored them. I cannot speak for the arrangements of other jurisdictions.

The Ghost Burglar cases were assigned, at least in Montgomery County, as any other burglary would be. Of the two dozen detectives in the Crimes Against Property Unit, six were assigned to cover the Bethesda District. This district comprised the wealthiest area of Montgomery County. At the time, Montgomery was considered one of the richest counties in the nation. All of Montgomery's Ghost Burglar cases, rapes, and assaults occurred in this high-dollar area. The six Bethesda detectives specialized to some extent. One was assigned most of the arson and bomb cases. Another took most of the commercial burglaries. The rest handled most of the major theft and residential burglaries. I was often given the cases in which antiques and art were stolen. There was a reason for this.

I received my BA in Criminology and Psychology from Maryland University. I had previously majored in history and taken art history courses. This qualified me to know the difference between an oil painting and an Oriental carpet. Then in the mid-1970s, William Blair Antiques of Bethesda was burglarized. Mr. Blair's shop contained the finest of 17th and 18th century British antiques and maritime art. I was assigned the case. What was most baffling was that only the most mundane of Mr. Blair's stock was taken, not the rare, expensive items. This was the reverse of what was normally expected. I was stumped. None of the stolen goods ever showed up in the DC area. I could only conclude that the stolen antiques were taken precisely because they were ordinary and therefore difficult to trace. Further, they must have gone out of the area, probably to New York City. I was right, and I was wrong.

Today, I am almost certain that the culprit was Bernard Welch. This was the period when Welch was mainly operating in Richmond, Virginia, occasionally the Washington, DC, area, and transporting the stolen antiques to Pennsylvania. There was no other commercial burglar who stole antique furniture in the neighborhood at that time. Welch had a record of breaking into antique shops and stealing furniture. He was arrested in West Virginia for this practice and sent back to prison in 1966. I was not aware of this information until a few years later.

Interestingly, because of this crime I became intrigued with art and antiques as an international criminal commodity. I became friends with William Blair. Bill was a true gentleman and a great expert in fine antiques. He gave me instruction and access to his reference library. Over the period of a couple of years, I became conversant in the general field.

Just up the street from Blair's Bethesda shop was Limon's Jewelers. Robert Limon was a gemologist and a fine, gentle man of the old school. He patiently instructed me on the ins and outs of the jewelry business. He had been a jeweler for over fifty years, and there was little he did not know.

On duty and off, I began to haunt antique shops, antique shows, flea markets, and museums. In short, I became the closest thing to an art, antique, and jewelry expert that the Washington area police departments had. Was I an expert? Not really. But in the land of the blind, the one-eyed man is king. Truth be told, I didn't really have to be an expert. My real expertise was the theft and disposal of these items. Art and antiques are not things a run-of-the-mill thief would recognize or knowingly steal. This class of property is not easy to dispose of. It is a specialized crime with a specialized market. I began to keep tabs on those who were known to steal antiques and art and those who would buy these items without question. Area police agencies began calling me for advice when they had such a theft. I began writing the occasional article for the New York-based "Art Theft Archive Newsletter."

Of course, Bernard Welch was not the only silver thief in the area. There were hundreds, and police departments were being overwhelmed. With the rising price of silver and gold, every thief who could was stealing sterling silver and jewelry. Even legitimate owners were selling the family tea service. As the price of silver neared fifty dollars an ounce there was a rush to the precious metal buyers. A sterling silver fork or spoon weighs in at one-and-a-half to two-and-a-half ounces. The precious metal of a knife weighs about one ounce because only its handle is silver. Therefore, grandma's twelve place settings of sterling might fetch four thousand dollars or more, with serving pieces. In the late 1970s that was a lot of money. It still is.

The selling and buying of silver became increasingly frenetic. I actually observed people going into antique shops and buying old sterling silver pieces. They would produce a small hand scale and weigh the piece. If the silver weight value exceeded the retail price, they would purchase it and quickly resell it to a precious metal dealer to be melted. Some thieves began stealing X-rays from medical offices. They had discovered that there was a half an ounce or so of silver in each large X-ray negative. The stolen film would then be sold for a few dollars each to dealers for silver extraction.

Precious metal buyers began popping up everywhere. The worst part of the whole madness was that only the cities of DC and Baltimore had pawn laws. The states of Maryland and Virginia did not. Items were being stolen in the morning, sold in the afternoon, and melted by dealers at night. It was a cash business without records. Unless a criminal was caught red-handed with the stolen goods, there was no proof, no sales records, and no recovery.

When we had time, we would stake out a precious metal dealer whom we suspected and watch who went in. If we saw somebody enter that we knew to be a thief, we would march in behind them and attempt to recover the items before they could be melted. This was difficult, because we usually would get to the stolen goods before the victim could report the loss. We, therefore, had no legitimate cause to seize the items. We could only rely on the dealer's cooperation to hold the goods for a period of time. We often received this cooperation because dealers hoped to maintain police good will and avoid the threat of future legal actions. We did our best, but it was a frustrating time for both police and victims.

It was for this reason that in 1977 and 1978, I began efforts to get the Montgomery County Council to pass a law regulating the purchase of precious metals. This law required the buyer to record the seller's name and address, obtained from proper identification. The buyer was required to hold the property, unaltered for fifteen days before resale. The dealer was further required to mail a list to police of the purchased items with the seller's ID information. It was a simple, commonsense law for the public benefit. Who would oppose it? I should have known better.

There was a chorus of opposition from coin dealers, antique shops, jewelers, secondhand stores, and precious metal buyers. Their complaint was that this law would be another onerous government regulation, right up there with income tax and parking tickets. When I discovered the strength of the opposition, I asked police officials for help. They turned me down. They did not believe that the law could be passed, and they did not desire the political heat its proposal was generating. They knew I was the prime mover of the effort. As I was doing this on my own time, they couldn't stop me, but they didn't like it.

To counter the opposition I was forced to do something that police officials—the old-timers—hated above all other things. I went to the media to publicize the need for the law. It wasn't hard to get the media's interest. The TV news paired film footage of people lined up to sell at silver-buying shops with interviews of the victims of silver burglaries. At open county council legislative meetings, I testified and was able to find silver theft victims to testify. The buyers of precious metals also testified. The news reporters were there to record it all. The law passed. Within one year, I was called to Annapolis, the state capital, to testify before a Maryland state legislative committee. A state law was passed based upon the Montgomery county law. The State of Maryland even adopted the buyer reporting forms I had designed for Montgomery County.

As an aside, the Montgomery County government awarded me a small cash award for my efforts, $450 as I remember it. The ranking police officials never said a word. They kept their silence and waited. When it came time to appoint a police administrator for this new precious metal law, another, apparently more deserving than I, was selected. I continued as an investigator in the trenches. I kept my position, but I had been labeled a showboater. This was a badge of dishonor for violating the old-timers' code.

Northern Virginia took similar steps to those of Montgomery County. These laws, along with the falling price of silver, slowly put a damper on the silver thefts. After the capture of Bernard Welch, there was also a great reduction in the theft of art and antiques. My specialized knowledge was no longer needed.

With the slowdown of burglaries, the centralized Crimes Against Property Unit detectives became obsolete. We were reorganized to station house detectives, investigating almost anything that came in. We handled all the cases we used to, and we were assigned to help on murder, rape, and robbery as well. I was not happy.

Police are humans, too, and have personal lives. Mine was becoming a nightmare. My wife, Joanna, and I had designed a home and bought a piece of land in the country. It would be a great place to raise children. In mid-1977, we had the house built and moved in with our two children—Deanna, age 6, and Dan, age 3. To make ends meet, I depended on some overtime and a part-time job. Life was good, at least until Christmas 1977. Our six-year-old daughter, Deanna, was diagnosed with brain cancer.

Over the next three years, life at work—because of Welch—and life at home was difficult. It became an onslaught of brain surgeries, chemotherapy, radiation treatments, hospitals, doctor visits, wheelchairs, rehabilitation, special schools, gasoline shortages, nights at home after chemo treatments holding my daughter's head while she vomited, or spending the night in a chair beside her hospital bed, then going to work when the nurse woke me. Every day it was something else. Looking back now, I don't know how my wife and I did it all and continued on as a family, but we did. Many others helped where they could. My friends at work collected enough money to send us to Disney World for a week. They made all the arrangements. It was the one thing my daughter wanted to do, and they granted her wish. For that I will be forever grateful. She would smile when I told her Heaven was like Disney World. I had stopped my part-time and most overtime work to be home as much as possible. The medical bills and associated expenses grew. Our church, St. Mary's of Barnesville, Maryland, paid our home mortgage a couple of months when I could not.

Our daughter passed away in our arms on October 8, 1980, and I slowly sank into a deep depression. I kept going because of my wife and son, but I was in a fog. At work, I acted more the robot than the detective. With the reorganization, I was transferred to police station detective duty, which compounded my depression. I couldn't go to sleep at night, so I drank until I fell asleep. To stay awake at work, I drank dozens of cups of coffee. I was smoking three packs of cigarettes a day. I stopped eating. My insides were in an uproar and my hands trembled. I was falling apart. Eventually, I was asked to transfer out of the detective bureau. I didn't care at the time, because my personal and professional worlds were in shards, like a broken mirror on the floor.

I went back on the road as a uniformed police corporal and slowly recovered over time. I was back to normal in 1985 when our second daughter, Amanda, was born. She was a two-pound preemie and almost didn't make it. But she did, and became the new joy of my life. Then, later that year an annual police physical revealed I had a flunky heart. It was attributed to job stress. I was forced to take a disability retirement from the police department in late 1987. I continued working for Montgomery County, providing security at a middle school for the next twenty years. There my job was to ensure a safe learning environment for students and teachers. I helped where I could, talked to troubled children in the halls, and tried to make a difference. It's not much, but it's all I knew how to do.

Now, reviewing the notes I saved, along with old newspaper and magazine articles, I have tried to reconstruct what happened thirty years ago. Some memories are sharp. I see what some people are wearing, the type of chair they sat in, and the look of Bernard Welch when he was removed from the

DC police prisoner van. I cannot remember all of the words exactly, but I tried to recreate the conversations that took place as accurately as memory allows.

It has been said that "nostalgia is the sweetest of drugs." I do not find it so. In this recollection, I have been forced to revisit old wounds and old demons. It brings back pain I buried long ago. I find myself weeping for my daughter, who died in my arms, for my young son, who was ignored while I was under a dark cloud, and for my wife, who stayed with me despite my dismal mood. Joanna, my college sweetheart, is also gone now, taken by cancer and buried beside our daughter in the country churchyard at St. Mary's. I also mourn for the murdered Dr. Halberstam. We, the police, should have done more, sooner. I tell myself I did the best I could, but sometimes I wonder.

Now on summer evenings, I sit alone with a glass of wine watching the sun set behind Sugarloaf Mountain, as Joanna and I used to do. I try to remember only the good times as the sky darkens and the stars emerge. I watch the lightning bugs lift into the air and remember my children chasing them in the twilight.

James King

[1] This is the first time Bernard Welch claimed paternity for Susan Swanson's child. (page 201)

[2] The authors estimate the real number of "Ghost Burglaries" to be closer to 5,000. In this era before computers, most police departments were short of space. According to Detective James King, after a year, thousands of burglary cases are boxed up and put into storage. After another year, the boxes are taken to a warehouse. Within a few years, the boxes are buried and impossible to find. Police departments have neither the time nor manpower to search old files. (page 201)

[3] According to Detective James King, "The jurors looked across to Welch at the defense table. He sat there staring at her without any emotion on his face. His eyes were like a reptile's, watching, unblinking, uncaring. The contrast between the two was stark as the jury began to understand the nature of man they were judging." (page 206)

[4] There is no evidence that Welch was ever a member of the Ku Klux Klan. Later he did affiliate with the Aryan Brotherhood, a racist prison gang. (page 213)

[5] Detective King, having worked at Lorton Reformatory as a college intern caseworker for several months, agrees with Welch's assessment of the facility's security. "Escape attempts from the medium-security institution were frequent and usually successful." (page 216)

[6] Manslaughter is considered a lesser crime because it is not a premeditated or malicious act. (page 223)

[7] The Rochester, New York, pin and the stolen New York plates could indicate that Welch did visit his family home after his escape. (page 248)

We are grateful to these individuals, and many others who wish to remain anonymous, for your generous contributions to this book. Your stories and insight were crucial in helping us sort through the volumes of information on Bernard Welch and those affected by his life of crime.

Jack Burch and James King

Tom Bailey
Charles Baxter
Sue and Bob Bennet
Marion Burch
Paul Burkey
Paul Cycak
Mr. Dickerson
Kim Faith
Kay Gower
Priscilla Gunderson
John Hamilton
David Hammerstrom
Daniel Kalstadius
Jerry Kaufhold
Sally Kirk
Scott Lyons
Kathleen Kiebler Mahoney
Tony Marcocci
Tony McWhorter
Alan Mitchell
Alexia Morrison
Joe Niedzalkoski
Rich Perez
Mr. and Mrs. Gene Pisodi
Dave Roberts
William C. Rollins
Sol Z. Rosen
Linda Siegel
Alan B. Sochin
Brian Stegeman

Jay Stephens
Thomas M. Stephens
Stan Sunde
Don Tibbs
Dave Turk
Joan S. Wolf

Special thanks to the following reference and research librarians and libraries for your invaluable help and support:

Beth Anderson, Dallas Public Library, Texas
Faye Haskins, Martin Luther King Library, Washington, DC
Debbie May, Nashville Public Library, Tennessee
Ellen Pioro, Duluth Public Library, Minnesota
Susan A. Washington, Rochester Public Library, New York
Wilson Library, University of Minnesota, Minneapolis
William Mitchell College of Law Library, St. Paul, Minnesota
Anoka County Library System, Minnesota

James D. King was one of the chief investigators of the Ghost Burglar cases for the Montgomery County Police Department in Maryland. From his work on various robberies, King developed an interest in antiques and art theft. After extensive research, he wrote several articles for the *International Archive of Art and Antique Theft*. This research, combined with his work on the Welch case, led him to write and champion a Montgomery County law that required sellers of precious metals and antiques to produce identification and the buyers to report the purchases to the police. This law became the model on which a Maryland state law was based, on behalf of which King was called on to testify.

After retiring from the police force, King became a security specialist with Montgomery County public schools. He was also a contributing editor for the trade magazine *American School and University*, writing monthly articles on educational security issues.

King retired from school security after twenty years and is now a full-time author. He lives in Maryland, and *Ghost Burglar* is his first book.

Jack Burch was the photo chief for Channel 9 Fox News in Minneapolis and a part-time filmmaking instructor in the Journalism Department at the University of Minnesota. He then spent 30 years as the owner and operator of Burch Communications, a Minneapolis-St. Paul video production company. His clients have included ABC News, Boy Scouts of America, the Discovery Channel, ESPN and ESPN2, Fox Network Sports, HBO, Johnson & Johnson, the Learning Channel, the US Army Corps of Engineers, and the US Marine Corps. He received the *InterCom Award* at the Chicago Film Festival (1982) and the *Keith L. Ware Award*, the US Army's equivalent of an Emmy. Burch lives in Minnesota. *Ghost Burglar* is his first book.

TO ORDER ADDITIONAL COPIES OF

Ghost Burglar

Call

218-391-3070

or

E-mail:

mail@savpress.com

Purchase copies online at
www.savpress.com

Visa/MC/Discover/American Express/
ECheck are accepted via PayPal.

All Savage Press books are available through all chain
and independent bookstores nationwide.
Just ask them to special order if the title is not in stock.